SUCHITRA SEN

Shoma A. Chatterji, film critic, journalist and author, won the National Award (1991) for Best Film Critic and the Best Film Critic Award from the Bengal Film Journalists' Association (1998). Her book *Parama and Other Outsiders: The Cinema of Aparna Sen*, won the National Award for the Best Book on Cinema in 2003. She won a research fellowship from the National Film Archive, Pune, in 2003–2004, and a senior research fellowship from PSBT (Public Service Broadcasting Trust), Delhi. She won the second prize in the Sahitya Akademi's Golden Short Story Translation Contest in 2007. She is has done her PhD in History. She was Senior Research Fellow of ICSSR for post-doctoral research on working women in Bengali cinema. She writes extensively on cinema and gender issues. She also covers media, human rights, development, child rights and contemporary issues in several print and electronic media publications across India. She has been on the panel of film juries at international film festivals and has presented papers on television and cinema at Thessaloniki, Greece, Mannheim, Stuttgart and University of Heidelberg, Germany; School of Sound, London; and Asian Film Centre, Colombo, Sri Lanka. Besides contributing to many edited compilations on Indian cinema, she has singly authored twenty published titles on cinema, gender issues, short fiction and urban history. She currently contributes to *The Statesman, The Tribune*, www.upperstall.com, www.IndiaTogether.org, *One India One People, Vidura, Media, Screen, Trans World Features* and *Free Press Journal*. She has been writing for thirty-five years and is based in Kolkata.

SUCHITRA SEN

The Legend and the Enigma

SHOMA A. CHATTERJI

HarperCollins *Publishers* India

First published in India in 2015 by
HarperCollins *Publishers* India

HarperCollins Publishers India, Cyber City, Building 10-A, Gurugram,
Haryana-122002, India
www.harpercollins.co.in

P-ISBN: 978-93-5177-638-3
E-ISBN: 978-93-5177-639-0

2 4 6 8 10 9 7 5 3 1

Typeset in 11/14.5 Apollo MT Std
By Saanvi Graphics Noida

Printed and bound at
MicroPrints India, New Delhi

MIX
Paper
FSC FSC® C218906

This product is made of FSC®-certified and other controlled material.

HarperCollins Publishers, Macken House, 39/40 Mayor Street
Upper, Dublin 1, D01 C9W8, Ireland

To my late mother, Sumita Gangopadhyay, who had her first book of poems published when she was forty-eight and already a grandmother, for triggering in me the spirit of creation and competition

And

To my late father, Ashok Kumar Gangopadhyay, who introduced me to the world of cinema by taking me for Sunday morning shows every week when I was barely four to watch Mickey Mouse and Donald Duck cartoons on the wide screen followed by the silent movies of Charlie Chaplin

CONTENTS

INTRODUCTION

BIOGRAPHY OR ANALYSIS?

Is it possible to write the life story of a person the writer has never met in flesh-and-blood, and spoken to over the telephone only twice? How honest is it to indulge in this second-hand biography? Is a biography a chronological sequence of events described with elaborate ornamentation based on research, hearsay, books and magazines? Or does it delve deeper into the psycho-socio-professional analysis of the person being written about? Arguments such as these are rendered null and void when one is writing a book on an enigmatic screen persona like Suchitra Sen.

This book emerges from the writer's passion for cinema in general, and the star-persona of a legendary actress in particular. Also, though there are many books in Bengali on this iconic actress, there is almost no comparable study in English for a larger reading audience that might be interested in knowing and learning more about this star-actress. The attempt is to present and portray Suchitra Sen from the standpoint of an avid viewer of films, a film critic and an author. As a critic experienced in analysing various features and parameters that relate to feminist-film criticism relevant to Indian cinema, the challenge is to find out whether the film portrayals of Suchitra Sen, with and without the solid support of Uttam Kumar, lend themselves into a deconstructionist, feminist reading. Or whether they are an exploration into one of the most successful and celebrated stars in the history of Bengali cinema. But this will form only a part of this study.

The study has tried to explore how, in a majority of her films, she played the perfect foil to the hero and his romantic interest, which is one of the reasons for her charismatic appeal for viewers of either sex, all ages and from across borders of social and financial status. There are some films where one can read between the lines to find out if there were any discrepancies in films that could offer a feminist reading that would reflect not only on Sen's versatility but also her screen image. This necessitated the urge to read some films against the grain, so to say, which revealed some interesting results. In other words, from a different perspective, films featuring Suchitra Sen, with or without Uttam Kumar, read in retrospect, reveal quite often that the character(s) given to her is (are) mainly traced back to her beauty and her screen charisma. But beneath that surface of beauty, grace and femininity, those characters were no less significant within the script and the film than that of the hero, be it Uttam Kumar or any other actor.

These questions do not arise when one is writing a biography of a historical persona like Adolf Hitler or Mahatma Gandhi, or a painter like Picasso, or a poet like Sunil Gangopadhyay because they lived a single life spanning several dimensions minus an illusory and parallel presence created on screen. Besides, sometimes, an author trying to write about the life and works of a legendary actress who remained in the news much after she became a social and professional recluse could fall prey to what might be termed 'celebrity voyeurism'. This needs to be avoided, and is difficult in the case of a matinee idol like Suchitra Sen, whose self-willed social seclusion, which began in 1978 and continued till her demise in January 2014, led to much conjecture about its hows and whys.

A detailed work on her life and films could almost naturally become embedded with what might be termed 'celebrity voyeurism' though there is no design, covert or overt, on the part of the writer to make the work an example of the same. It is the 'reading' of the text that might be interpreted so. In order to steer clear of this debate, the author has not probed into the minute details of her personal life that remained as private and intimate as Mrs Sen could have possibly kept it. This is also because the subject's self-willed privacy needs to be treated with the respect and dignity it deserves.

THE DUALITY OF EXISTENCE

When one is trying to explore the life of a phenomenal screen persona and icon, one is constantly attacked by questions triggered because of that very persona. Is one writing about the persona one has been used to watching on screen—shedding tears when sad, laughing when happy, subtly romantic when in love and angry when betrayed? Or is one writing about the real flesh-and-blood person hiding behind the screen and the camera-captured image of a woman who was born, grew up, got married, appeared in films, became a mother and grandmother, and then passed away? Who is this woman behind the tears and the laughter, the make-up and the flowers in her hair, and the costume? Who remains hidden behind the character she is portraying on screen, emoting responses as diverse as laughter and tears? How does one break through these layers of the screen image built slowly and steadily, brick by brick, if one has never had the opportunity of seeing the real woman behind that image?

Suchitra Sen's story is one of a long series of impersonations created first for the screen, and then for the audience. It is a dual life, one lived off screen and the other on screen. If she was Roma at home to her daughter Moonmoon, whom she brought up almost single-handedly, she became Radha on screen, in *Deep Jele Jai*, playing the dedicated nurse brainwashed to masquerade as a lover to cure a patient. If she was the wife of her husband at home, as if by the touch of an invisible magic wand held by a director who knew his job, she turned into Roma, the doctor, who, in *Harano Sur* (1957), falls in love and impulsively marries her amnesiac patient who forgets that she exists when he regains his original memory.

Sen lived a high-profile life of glamour, within the flashbulbs of photographers, defined by the headlines of the print media, put up on huge hoardings at every street corner and featured in gossip columns of every imaginable glossy magazine. She was chased by the paparazzi even after she disappeared from public space. No one is quite sure about where the screen persona ends and the real person begins because the blurring between the screen image and the real woman is so overlapping and vague that at times the two appear to merge into one and then suddenly move in different directions just when you feel you have enough grip on both personalities to create a cohesive whole.

In an article, Maarten Reesink[1] raises questions on what makes some people so attractive for mass audiences. Two arguments are forwarded. The first is the concept of authenticity. A star has to convince the audience, in one way or another, of being 'real', to show something interesting that is inherently his or her own in the public appearances. In other words, there are two sides that need to be balanced delicately. One is Suchitra Sen, the star as the '*image*' created, sustained and perceived by the media, by publicity strategists and by the audience alongside the characters she has portrayed in her films. The other is the real woman Suchitra Sen whose real name is Roma, the private individual, wife, mother, et al.

The star 'image' is surrounded by an aura otherwise called charisma, the 'X' factor that a person has in him or her to make it as a star. What is 'charisma'? Charisma is not as enigmatic as most artists and film-makers have made it out to be. Richard Dyer[2] has put forth the argument that charisma stands for very concrete norms and values as well as the tensions in a society at a certain point in time that a specific person seems to embody. Dyer offers Marilyn Monroe as an example and states, 'Her image was to be situated in the flux of ideas about morality and sexuality that characterized the Fifties in America. Thus, she seemed to "be" the very tensions that ran through the ideological life of Fifties' America.'[3]

Does this argument stand the test of time, culture, geography and history when Suchitra Sen is placed at the centre? Yes, she does, by virtue of her durability as a star, much later as an actress in her own right. Also, if one took the entire range of her films into consideration and then broke it up into genres, she defines a microcosm of the 'ideal' woman men would be ready to swoon over, fall in love with and marry, while women would love to identify with and/or idolize her as the ideal woman. Moreover, the nostalgia she sustained through her films continued during her lifetime as well as after her death despite her voluntary withdrawal from films and from public life. Bengali television satellite channels virtually run a race to telecast films featuring her in the lead role, with or without Uttam Kumar by her side. One has no idea about the TRPs of these telecasts, but the proof of repetition and sponsorship stand testimony to the timelessness of her charisma and hold over a large section of viewers.

One must admit, however, that the trigger for choosing to write an analysis of the works of a particular cinema icon over others comes from personal feelings, teenage nostalgia, expectations and reactions that are rooted in the subjective response of the writer. But that is just the beginning of the story. This needs to be followed by an intelligent critique of the personality's contribution to Indian cinema in general, and to Bengali cinema in particular. One needs to try one's best to sustain a balance between the subjective response of a fond critic and the objective analysis of a writer who desires to place the person's work and contribution in perspective. In other words, one needs to reflect upon feelings of nostalgia, of wonder and awe about what endeared the persona of Suchitra Sen to the writer in the first place, followed by an exploration of how these relate to more objective factors concerning the star-actress in question.

REVIEW OF RELATED LITERATURE

The author has tried to remain as objective as possible while writing this book. This has been easier than one felt it would be because there has never been any direct interaction between the writer and her subject. The direct analysis of Sen's work is gleaned from having watched her milestone films again and again. The secondary information about the various shifts in her personal life have been collected from her childhood schoolmate, Phoolrani Kanjilal, who wrote a book in Bengali entitled *Amar Ballobondhu Mayanayika Suchitra Sen* followed by one-to-one interviews with Kanjilal. Another work called *Suchitra-r Katha*, by her long-time friend and veteran journalist, Gopalkrishna Roy, was consulted. This book, however, is a collection of reminiscences and anecdotes from his many sittings and interactions with the elusive actress and star. There are very few references or anecdotes relating to her films and to her work as an actress.

Abhijit Kundu's PhD thesis[4] explores the changing portrayal of women in Bengali cinema spanning the last five decades of the twentieth century. The study is about whether stereotyped images of women drawn from family institutions have been transcended on screen and 'to locate how, over a period of time, alternative subjectivities for women are involved through filmic enunciation'. The focus is on the conflict between tradition and modernity, and whether this conflict is resolved through an exploration focussing on the historical and social conditions which produce such changes.

This is an extremely broad-based study on the historiography of the position of women in Bengal. The researcher has chosen two Suchitra-Uttam starrers from the 1950s, namely *Agnipariksha* (1954) and *Harano Sur*, and the focus gravitates towards three films—that of Satyajit Ray, Ritwik Ghatak and Mrinal Sen—followed by a film by Rituparno Ghosh. The two films starring Suchitra Sen and Uttam Kumar occupy a very small space in the entire study and, sadly, there is no analysis of any film in which Suchitra Sen is presented without

Uttam Kumar, which leaves an unexplored vacuum in the image of women in Bengali cinema in the 1950s. These two films have been juxtaposed against *Charulata* by Ray and *Meghe Dhaka Tara* by Ritwik Ghatak, though these films belong to the 1960s. He writes: 'If in *Agnipariksha* the battle between tradition and modernity is narrativized by invoking the female protagonist as the site for a resolution of the two contending world views, in *Harano Sur* modernity is achieved "in a fantasy space outside society, a fantasy underlined by our inability to apprehend it through a method not normally productive for understanding Indian popular films". It is all about establishing the importance of conjugality as a marker of modernity.'[5] Kundu's analysis of the two Suchitra-Uttam box office hits is used as a secondary frame of reference for the Ray and Ghatak films and not as independent films to explore the magic of their screen romance, melodrama and plot significance.

An interesting study can be found in the PhD thesis of Smita Mitra.[6] According to the researcher, the work 'focuses on a specific cinematic fragment of the post-Independent Bangla Cinema in the 1950s–70s, a period referred to as the "golden age". I read the constellations of the narratives, genres and two stars, Uttam Kumar and Suchitra Sen, to delineate post-colonial cinematic modernity through melodrama to analyse the experiences of the middle-class Bengali, modern, urban-self. This period is also known as the Uttam-Suchitra Yug (The Era of Uttam Kumar and Suchitra Sen) as these two stars ruled the industry and were seen as the most successful stars. Both these stars constitute a "phenomenon" that has acquired "iconic" status not only within the Bangla film industry but also within the popular imaginary of the Bengalis. My work maps the iconicity of the two stars from 1950s–70s and beyond.'

In another detailed essay 'Mahanayika Madam', Smita Mitra sheds light on Sen's personal and private life, and her fierce guarding of her privacy. Mitra writes that her paper 'foregrounds the non-cinematic processes by which her star persona was created and their resonances in the filmic narratives. Finally, it attempts to understand the nature and materiality that constituted the "star text" of Suchitra in the early phase of her career while she was still in the process of forging her star persona.'[7] Mitra's paper maps two of Suchitra's performances—*Agnipariksha* (directed by the collective Agradoot) and *Sagarika* (directed by the collective Agragaami, 1956)—that catapulted her to stardom with Uttam as her romantic lead. She has analysed the films within a cluster of films that Moinak Biswas refers to as the 'new melodrama' of the 1950s. She asserts that this was a reinvented form of screen melodrama distanced from earlier feudal melodramas that were produced during the studio era. These two films have been chosen because they were made during the earlier period of the Uttam-Suchitra 'golden era' that charted the emotional journeys of the middle-class woman that combined within the same persona both the star presence and charisma of Suchitra Sen's personality.

'She was persistently cast as an educated professional woman—doctor, lawyer, teacher, social worker—traversing vast social and spatial distances. Romantic love and its various possibilities—normative and transgressive—acquire interesting resonances in the articulation of the woman's place and space in these melodramas,' writes Mitra. She further adds, 'In my opinion, Suchitra's "star persona" is constituted by a certain trope of middle-class "femininity" that became part of her popular appeal. It is within this larger social and cultural matrix of meaning and signification that her "mahanayika" (the great actress) tag needs to be located and understood. In Bangla, "nayika" is considered a more respectable term than the popular but lowly *taraka*. This term "taraka"—a mere popular star—was considered inadequate and not evoked for accommodating Suchitra's "extraordinariness" and "greatness". It is almost as if the semiotics of naming had to foreground her great stature along with her immense popular appeal, in addition to her acting abilities.'

In another talk, Mitra maps the accretion of 'iconicity' of the well-known popular female star of the 1950s and '60s from Bengal,

Suchitra Sen. She is an important figure for popular cinema in Bengal as she became one of the most successful female stars who commanded a status that is very often compared to Kanan Devi, the erstwhile star of the 1930s–40s. The circulation of nostalgia around her seems to haunt the contemporary as well. Her talk focuses on certain cinematic moments from Suchitra's career, the first phase in the 1950s in which she became known for her romantic roles opposite Uttam Kumar, followed by the break-up of their pairing in the 1960s to her charting of her individual star text where she consolidated her position with the first-ever international award won by an Indian actress at the Moscow film festival in 1963, with *Saat Paake Bandha*.[8]

In her book, *Bengali Cinema: An Other Nation*, Sharmistha Gooptu devotes nearly a hundred pages to Uttam-Suchitra films. But the focus is distributed more between Uttam Kumar's screen charisma and the Uttam-Suchitra magic than to Suchitra Sen's emergence as an actress in her own right to which she devotes just two or three pages, concentrating primarily on comparisons with Nargis and the Raj Kapoor-Nargis romance.[9]

However, one must concede that she elaborately analyses some Suchitra-Uttam films and places the success of the pairing to 'identification that was rooted in the figures of an idealized female and an idealistic and ethical male, embodied respectively by Suchitra Sen and Uttam Kumar, and their romantic love became the stuff of intense emotional identification among Bengalis of the post-Independence generation'.[10] She goes on to explain how 'against the rapidly transforming backdrop of Bengali society, the world of Uttam and Suchitra signified the perfect balance of permanence and change in Bengali life. It made for a new sense of modernity, and a sense of self which stood over and above the contemporary ideal of the nation. At a time when the spectre of Bombay cinema loomed large, the Uttam-Suchitra films created a niche audience which sustained the Bengali film industry for more than two decades.'[11]

However, one would like to point out that Uttam-Suchitra films did not create a 'niche' audience but slowly and surely commanded a mass audience with every show running houseful at a time when television had not made its presence felt in the national and regional scenario. This happened in theatres within Kolkata (erstwhile Calcutta), in the suburbs, and in the villages of West Bengal. Suchitra-Uttam films began to beat the Mumbai (erstwhile Bombay) films hollow at the box-office pickings even at repeat releases. *Harano Sur*, for example, ran to a full house for every Sunday morning show at Mumbai's Chitra Talkies that ran Bengali films only on Sunday mornings. Similar records were created for other Uttam-Suchitra films released in Mumbai either at Lotus Cinema, Worli, or at Ganesh Talkies in Parel, both theatres no longer in operation. In terms of the box office, even Satyajit Ray's films released at Lotus could not compare with those of Suchitra-Uttam films. The audience cut across age, class and sex, and even children craved to watch these films not only because of the lead pair but also because of the storyline and the music.

Maitreyee B. Chowdhury's book *Uttam Kumar and Suchitra Sen: Bengali Cinema's First Couple*, is a reader-friendly, fast-paced primer on the star pair that does not go into great depth but at the same time, offers unusual insights into several phases of their celluloid partnership and some offshoots this pairing brought out that have left their footprints on the sands of Bengali cinema. Two chapters, 'Memorable Films and Scenes' and 'If Music Be the Food of Love', throw up shades of the writer's insights into distinguishing features of the cinema partnership of this magic pair, albeit without delving into the depth and archival value of the films and the music. While the first chapter merely skims the surface of a few films, the chapter on music and songs is significant in highlighting how music played a very important role in taking all films pairing Uttam Kumar with Suchitra Sen to a different level altogether. Songs such as '*Shono bondhu shono*' in *Shaap Mochan* (1955), '*Ei poth jodi naa shesh hoi*' in *Saptapadi* (1961), '*Tumi je amar, ogo tumi je amaar*' from *Harano Sur*, '*Nir chhoto khoti nei, akash to boro*' from *Indrani* (1958) or that melodious '*Jodi bhool kore bhool modhur holo*' from *Agnipariksha* and

'*Amar shopne dekha rajkanya thake*' from *Sagarika*, are milestones in the history of lyrics and music in Bengali cinema.

Chowdhury maps out a historical perspective of music and playback music in Indian cinema, followed by Bengali cinema, drawing on the work of stalwarts who initiated the movement of music in cinema, paying tributes to lyricists, music directors and singers who contributed to the rich musical history of Bengali cinema. She finally arrives at a brief analysis of songs and music in Uttam Kumar-Suchitra Sen films. She also analyses how the voice of Hemanta Mukhopadhyay began to be identified with the face and screen persona of Uttam Kumar so much that it became impossible for the audience and for music lovers to imagine any other singer lending his voice to Uttam Kumar during the time he worked with Suchitra Sen. Chowdhury also elaborates on similar identification between the voice of Sandhya Mukherjee and the screen image of Suchitra Sen. Interestingly, both Hemanta Mukhopadhyay and Uttam Kumar on the one hand and Sandhya Mukherjee and Suchitra Sen on the other became lifelong friends. This signifies the kind of close bonding people within the industry shared with one another beyond their professional bindings. Sandhya Mukherjee and Suchitra Sen perhaps is the only singer-actress pairing in the history of Indian cinema in general and Bengali cinema in particular that defines a unique representation of the complete symphony between 'voice' and 'image' on screen and the symbiosis remains not only beyond comparison but also offers scope for research.

Himangshu Chattopadhyay, a senior film journalist, critic and editor, has written *Tollywooder Greta Garbo*, a biography of Suchitra Sen, which offers information not available elsewhere. For example, Chattopadhyay states that film-maker Arabindo Mukhopadhyay had seen Suchitra Sen as a junior artiste in a film called *Atom Bomb* (1954) being shot at Indrapuri Studios. Then Nirendra Lahiri thought of casting her in the female lead in a film called *Kajori* (1953), directed by Biren Chatterjee. Later, Sabitri Chatterjee was chosen to play the lead and Suchitra Sen played the second lead. Since Sabitri Chatterjee was an established heroine of the time, Suchitra Sen's image did not even appear on the posters of the film!

Filled with a plethora of photographs, the book is a collection of reminiscences, anecdotes and biographical information available to the author himself as well as gathered from people who worked with Sen and knew her professionally. The author digresses into other subjects such as the serious tiff that Uttam Kumar had with his wife Gauri Debi, as a result of which he left home one night, never to come back. Such descriptions of incidents that do not have any direct connect with Suchitra Sen dilute the essence of the subject and the writing. The text does not have any chapter breaks and is organized as a continuous read. This sometimes leads to confusion, especially because the narrative winds its way between the past and the present, after Suchitra Sen went into social seclusion following the commercial disaster of *Pronoy Pasha* (1978). There is a long and nostalgic description of how Bhupen Hazarika met Pramathesh Barua, which meanders without linking itself to the subject of the book. The link with Greta Garbo, whose name has been used in the title, is hardly explained. The quotes of other personalities who knew the actress are encrypted into the narrative without making any connections, and this only adds to the confusion.

An illuminating and well-researched analysis is found in Bhaskar Sarkar's *Mourning the Nation: Indian Cinema in the Wake of Partition*. In the third chapter, Sarkar, associate professor of Film and Media Studies, University of California, Santa Barbara, offers a different perspective on the Suchitra-Uttam romantic narratives which, according to his understanding, 'helped an enervated population to dream again. This refers to a cluster of romantic melodramas, the most celebrated of which featured superstars Uttam Kumar and Suchitra Sen.' The book is not about Uttam Kumar and Suchitra Sen, but is about whether cinema in India was impacted by the Partition in 1947 and if it was, how this manifested itself in Indian cinema. Within this larger picture, the author analyses several films starring the magical pair, how the melodramas they featured in seemed to 'make sense of the social upheaval by mediating it within the private context of the home and eventually to impose order through the resolution of crisis and the reconstitution of the family.'[12] He elucidates his argument with detailed examples from films like *Sadanander Mela* (1954), *Agnipariksha, Ora Thake Odharey* (1954), *Sabar Uparey* (1955) and others. His is the only work on Suchitra-Uttam films that questions and discusses the violation of women, which was one of the main problem areas of the Partition. He questions the rare reference to atrocities on women that have been touched upon only in passing, 'as a shameful acknowledgement of an experience that did occur (a realist gesture aimed at establishing a historical milieu), but is too painful to be dwelt upon'.

Sarkar extends his argument to certain popular films following the civil war in 1971, in East Pakistan, that led to the formation of Bangladesh. He states that *Alo Amar Alo* (1972), which turned out to be one of the last films casting the Suchitra-Uttam pair 'evoked painful memories of Partition violence to establish the persistence of certain conflicts and structures of exploitation'.

The Indian Partition in Literature and Films: History, Politics, and Aesthetics, edited by Rini Bhattacharya Mehta and Debali Mookerjea-Leonard, devotes a solid section on the Uttam-Suchitra films. The chapter discusses two primary films—*Nabaraag* (1971) and *Alo Amar Alo*—which are based on romantic novels by Ashutosh Mukherjee and Pratibha Bose, respectively. The former was directed by Bijoy Bose and the latter by Pinaki Mukherjee. These two films, states the book, 'were made in the mould of romantic melodrama, with the conscious choice of casting Sen and Uttam Kumar in the leading roles. The interjections and the eventual sublimation of the trauma of Partition into the romantic fantasy this on-screen couple embodied were part of a complicated passage of the plot from the novels to the films.' The author insists that the reading of these two films is with an eye 'on the shift in the relationship between private desire and anxiety on the one hand and the political expression of the same on the other'. The author insists that in the twenty-two years between 1953 and 1975, Suchitra Sen and Uttam Kumar played the lead roles in about thirty Bengali films produced in Kolkata. Out of these, the ones made in the 1950s and '60s form the definitive core of the '"golden age" in Bengali cinema'.

One begs to differ with the exaggerated emphasis on Partition in the above two books because if one considers the entire oeuvre of Suchitra-Uttam films made in that period, there are many films that do not fit into the 'Partition' story of melodrama. Melodrama was a mandatory feature of almost every Bengali film in general, and every Suchitra-Uttam film in particular. But this does not necessarily mean that the tremendous iconization of the couple is due to the audiences' mood immediately after Partition, and for films that placed them in some way against the backdrop of the Partition. The films explored and analysed in this book, and also in the book by Bhaskar Sarkar detailed above, can perhaps be read against the backdrop of the Partition. But this does not apply to most of the other films they performed in during the same period. No one can generalize that part of the Uttam-Suchitra charisma was the result of placing their romantic love, stripped of sexual innuendo and eroticism, against the socio-historical backdrop of the Partition.

Sadanander Mela features Suchitra Sen and Uttam Kumar in a subplot secondary to the protagonist Sadananda (Chhabi Biswas). The love story of the younger couple comes much later in the film which is less important than the main story. Interestingly, however, Suchitra Sen has a more dynamic, slightly rebellious and bold character to play as Sheela, a millionaire's daughter, who believes in living by her own rules than Uttam Kumar, as Ajit, whose character is more static. *Agnipariksha*, the film that catapulted the pair to overnight stardom and fame, had nothing to do with Partition but was a story that began as a kind of indictment against child marriage to later evolve into an argument for love in an arranged marriage that arrived later in the life of the couple.

Shaap Mochan was based on a novel by Falguni Mukhopadhyay, one of the most populist writers of his time, with whom a parallel may be drawn with Gulshan Nanda, a favourite of Hindi film-makers. This film, too, had nothing to do with the Partition. Replete with coincidences and melodramatic twists, the film features Suchitra Sen as Madhuri. Her father is a family friend of Mahendra's (Uttam Kumar) father. Madhuri is Mahendra's support system and moral back-up. She persuades him to transcend the so-called 'curse' he believes his family is under. She constantly eggs him on not to believe in the curse imposed by the guru on this musically talented family. The curse maintains that anyone in the family who continues to practise music will die. Madhuri is rich, educated and beautiful compared to Mahendra who is very poor, and is unable to make a living out of the music he is gifted with. How the curse is finally broken with the help and support of Madhuri, who overcomes obstacles in love, makes for a melodramatic and heightened climax. The film is still remembered and watched for its beautiful music composed by Hemanta Mukherjee, to lyrics written by Bimal Chandra Ghosh. The songs were sung by Pandit D. V. Paluskar, Hemanta Mukherjee, Chinmoy Lahiri, Shyamal Mitra and Pratima Banerjee. The film's archival value is mainly due to its rich music. The very timelessness of the romance in these films proves time and again that it is not confined to any definite socio-historical backdrop, though one must concede that perhaps, in the beginning, the post-Partition chaos in Bengali society did welcome the screen romance of this extremely handsome couple as a balm to soothe frayed nerves.

This writer is constrained to state that barring a few exceptions, most Bengali titles available in the market on Suchitra Sen are based on hearsay, conjecture, speculation, personal comments, implications, interviews, interactions and suggestions. In this sense, the authenticity that must back a biography or even a cinematic history of a famous actress, is missing. Gopalkrishna Roy's two noted books on Suchitra Sen in Bengali show how the star gives evasive answers to all his questions, never mind whether they are simple, straightforward, round-about or complex. These books are

– *Suchitrar Katha* (1998), which has gone into many editions, and *Anyo Ek Suchitra* (2009).

I have tried to create new areas and spaces while exploring and analysing the enigma called Suchitra Sen differently from how she has been fleshed out in other books. This has been done without marginalizing the works of others that have contributed significantly as frames of research and reference.

1

AN OVERVIEW

BACKGROUND

'Suchitra Sen was an era,' writes journalist Ranjan Bandopadhyay in *Suchitra Sen Ebong Ananya*. It is a term that has never been used to define any film persona in the country, not even Uttam Kumar or Amitabh Bachchan. Yet, Suchitra Sen never won the National Award. Suchitra Sen was the most charismatic actress Bengali cinema has ever seen. Her ethereal beauty, coupled with her phenomenal acting and immense box-office popularity, particularly her on-screen pairing with the late Uttam Kumar, gave her legendary cult status in Bengal. She created a new image in Bengali cinema, one that evolved over time. From a beautiful face ideal for the celluloid close-up in black-and-white, shot with chiaroscuro light effects, she graduated to the silent victim of circumstance or love, or both. She then transcended these celluloid stereotypes to become the articulate and tragic actress who capitalized on her tragedy, which was twofold—it was drawn from personal life and from the characters she portrayed. She occupied an independent and unique space within cinema, and outside of it. Within cinema, she was the star-actress no one could hold a candle to. Outside the world of cinema, as a woman, she broke many rules in the book of the Indian woman stereotype she so smoothly moulded herself into, for many of her screen roles opposite her screen heart-throb Uttam Kumar.

She made her debut in the unreleased *Shesh Kothai* in 1952. The following year saw her act opposite Uttam Kumar for the first time, in *Saare Chuattar*. The film, an effervescent comedy, was also the breakthrough film of director Nirmal Dey. It was a reasonable hit at the box office. However, it is remembered more for launching the pair of Uttam Kumar and Suchitra Sen. They went on to become icons of Bengali romantic melodrama for more than twenty years, creating a distinct genre unto themselves. Their films were famous for the soft-focus close-ups of the stars, particularly Sen, and lavishly mounted scenes of romance against windswept expanses and richly decorated interiors with fluttering curtains and such mnemonic objects as bunches of tuberoses, etc.

Suchitra never remained static as an actress. With newer roles, her multifaceted talent bloomed in different ways. 'She is the face that launched umpteen hits. She was a rage, the kind that only Marilyn Monroe succeeded to be in Hollywood,' a film critic had once surmised. But she is more often compared with the great Greta Garbo in the sense that like the famous Garbo persona, no one except her immediate family members, consisting of daughter Moon Moon, son-in-law Bharat Dev Burman and granddaughters Riya and Raima, has seen Suchitra Sen in flesh-and-blood, except once or twice, since 1978. She continued to live, safely cocooned within her small island of private sunshine, surrounded by her daughter and two granddaughters, in a spacious and beautifully appointed apartment at Ballygunje Circular Road, an elitist pocket in the southern parts of Kolkata. The apartment is one of the four she acquired when promoters brought down her original home at the same venue to erect a series of high-rise apartments. She bequeathed the three other apartments to her daughter and granddaughters.

However, when probed deeply, the comparisons with Greta Garbo do not quite jell with the life and times of Suchitra Sen. This has been explained and argued in greater detail in a later chapter. This writer has tried to argue that there simply cannot be any comparison between Garbo and Sen based on their stepping away from public life because their reasons were different, they belonged to different cultures and different cinemas, and their life stories charted different territories.

THE TRANSITION FROM ROMA TO KRISHNA TO SUCHITRA TO MRS SEN

How did Roma become Suchitra Sen? She was encouraged by her husband Dibanath to step into films. The story goes that she was initially offered a singing assignment at a recording studio in Park Street. She was introduced as Roma Sen. But that assignment was shelved in favour of the female lead in a film to be directed by Sukumar Dasgupta, a noted film-maker of the time. Dasgupta put Sen through a screen test. The film was *Saat Number Koyedi*. One of his assistants, Nitish Roy (not to be confused with the Mumbai-based production designer Nitish Roy), rechristened this new actress Suchitra. In 1952, she signed three more films. One was *Kajori*, directed by Niren Lahiri; then there was *Saare Chuattar*, directed by Nirmal Dey; and then *Bhagawan Sri Sri Krishna Chaitanya*, directed by Debaki Bose in which Basanta Choudhury made his debut in the title role. Her hero in *Saat Number Koyedi* was Samar Roy, while in *Saare Chuattar* it was Uttam Kumar.

The number of people in the industry who could call her Roma could be counted on one's fingers. Uttam Kumar was one of them. Among the few others were producer and distributor Asit Choudhury, and Anil Bandopadhyay, the DCP at the time. These three friends were influential in Mrs Sen's life and career. Till date, everyone in the Bengali film industry refers to her either as 'Madam' or 'Mrs Sen'. From the outset, she had a reserve about her that wrapped her like an aura, automatically vesting her with a dignified distance not usually seen or recognized in film stars those days, particularly in the women.

There was one group that addressed her as 'sir'. Film-maker Gulzar, who directed Suchitra Sen in *Aandhi*, leads that group. He continued to address her as 'sir' in a military tone of voice until her last days; this had remained a mutual joke between them since the making of *Aandhi*. 'Though I was much junior to her in experience and in age when she was working in *Aandhi*, she insisted on addressing me as "sir". We went on location with Raakhee and with Meghna, who was then a toddler. She became friends with Raakhee but continued to call me "sir". Then, one day, I warned her that if she did not stop calling me "sir", my entire unit would address her not as "madam" but as "sir". This form of address sustained,' reminisces Gulzar.

CHILDHOOD, MARRIAGE AND SOME SWEET MEMORIES

Suchitra Sen was born in Pabna, originally in the northern parts of undivided Bengal, and now in Bangladesh, on 6 April. The year of her birth is somewhat clouded because some sources trace it back to 1931 while others say the year was 1934. This is a part of the mystique that adds to the enigma called Suchitra Sen. She was the fifth among three brothers and five sisters. Her father's name was Karunamoy Dasgupta, and her mother's name was Indira. Her nickname was Krishna. She grew up in distant Pabna, miles away from Bolpur, in Birbhum district, presently in West Bengal. Her childhood is shrouded in mystery; some say she studied in Santiniketan. During her time, daughters of middle-class Bengali families did not go to boarding school. But then, her maternal uncle B.N. Sen lived in Bolpur with his family, and she would often come to stay with them. For some time during her early childhood, she lived with her maternal uncle's family in Patna. When she was admitted to Pabna Girls High School, her father entered her name as 'Roma' in the admission form. She was noted for her beauty right from her childhood. It was perhaps her beauty that heralded an early marriage, in 1947, to Dibanath Sen, son of an extended joint family that migrated to Kolkata. Suchitra is perhaps the first Indian actress in Bengal to have made her film debut after marriage and motherhood. In a nostalgia piece penned by journalist Amitabh Choudhury, Suchitra Sen is quoted recalling an interesting anecdote from her childhood.

> Listen to this incident from my childhood. I was in Patna, staying with my Mama's family. I was about three then, playing in the field, clad only in a pair of tiny panties. A naga sanyasi arrived at my Mama's house. Some time later, I was summoned to show myself to this sanyasi. The man kept staring at me for a long time. Then he said, this girl will become famous when she grows up. Her name will become a household word. I do not know whether you will believe this. But it is true.

Phoolrani Kanjilal (nee Choudhury), a classmate of Suchitra's at the Pabna Girls High School, says, 'We formed a group of five girls chirping away merrily during the school recess. The girls, besides Roma, were Moloya Sarkar, who topped the class, two sisters Reba and Rekha, and I. I met her when I changed schools quitting Mahakali Pathshala to join Pabna Girls High School in Class IV. She was already a student there. We would take active part in the cultural programmes of the school. Though she was never very good at studies, she wrote a beautiful hand and was quite conscious about her appearance, her hair plaited down just so, her sari pleated right, always prim and proper in school or at home.' Roma enjoyed decking up for marriage functions and drew a lot of male attention, but did not respond, as those were times when interactions between girls and boys were frowned upon. Kanjilal recalls Roma teaching girls to dance to the lines of a popular Tagore song that went, *'Hriday amaar naacherey aajike moyurero moto naacherey'*. Kanjilal and Roma studied together in the same class for six years. 'She was warm and friendly, a girl with good taste and decent manners. No sign of the famous Suchitra Sen "moods", when she became a star, was evident then,' says Kanjilal. 'But there was something different about her, something we could not quite put our finger on but could feel. So, when I saw her after a long time on screen and realized that Suchitra

Sen was none other than my school friend Roma, it was not as big a surprise as it ought to have been. The biggest surprise during our school days was when Roma came back from a holiday in Puri, a seaside resort in Orissa, where she had gone with her grandmother, and declared, "My marriage has been fixed."'

The boy was Dibanath Sen, son of Adinath Sen, Bar-at-law, who lived in Kolkata. The groom's family placed no demands for dowry—unthinkable in those days—and Roma got married to Dibanath in 1947. 'I attended her marriage. She looked beautiful as a bride and contrary to convention, did not cover her head with the bridal veil,' reminisces Kanjilal. 'But my introduction to Suchitra Sen, the star, was in 1954. I was a newly married bride. The whole family had booked in to watch a newly released film called *Ora Thakey Odharey*. I did not recognize her at once, though. I found a strong resemblance between the actress who played the female lead and my classmate Roma. My sisters echoed my feelings. We asked one of our older brothers who was a technician in Bengali films. He confirmed that Suchitra Sen and my classmate Roma were one and the same person. I could not believe my ears. Several years later, when I saw her with Uttam Kumar in the film *Saare Chuattar*, much after the film was first released, I noticed that her bridal make-up and attire were a celluloid replication of her own marriage,' sums up Kanjilal.

'We did have a face-to-face encounter many years later, in the late 1960s. Roma had invited me to her Ballygunje home through an actor we both knew well. Parijat Bose, the actor, said he would pick me up and take me to her home. I found two watchmen guarding the entrance. One of them asked me to fill in a slip. But before I could fill it, Roma came down herself and gave me a big hug. She refused to let Parijat leave without taking some sweets because, "you have brought back an old friend of mine", she said with her magic smile. She wore no make-up and was draped in an ordinary cotton sari. It was some time after her film *Fariyaad* was released and she had cut her hair short, I noticed. We exchanged nostalgic memories about our childhood and she expressed a wish to meet the other three girls of our gang—Moloya, Reba and Rekha. When I expressed a desire to watch her shoot for a film, she refused. She said, "If you watch the shooting of a film, *any* film, you will lose all the charm of watching a film." I went there a couple of times more because she had already told me that I needn't call before visiting. But then I stopped, because our worlds were too different, and though she was always warm, I felt neither of us had anything more to contribute to our relationship, or the need to sustain it,' says Kanjilal.

Dibanath is said to have noticed his wife's artistic potential as soon as they were married. Being culturally inclined, he wished his wife to be a part of the cultural world. His father Adinath Sen's first wife was Bimal Roy's sister. Though the sister passed away quite early and Adinath married again, the family continued to keep links with Bimal Roy and the children continued to address him as 'Mama'. This link came in handy when Dibanath wished to initiate his wife into films. This led to the recording studio event and finally to *Saat Number Koyedi*. Before shooting was to begin, a big hurdle had to be crossed. Who would talk to Adinath Sen and ask for permission to permit his daughter-in-law to act in films? Dibanath did not have the guts to approach his father, so he pushed his wife to do so. Roma took courage, approached her father-in-law, and told him everything. 'If you have the talent, I have no right to destroy it. So, if you wish, I will not stop you from fulfilling your dream.'

Much later in her career, when she was the most sought-after star-actress in Bengal, Suchitra Sen's marriage ran into stormy weather till the couple finally decided to part, with Suchitra taking the responsibility of daughter Moon Moon. A few years after the separation—one is not sure if they had divorced—Dibanath Sen passed away in the US where he was working for a merchant shipping company. Moon Moon is said to have woken up from a nightmare the day before. On the morning of 28 November 1969, a long-distance telephone call informed Suchitra Sen of the untimely and tragic death of her husband in an accident. She insisted on having his body flown down to Kolkata to allow Moon Moon to have a final glimpse of her father whom she loved very much. Producers and directors who were close to her and had worked with her during this phase say that she purged her inner pain by giving of herself to her work completely, and this brought out the best of her talents. No one ever heard Suchitra pour out her heart about her personal problems while she was working. A slice of reality was revealed in the way she portrayed the role of Archana in *Saat Paake Bandha*. This was the time when the trouble in her married life had reached a peak.

Several years later, in the late 1980s or early 1990s, Suchitra Sen brought her ailing mother down from Bhubondanga, near Bolpur, in Birbhum district, to her residence in Kolkata. An acquaintance had called her up after a visit to Bhubondanga to inform her that her mother missed her famous daughter and wished to see her. Indira Dasgupta was residing with one of her sons at that time. The person who called her suggested that Suchitra bring her mother down to stay with her. Sen thanked the lady and brought her mother to live with her. Her mother passed away some time later of cancer, at her daughter's home, and with her daughter by her side until the very end. She personally attended to her last rites at the city's Keoratala burning ghat.

Dhiren Deb, known to be Suchitra Sen's personal photographer (a label he refuses to acknowledge) during the entire course of her career, knew her well. He has a rare collection of photographs of some of Suchitra's most private and personal moments. For instance, there is one picture of Suchitra sitting on her haunches, her face split up in an ear-to-ear grin, sari jacked up to the knees, chopping fruits for a puja in her home. Another one shows the actress with the little Moon Moon wearing a frock, standing by her side. The backdrop shows a small Dakota from which the trio has just landed at Santa Cruz airport in Mumbai to report for the shooting of Bimal Roy's *Devdas*. 'The date was 2 June 1955 and at the time, there were no direct flights from Calcutta. We had to change aircraft at Nagpur and it took around seven hours to reach Mumbai,' said

Deb. 'We were in the same flight for different reasons though. She was reporting for work on *Devdas* and I was on my professional assignment as photographer. Our relationship reached far beyond the constraints of the normal photographer-subject relationship. But the entire credit for this bonding based on friendship, pure and simple, goes to Madam alone. In all these years of my life as still photographer in films, I have never met a woman more decent, warmer, more beautiful, more complete and ideal than Madam. Her outstanding personality finds no comparison with any star-actress in the country. I have taken photographs of Suchitra Sen right through her career in films. No photographer, press or otherwise, was permitted on her sets during a shooting. She is one of the most dedicated artists of Indian cinema. She would report to the studio at least five minutes before reporting time for shooting, so punctual was she. In my opinion, it is this dedication that makes her reign supreme as the queen of Bengali cinema more than twenty years after she called it a day.'

Gulzar and Suchitra developed a lasting friendship during the shooting of the film *Aandhi*. 'She was a warm human being. I never knew she had noticed and remembered that I like a glass of cold milk every morning. There was not a single occasion when she forgot to give me a glass of cold milk each time I went to visit her at her residence in Calcutta. Once, I had gone on a very short trip and was staying at the Grand. I could not make the time to meet her. Then, Barin-da [Barin Dhar], a close associate of Suchitra, who was married to her younger sister, Runa, came up to my room and said that "Sir" was waiting for me in the car in the parking lot downstairs. I rushed down to meet her. "How can you leave without taking your glass of cold milk?" she asked. She took me home and did not allow me to leave until I had taken that glass of cold milk she served me herself. She was a lovely human being with a fine sense of humour. I believe she had the right to choose her friends. She was very hospitable, too, and if she chose to guard her privacy, I don't think there is anything wrong in that.'

Another interesting anecdote he shares is that Suchitra Sen had the rather unusual gift of feeding crumbs to crows out of her own hands. 'Feeding pigeons or parrots is a usual sight. One does not usually see *crows* being fed by people. But Suchitra Sen had this fondness for feeding crows. I have seen a crow perch on her shoulder, then clamber down near her hand, and she would feed crumbs to the crow with her own hand,' says Gulzar.

Narratives available on her life tell us of the terrible struggles and hardship that she had to undergo to realize her dream of breaking into the industry and how, in the initial phase of her career, she was badly treated by producers and directors. She soon gained notoriety by getting into a well-documented and publicized spat with editor Kaalish Mukherjee, who ran a popular film magazine, *Rupmancha*, and was known to give photo publicity to young and emerging actors, the only stipulation being that they come to his office-cum-studio for the photo shoot. Suchitra refused to have her photo shoot and was extremely curt with him. Angry and humiliated, Mukherjee printed a scurrilous piece about her in the next issue, chiding her for being haughty and proud, ending with the lines that *nati* (public woman) should remain in her place: 'We want to see her where she belongs and not try to be above her station.' This episode, and the rumour-mongering unleashed by a miffed Mukherjee, are often cited to justify not only her 'difficult' and strained relationship with the popular press but also gave valence to her 'moody and stern personality'.

A STORY OF MISSED CHANCES AND LOST OPPORTUNITIES

The Suchitra Sen story remains incomplete without mentioning the gaps in her career. Having redefined the meaning of mainstream cinema for the mass audience, Sen never got the chance to work with the three pillars of parallel cinema in Bengal, namely, Satyajit Ray, Ritwik Ghatak and Mrinal Sen. Her image was so larger-than-life, that, somehow, a Suchitra Sen without glamour could never be imagined till Gulzar's *Aandhi* appeared on the national scene. Satyajit Ray did approach her for the title role in Bankim Chandra's historical fiction *Debi Choudhurani*. She initially agreed, but later backed out of the project. 'He had asked for dates at a stretch without a break. I could not possibly agree because this would have placed all my other producers in trouble whose films I had either already signed for, or whose films were under production. I could not agree to the exclusivity clause which producer R.D. Bansal later put into the contract,' she is reported to have said to journalist Amitabh Choudhuri, personal friend of Suchitra Sen. She later did the same film in the title role directed by Dinen Gupta, in 1974, opposite Ranjit Mullick, but neither the film nor her performance has endured in public memory.

Sen never ever acted in a film based on a Tagore classic. Actresses not as talented and experienced as she was have had the opportunity of enacting a character from a Tagore story. Suchitra Sen is not one of them. She was once chosen to act in the female lead, Damini, in a celluloid version of Tagore's famous classic *Choturango*, to be directed by painter-director Purnendu Pattrea. She had agreed to work in the film because noted writer Premendra Mitra had personally requested her to take on the project. Besides, for her, to bring a Tagore character alive on screen was a dream come true. But the suicide of Hemen Ganguly, the producer of the film, put paid to all hopes and the film was shelved for good. She was also supposed to portray the famous theatre actress Binodini opposite Rajesh Khanna. This too did not happen. She had agreed to do one of the two important female roles in a film adapted from Bankim Chandra Chattopadhyay's *Krishnokanter Will*. The film did not even begin shooting and was subsequently shelved.

Her beauty and her stylized performance often came in the way of a complete character identification. Her acting *appeared* to have shades of Stanislavsky—the ability to go under the skin of the character. But in the ultimate analysis, they all boiled down to one woman—Suchitra Sen. Shades of Bertolt Brecht's distancing the character from the actor could also be seen—because beyond the make-up, the costume and the ambience, it was Suchitra Sen *being* Suchitra Sen. Perhaps she did this more by design. With her performance in *Aandhi*, she proved how deeply she could imbibe Stanislavsky into her system if she wanted to. Perhaps it was commercial cinema's near-total dependence on her star value that drove her. The fact remains that despite her brilliant performance as Rina Brown or Archana or Kamallata or Roma, the lowest common denominator that characterized these screen characters was a single star—Suchitra Sen. She lost out on the golden opportunity to 'live' those characters on screen. That is why she decided to strike it out on her own without the support of Uttam Kumar. She lived the characters all right, but the common link was the star persona of Suchitra Sen. Strangely though, instead of diluting their intensity, her star aura invested them with richness unknown before, or after her. In retrospect, what seems to be a problem could really have been Suchitra Sen's unique selling point—her charismatic screen image as star that eventually linked itself and became Suchitra Sen, the actress.

MOTHER AND GRANDMOTHER

'My mother never ever made me feel the pressure of being her daughter. I cannot say the same for the Bengali film industry though. Mother permitted me to do whatever I wanted to do, she let me play, she encouraged me to paint and draw. I did not miss her much as I was in boarding school and learnt to live independently. I just enjoyed being her daughter. The only thing she did not wish me to do is to join films. When I announced I was going to do jatra, she just freaked out. But in the end, she accepted my choice and she encouraged both my daughters,' says Moon Moon Sen. 'The two things she emphasized through my growing up years were a solid education and a stable family life. I have tried to live up to both.

She gave me the best of education one could dream of. I was good at art and she kept one of the best artists to coach me in drawing and painting. And my husband and daughters have given me the happiest moments in my life.'

According to the granddaughters Riya and Raima, 'We have never really idolized our grandmother though she was always around to guide us and show us the way. But for us, they are just mother and grandmother, not Moon Moon Sen and Suchitra Sen. We've never bothered about going along with Maa to her shoots. But we do regret having missed out being on grandma's shoots, we weren't born when she quit.'

When asked how she felt about stepping into a Bengali film as leading lady, Raima said, 'I felt my flesh tingle and my skin break out in goose pimples when I found myself facing the camera on the same studio floors where my granny did such great work in Bengali classics. At certain moments, I just could not believe myself. Tollygunge has a special place in my heart because I am linked to it through blood ties. At the same time, I understand the disadvantage of being Suchitra Sen's granddaughter. There will be the inevitable comparisons I will never be able to live up to. Times have changed. Film-making has changed. Cinema itself has undergone a dramatic metamorphosis over the years. But it's all in the game.'

Will she be able to hold back that unshed tear on her heavy eyelashes before it can drop? Can she break her body language into fragments to express the emotional pain of the character she portrays? Has her grandmother taught her the grammar of expression, body language, look and emotion she had learnt so well? She is in no position to respond to these questions now. For, unlike her reclusive grandmother, she has time on her side.

2

UTTAM KUMAR AND SUCHITRA SEN: A MAGICAL SCREEN CHEMISTRY

BACKGROUND

From the 1950s through late '70s, Uttam Kumar was to Bengali cinema what Amitabh Bachchan has been to mainstream Hindi cinema, in a much later period, though. With this single star, Bengali cinema saw the sustained commercial viability of its films, both commercial and offbeat. Whether he was cast opposite his popular co-star Suchitra Sen or a newcomer like Anjana Bhowmick, Uttam carried the entire burden of Bengali cinema on his strong shoulders until his death. More than twenty years after his death, all the Bengali heroes of the mainstream—from Prasenjeet to Chiranjeet to Tapas Paul—cannot *together* produce the charisma and the versatile performances this single man was capable of. Till this day, theatres screening films starring Uttam Kumar draw full houses. All Bengali channels thrive on films starring him. Even Satyajit Ray created a special script with Uttam Kumar for one film, *Nayak* (1966). An important element of writing a biography of Suchitra Sen is that it must feature Uttam Kumar. The same applies to any work on Uttam Kumar: it can never be complete without analysing the role of Suchitra Sen as his screen partner.

UTTAM KUMAR

Uttam's first film *Dhristidaan* released in 1948. Some say that he made his debut as an 'extra' in a film called *Mayadore*, in 1947. His last film, *Ogo Bodhu Sundari*, loosely adapted from *My Fair Lady*, hit the screens in 1980. He suffered a massive stroke during the shooting of this film and passed away a few days later, on 24 July, at the ICU of a leading nursing home in Kolkata. Over more than three decades, he acted in not less than 159 Bengali films, investing the characters he played with a unique charm, whether he played an old, faithful servant in *Khokababur Pratyabartan* (1960), based on a short story by Rabindranath Tagore, or as an amnesiac industrialist opposite Suchitra Sen in *Harano Sur*, inspired by the famous Hollywood hit, *Random Harvest*. As he mellowed into character roles with age, his performance matured and his screen persona took on a new look, though he continued to dominate the screen in mature roles such as the committed manager in *Agnisankar* (1961), or as the strange villain in *Aparachito* (1969), or as Chunilal in Dilip Roy's *Devdas* (1979).

His success lay in his complete Bengali-ness. Another reason for his popularity was that he never tried to imitate the style or mannerism of any actor—Bengali, Indian or foreign. He treated every character he played as a Bengali first and as a character later. This made his portrayals original and inimitable. Chhabi Biswas, a great actor, delivered his English lines by imitating English spoken by the British. They came out distorted and unreal. Uttam Kumar delivered his English lines exactly like Bengalis speak English. Yet another reason for his success and popularity was that his research and homework for every character—big or small, hero or cameo—was without parallel. If he took wrestling lessons in an akhada for a few scenes in a given film, he took riding lessons for another till he had almost mastered riding and did not need a double for Tapan Sinha's classic period film *Jhinder Bandi* (1961). He was a trained and talented singer, therefore his lip-sync to his songs in films could not have been better. He knew to play the tabla very well; once he even went on-stage to play the tabla for a close friend because the regular tabalchi had failed to appear.

Uttam Kumar was brilliant in negative roles, too. He played the villain obsessed with his love for a young woman in *Aparachito*. When he discovers that the woman is in love with his naïve and innocent friend, he kills her. In *Baghbondi Khela* (1975), Uttam Kumar as the middle-aged hero plays a debauch whose way of life makes his wife leave him. Though he is a wealthy man, he traffics young girls from poor families. The mature Uttam Kumar put in an unforgettable performance in the film. In *Stree* (1972), Uttam Kumar as the villainous landlord is shocked to discover on the day of his son's wedding that he is not the father. He rides on horseback to the home of the family photographer, the real father, and shoots down the already dead man. He rides back and shoots himself. In *Lal Pathar* (1964), he evolves from a cold-blooded, cruel and oppressive zamindar into a mentally deranged, doddering old man, a ghost of his former self, cared for by the woman he had kidnapped and kept in his home, but had never married.

His smashing looks were conducive to any costume, be it a three-piece suit, a dhuti-punjabi worn Bengali style, a nightgown, a naval uniform or the elaborate costume of a Mughal emperor. He slipped under his costume and make-up and closeted himself in his make-up room, concentrating on the shot for the day, sometimes for hours at a stretch till the spot boy came to tell him that the camera was ready to roll. When Satyajit Ray directed his make-up man, Ananta Das, to inform Uttam Kumar that the actor would not wear any make-up for his title role in *Nayak*, Das was scared. When the actor sat in his make-up room on the first day, shouting out for Ananta to begin, Ray told him that there would be no make-up for him, except for a little padding on the face for the flashbacks showing the hero as a young man. Uttam Kumar was not exactly overjoyed. But after the film was complete, he told Ray that for the first time, he could act naturally without the baggage of make-up. 'Acting without make-up was a different cup of tea; my facial expressions were smooth, seamless and spontaneous, which would not have been possible under the weight of heavy paint,' said the actor in a conversation about his work in *Nayak*.

SUCHITRA SEN

Suchitra Sen made her debut in *Shesh Kothai*. She was paired opposite Uttam Kumar for the first time in *Saare Chuattar*. The two turned into overnight icons of Bengali romantic melodrama, sustaining the on-screen chemistry for more than twenty years. They starred in thirty films, beating the Spencer Tracy-Katherine Hepburn pair hollow. When the young and beautiful Suchitra Sen emoted a love scene with Uttam Kumar in *Chaoa-Paoa* (1959), *Pathey Holo Deri* (1957), *Alo Amar Alo* (1972), *Saare Chuattar* (1953), *Kamallata* (1969), the charged feelings between them came across so tangibly that one could stretch one's hand to touch them.

Suchitra Sen became a nationally renowned actress with some meaningful Hindi films. Two of them are Gulzar's *Aandhi,* based on an original story by Kamleshwar, and *Mamta*, directed by the late Asit Sen, where she portrayed the two diametrically opposite characters of the kothewali mother of a sophisticated daughter who is a barrister. The film was the Hindi version of the original Bengali film *Uttar Phalguni* that turned out to be a box-office hit. In *Aandhi,* one could see in the character she played, glimpses of the mannerisms and characteristics of Indira Gandhi. Released during the Emergency, the film created a storm within the prime ministerial office and was briefly banned because Mrs Gandhi who was the prime minister felt it could reflect badly on her. When this writer spoke to Kamleshwar about who his inspiration for the story really was, he had a good laugh and confessed that it was fashioned after Rani Gayatri Devi of Jaipur, and Mrs Gandhi was nowhere in his mind when he wrote it. Suchitra Sen insisted that she did not fashion the character after Mrs Gandhi.

THE MAGICAL SCREEN CHEMISTRY

Historically, these two as a star couple arrived on the cinema screen at a critical time when Bengali cinema was going through a bad phase. New Theatres that had reigned supreme for many years, gifting Bengali cinema with some of its best actors such as Pramathesh Chandra Barua, Kanan Devi, Pahari Sanyal, technicians like Bimal Roy and Nitin Bose, and music directors like R.C. Boral and Pankaj Mullick, had pulled down its shutters with *Bokul* (1954). Interestingly, Uttam Kumar featured in its last two productions. Bengali cinema was, at the same time, going through marketing troubles as the long-term consequence of Partition when East Bengal became a part of Pakistan. There was a subsequent dearth of new faces and talent and in terms of technique; many had migrated to Mumbai to seek greener pastures and production values began to decline because of budget cut-downs and lack of commanding technicians. Bengali cinema was losing glamour and Hindi cinema was rising in popularity. In this grey phase, a film called *Agnipariksha* ended the downswing with the introduction of a star couple—Uttam Kumar and Suchitra Sen.

Uttam Kumar and Suchitra Sen formed one of the most formidable romantic pairs in the history of Bengali cinema. At their best, the pair made the likes of Raj Kapoor-Nargis, Spencer Tracy-Katherine Hepburn pale in comparison. Together, the Uttam-Suchitra pair heralded the golden age of Bengali cinema. They brought spring, and a breath of fresh air, that lasted over two decades. Every member of the audience would wait with bated breath for the typical climax of a Suchitra-Uttam film with the two embracing each other, with the 'The End' sign superimposed on the embrace. Some say in one of these films, *Shilpi* (1956), the hero dies in the end. The film flopped. Between them, the two wrote a new chapter in the history of Bengali cinema. There hasn't been anything remotely close to this celluloid chemistry either before or after.

Their physical beauty, their style of expressing romance on

screen, and finally, their glamour came like a life-saving drug for an industry gasping for breath. Lovers tried to identify with the love they projected on screen. During this phase, Uttam Kumar was paired with other actresses also. He acted opposite Sabitri Chatterjee in twenty-seven films. Most of them were commercial hits. But they failed to create or re-create the magic Uttam could bring on-screen with Suchitra.

The Suchitra-Uttam pairing had another rare quality. The two could change the magic of their screen romance in keeping with the changing needs of a different script or director or role. In their earlier phase, the Suchitra-Uttam on-screen romance was noted for the intense passion it generated visually, through dialogue and through imaginatively choreographed song sequences. The love songs lip-synced by them, together or individually, or even in the soundtrack, continue to be big hits in the music industry to this day. For the four film versions of the Sarat Chandra classics they acted in—*Chandranath* (1957), *Rajlakshmi O Sreekanto* (1958), *Kamallata* and a *Grihadaha* (1969)—they changed the very definition of romance from the passionate to the subdued, in full control of their emotions, mature. Love, separation, reunion, and a happy ending were the four stereotypical phases redefined for cinema by Suchitra Sen and Uttam Kumar. *Pathey Holo Deri*, re-released in late 1982, two decades after its first release, celebrated a silver jubilee run!

They shared an excellent rapport on the sets though they were never known to have fallen actually in love with each other, despite what the gossip magazines then would often insist. Both began their careers after their respective marriages to their partners. This did nothing to spoil the magic of their box-office charisma. Though they appeared together for the first time in *Saare Chuattar*, the film that actually established the two as the best box-office pair in the history of Indian cinema was *Agniparíksha*, directed by Bibhuti Laha.

In an interview,[1] director Bibhuti Laha said, 'When I chose this pair for *Agniparíksha*, everyone said I was crazy to have paired a flop master with a dumb doll. These were euphemisms the film industry used for them at the time. The only thing both Uttam and Suchitra had going for them was their face. I concede that it was a considerable risk I took in taking them on to play the two leads in a film that called for considerable acting talent. Till the last minute, everyone persuaded me to change my mind and cast Bikash Roy and Anubha Gupta in their place. But I was determined to cast new faces in my new film. I called them up and they happily came in to sign their contracts. The rest, as the clichéd saying goes, is history. They won hands down with this film. The film proved to be their starting point. My only credit lies in that I played the first tunes on the flute.'

Late Anup Kumar, the character actor who passed away some years ago, said, 'During the 1960s, the entire audience in Bengal was convinced that Uttam Kumar and Suchitra Sen were lovers in real life too. Producers and directors cashed in on this popular notion as much as they could, and almost always, with happy results. Young boys and girls would use their names together as "Uttam-Suchitra", so complete was their popularity and identification with the masses. I worked with them in many films. While I waited for my shot on the sets, the perfect rapport the two shared amazed me again and again. Roma-di knew precisely how Uttam-da would respond to what line of dialogue. Uttam-da too understood her moods completely. This chemistry between them brought out some of the best romantic performances in Bengali cinema. Thus, one cannot really blame the middle-class audience. No one had ever seen such spontaneous, such real-life romance on the screen ever before. Everything appeared larger-than-life, meaning, each film show was like a beautiful dream, when the show came to an end, so did the dream.

'The Uttam-Suchitra pair proved that it was possible to bring cinema right into the streets to touch the man out there. When the girl next door came to hang out the day's washing, the boy from the neighbouring terrace would belt out a song in typical Uttam Kumar style from an Uttam-Suchitra film. At times, such incidents even led to real love between the boy and the girl. This ability to identify so completely with the audience is an extremely difficult task. But these two had turned this near-impossible task into reality. This was backed by the fact that whatever ego hassles, problems linked to their acting together on-screen they might have shared in the course of their professional lives, they never once were rude to each other in public, on the sets, or in the studios. In all my years of having worked with them, I cannot recall a single incident where they exchanged strong or angry words on the sets, either during, before or after the shooting.'[2]

Uttam Kumar's younger brother, late Tarun Kumar, a noted character actor, said that to the best of his knowledge, the celluloid romance between his brother Uttam Kumar and Suchitra Sen never translated into their real lives. 'Every actor knows that it is easier to act out what the director says. But it is impossible to reproduce scenes from one's real life. Our lives may be filled with dramatic incidents, but this does not reduce our entire life into a drama. My own theory about the phenomenal popularity of the Uttam Kumar-Suchitra Sen pair is that almost throughout their career together, they shared a spirit of healthy competition and mutual respect. This did not sustain in the later years for many reasons. But even during this time, they never ever slighted each other,' said Tarun Kumar.[3]

Suchitra was almost always draped in a sari, with a sleeved blouse. She did not need to show skin, flash a thigh or reveal a cleavage to exude sex appeal. There was an instant audience identification with the Suchitra-Uttam pairing and that is why it was such a hit. Yet, not once did they kiss. 'It was all there in her beautiful face,' said Uttam Kumar once. 'She is so beautiful that thousands come to the theatres just to look at her face. Where can you get a photogenic face like that? Roma is the most beautiful, the most glamorous among all my leading ladies. I have been lucky to have been cast as the man she fell in love with.'

The pairing fell apart when they were doing *Saptapadi*, produced by Uttam Kumar. Sen had problems, and they did act later under other banners but somehow, the magic was lost.

Most of the plots chosen by film producers were noted creations of fiction authored by popular Bengali novelists like Sarat Chandra Chatterjee, Nihar Ranjan Gupta, Bibhuti Bhushan Bandyopadhyay, amongst others. Uttam and Suchitra could vividly personify the characters from the novels of Sarat Chandra Chatterjee, especially when the character of the female romantic interest conformed to the conventional expectations of the 'ideally moral' woman. There was the inherent conflict of being a beautiful woman and at the same time never swaying in her moral stance, forever functioning as a pillar of support for the love of her life.

In *Kamallata*, based on a segment of Sarat Chandra's four-volume autobiographical classic *Sreekanto*, Suchitra Sen portrays the title role of a child widow, who is almost totally engrossed in religious rituals. When she meets a wandering young man called Sreekanto (Uttam Kumar), who steps into the ashram, she falls in love with him though there is a huge gap between their social and financial status. Sreekanto belongs to an affluent Brahmin family of aristocratic stock, and she is a widow leading a life of an ascetic in a hermitage. But she declines his proposal for marriage and decides to go away to the city. Kamallata wishes to liberate him from any kind of commitment and bondage, even though she desperately needs his protection and shelter.

'Will you close your eyes to caste, culture, tradition and social norms? I am a widow. I love you deeply but I cannot tolerate your humiliation in the eyes of society,' she elaborates as explanation. The climactic shot shows Sreekanto standing silently on the platform at the railway station, as Kamallata bids him a sad goodbye. She stands at the door of the compartment, her eyes moist with tears, calm and quiet as the train moves away from the frame. Sen speaks through her large, almond eyes, rendering dialogue superfluous. The melodrama is present, but it is discreet and is subtly enhanced by the understated performances of the two actors. As Kamallata, Sen gave one of the most mature performances in her films that pitted her opposite Uttam Kumar in narratives where mostly the hero dominated the scenario. She looks beautiful even in a widow's weeds and the sandalwood markings on her face, a signature of the religious followings of the ashram. However, on hindsight, when one views the film again, one realizes that this film was made in the later stage of her career and therefore, it was the star Suchitra Sen who kept peeping out of the painted face of the character Kamallata. She looks beautiful in every shot, many shot in close-up, but it is Suchitra Sen one sees and not the Sarat Chandra character Kamallata. The story she narrates about her tragedy in the past when she played the piano, painted and lived a lonely life, emphasizes the melodrama in the story and the character.

It would be apt at this juncture to quote from Bhaskar Sarkar, who writes:[4]

> Her (Suchitra Sen) coupling with Uttam Kumar, indisputably the most popular star of the Bengali screen, allowed for the projection of a certain fantasy: the *adhunika*[5] could now desire within limits imposed by the narrative. Of course, the heroine's passion for one particular star-hero across so many narratives served to rein in feminine desire, domesticating it within a monogamous ambit, even de-eroticizing it by investing it with the aura of 'true love'.

However, one begs to disagree with Sarkar's labelling Suchitra Sen in Uttam Kumar films as 'adhunika'. The 'modernity' she defined in her films depended on the story on which the film was based. It was a time when the story was the 'hero' of every Bengali film. Yet, one must give credit to the director, the script and the two main actors—Suchitra and Uttam—for bringing to life a blend of everything that romance stands for, without trying to titillate or sensationalize. At the same time, sensuality prevailed and sustained the audience's intrigue to watch the next film in which they would be coupled in.

Their romance defined an ambiguous, ambivalent area of the screen surface, looking for a place to attach itself to, and this had an impact on the audience. In other words, their romance was all-pervasive on the cinematographic and narrative space of the screen, visually and in terms of the narrative. The romance grew within a context where sound, music, images, dialogue and silence kept moving ceaselessly. The 'off-screen' image of Uttam Kumar and Suchitra Sen continues to sustain and we try to situate them in a place contiguous with the screen in the present tense of the action. At times, such as in *Harano Sur*, after Alok Mukherjee, the amnesiac patient, suddenly leaves the home where he was living with his doctor wife Roma Banerjee, and buys a ticket to go back to Kolkata, his image keeps haunting the screen space without really being there. It is with these 'absences' substituting for the physical presence of the character that one can understand and acknowledge the specific power this magical couple held on its audience for around two long decades, where their 'ageing' did not create any dent on their charisma.

One socio-historical reason for the success of their screen romance could be surmised from the degree of the audience's identification with the 'happily-ever-after' mode the middle-class and lower-middle-class aspired to and dreamt about. New Theatres' history was filled with very serious subjects that sometimes led to tragic endings such as *Devdas* and *Mukti* (1937). Suchitra-Uttam romances ended in 'happily-ever-after' climaxes without the hero and the heroine having to kiss even once. This happy climax was preceded by long twists of conflict, confrontation, misunderstandings, family schisms, melodrama, class differences and so on. The happy endings came as poetic justice to what went earlier. None of the films show any transgression of middle-class morality in physical and sexual terms, and this might have created an additional appeal for the audience. The films belong to a social matrix where young love remained by and large confined to an exchange of meaningful looks across neighbouring terraces in urban and rural neighbourhoods, not necessarily ending in marriage.

SOME HIT FILMS OF SUCHITRA SEN AND UTTAM KUMAR

The criteria this author set to pick films of this couple for a detailed analysis could be said to have been based on the commercial success of the films. But that is debatable because among the thirty-odd films they did together, most were super hits. So, the choice could also have been subconsciously based on the historic popularity of these films that are still written about, watched and commented upon by film scholars and industry insiders as memorable films, films that represent the golden era of Bengali cinema and films that are crassly commercial without trying to pull the audience through compromising elements. Above all these is the fact that television channels are continually proving that among the audience, these films have tremendous repeat value. The films chosen for this chapter are: *Agnipariksha, Harano Sur, Rajlakshmi O Sreekanto, Saptapadi* and *Nabaraag*.

Agnipariksha

This has been chosen because this was the second film that the couple was paired in, but the first that triggered their tremendous box-office run that went on for two decades. Besides, it was the celluloid portrayal of a short novel by Ashapurna Devi, who later became a prolific, popular and much awarded writer in Bengali literature.

Jnanpith award-winning littérateur Ashapurna Devi's own life reads like an incredible novel. She is one of the most brilliant fiction writers in India who never stepped within the four walls of a school as a student all her life. Ashapurna grew up in Kolkata, where her father was an artist and her mother a literature-loving housewife. Married at a young age in a traditional family, she had free access to Bengali magazines and books. She wrote her first stories, for adolescents, during the 1930s. Her first adult work was *Swamir Premika* (1937) in which she touched upon the changing and contradictory expectations of men from women—as traditional, obedient wives and at the same time, as stimulating, glamorous lovers to be shown-off to others. Ashapurna Devi is known for her strong female characters. At times, some critics have downplayed the importance of her writing, calling her the 'kitchen writer'. But she proved them wrong by writing prolifically and courageously while she also ran a home with her husband and their three children with great success. She did her writing within the framework of the traditional family and had the steadfast support of her husband.

She wrote with great insight novels, novelettes, short stories and also delightful and satirical stories from the point of view of children. Most of her short stories and novels wove in strident attacks on patriarchy. Patriarchy victimizes men too in the sense that men are conditioned to believe they are superior to the female sex and, therefore, have the power to dominate, suppress and control women. Women are conditioned to believe that they are lesser than men and so can be dominated, suppressed and controlled by their male counterparts – father, husband, brother and son. The unequal power equation between men and women is largely sourced back to the social, cultural and historical conditioning of men and women both. Even *Agnipariksha* celebrates the sanctity of the eternal bond of marriage, though the two protagonists were married off as children at a time when they did not even know the meaning of the word 'marriage'. In this sense, *Agnipariksha*, in retrospect, encourages child marriage in a manner which is in sharp contrast to Ashapurna's bold and often radical literary oeuvre.

Tapasi is married off as a young girl to the teenage zamindar boy Bulu, on the insistence of her grandmother and against the express wish of her own mother. The mother is fleshed out in negative shades because she is against early marriage and wishes to bring up Tapasi through educated and westernized ways. Tapasi's angry mother brings her back from the ancestral home of Tapasi's in-laws and her father dies of shock. Destiny catches up when Tapasi meets a handsome, highly educated and westernized young man, Kiriti, during a visit to a hill station. Though the two fall in love, Tapasi is constantly disturbed by memories of her childhood marriage. Since she has no knowledge about her groom's current life, she is torn apart by the uncertainty of whether she is a married woman, an unmarried woman or a widow. 'Her subjectivity and her fulfillment are determined primarily in terms of relation to a male mate—current, future or past. Her female friends are, likewise, caught in a web of constant anticipation even as educated, cultured and socially adept young women, they are forever waiting to be discovered and claimed by some man.'[6]

The film is filled with moments of melodrama from beginning to end. But the melodrama defines the film's character and the interaction between and among the main people involved in the story. For instance, when Tapasi meets Kiriti and realizes that an emotional bond is being built between them, she seems to forget all about her marriage as a young girl. A small street scene she happens to see from inside the car in which she and Kiriti are travelling suddenly takes her back to her past and she is traumatized both by memory and guilt. The car stops because a marriage procession is passing in front and the bride is a small girl. One does not get to see the girl closely, but the damage is done. Tapasi is almost seized by a strange fear, and by feelings of deep guilt. From then on, she stops going out, stops meeting Kiriti, stops dressing up, leaves her hair loose and refuses to even step out of her room. Kiriti visits every day, but she does not wish to meet him.

The change in Tapasi's life affects the rest of the family and this is where one can glimpse sparks of good acting by Suchitra Sen, though in keeping with the acting style of the time, there is some element of overacting and exaggeration. As Kiriti, Uttam Kumar's performance is very balanced and credible. Suchitra Sen limited herself because she was conscious of how the camera would capture her face, and this was more than evident even among her peers of the time such as Meena Kumari. It was a time when the face of the beautiful heroine was more important than the body for the director, the cameraman and the actress. Right through the film—from the moment she meets Kiriti for the first time, at the hill station, till the last minute when the two meet in the ancestral village home—Tapasi looks beautiful. Her good-for-nothing brothers are quick to point out that she holds a master's degree in English with a first class, can speak English like an Englishwoman and can sing like a nightingale. This suits the purpose of the projected love story because Kiriti with his smashing looks, polished manners, high education and the elitist 'stamp' of a ten-year stay across UK, Europe and the USA is considered the perfect match for Tapasi as her husband.

But who is Kiriti? He is none other than Bulu grown up, adult and eligible. In other words, Bulu chooses to keep his true identity a secret from Tapasi and her family. This impersonation is triggered by his desire to see Tapasi go through *agnipariksha*—trial by fire—his true identity to be revealed only if and when Tapasi comes out of the agnipariksha successfully. This 'doubling up' as someone else that amounts to misleading the lady he has fallen in love with is not only marred by strong patriarchal notions but is also a betrayal of the trust Tapasi has placed in him because she does not know that this is the same young Bulu she was married to.

The film was made in 1954, when divorce was a sacrilegious term. Hindu marriages negotiated by the respective families were considered to be for 'eternity' or till 'death do us part'. No one questions Kiriti's wilful impersonation as a breach of faith because that is how patriarchal values dominated society and this reflected itself through cinema. Bhaskar Sarkar writes: 'Through her misrecognition, the narrative dramatizes the confrontation between tradition and modernity as the conflict between the "double" Bulu and Kiriti. Although much of the film unfolds from her point of view, ultimately she remains a pawn in the hands of the primary male subject. Since the audience realizes the truth before the protagonist does, the transgressive potential of her desire for "another" man is contained; it is her masochistic struggles that become the primary locus of spectatorial pleasure.'[7]

On hindsight, *Agnipariksha* threw up, perhaps for the first time, the complete screen compatibility of Uttam Kumar and Suchitra Sen, also unwittingly pointing out the difference between the two stars in terms of their screen image and command over acting. Suchitra Sen as the grown-up Tapasi enters the frame after a good twenty-odd minutes of screen time. The entire story is from Tapasi's point of view. Yet, once Kiriti steps in, she becomes the object of cinematic gaze. The story is manipulated on three fronts: one by her mother, brother, aunts and cousins, on another by her own traumatic past and thirdly, by Bulu pretending to be someone else. Uttam Kumar as Kiriti smoothly takes over the proceedings once he enters Tapasi's life. He is suave, charming, attractive and mesmerizing, and is in complete command of the drama he has created. Suchitra as Tapasi is like a beautiful counterfoil, in suffering and in pain, when her life changes with dark memories superimposed onto her present. The character of Tapasi as a child, portrayed by Shikha Rani Bag, is a classic performance that reaches beyond the adult Tapasi. The expression of complete puzzlement and confusion on her face as her eyes wander alternatively to the bed of the dying zamindar, to the chandelier hanging above, to her bridegroom not understanding at all what is going on, is very convincing.

Agnipariksha became a super-duper hit because it did not contravene audience expectations of conventional, middle-class morality. Tapasi ultimately goes back to the man she was married to as a girl, and there is no ideological conflict in this which might have steered the audience the other way. The music and the placing and orchestration of the love songs—*'Ke tumi amaare daako'*, *'Gaane more kon indradhanu'* and *'Jodi bhool korey bhool modhur holo'*—give an added dimension to the screen romance between Tapasi and Kiriti, both before and after Tapasi is disturbed by the trauma of her childhood marriage. The film set the pace for the electrifying chemistry between the lead pair portrayed by Uttam Kumar and Suchitra Sen and remains a milestone in Bengali cinema.

Abhijit Kundu[8] offers a different perspective that, if studied from another point of view, the film underscores the dilemmas of three women spanning three generations from the same family, and all three are linked closely to the institution of marriage. Kundu writes: 'In *Agnipariksha,* the subordination of woman is less signifying than representing the female protagonist Tapasi as the site of a contest between her mother and her grandmother over the ideal of femininity. In the contest between the grandmother's notion of femininity in tune with "traditional" Hindu custom and the mother's ideal of "modernity" of the emergent middle-class Hindu, Tapasi attains all the modern way of life, yet she finds solution to her dilemma taking recourse to the repertoire of tradition. In this sense, the film in its ideological agenda does not critique patriarchy as such. In fact, female subjectivity is espoused within the greatest institution of patriarchy, the family. Nevertheless, it does allow us to hear the female voice of the family. It vents out certain repressed female energies. Yet it cannot move beyond the parameters of patriarchy.'[9]

Harano Sur

Harano Sur is unique because it is an adaptation of a famous Hollywood film, *Random Harvest* (1941), based on the novel by James Hilton, starring great stars Ronald Colman and Greer Garson. Though Ajoy Kar, director and cinematographer of the film, was roundly criticized by many for having 'lifted' the story, the popularity of the film over time stands testimony to Kar's ability to give the film a completely Bengali identity, with generous medical loopholes and cinematic licenses taken on the 'amnesia' theory.

Ajoy Kar began his career as cinematographer and earned fame for his amazing command over lighting in an era when cinema was entirely black-and-white. As director, his repertoire might appear small, with twenty-six films between 1949 and 1989, when compared to the output of later directors. However, his films offer a glimpse not only into his versatility in choosing genres and stories that were different from one another but also in his innovative work with lighting, and with the camera. He worked with three generations of actors and technicians like Kanan Devi, Sandhya Rani, Bikash Roy, Dhiraj Bhattacharjee, Manju Dey, Sabitri Chatterjee, Uttam Kumar, Suchitra Sen, Soumitra Chatterjee, Aparna Sen, Sharmila Tagore, Lily Chakraborty, Tanuja, Tandra Burman, Victor Banerjee and Supriya Choudhury. His films were mostly based on rich works of literature, both Bengali and Western. His first big hit, *Jighangsha* (1951), a thriller, was a Bengali adaptation of Arthur Conan Doyle's *The Hound of the Baskervilles*, and brought him to the notice of the film industry and the audience in a significant way. Before this, his adaptation of Sarat Chandra's *Mejdidi* (1950) revealed his mastery over the creation of a powerful script and elegant story-telling, with Kanan Devi giving one of her most memorable performances in the title role. Kar shot over eighty feature films before turning to direction, with the Sabyasachi collective. The collective included Binoy Chatterjee (script), Jatin Datta (sound), Kamal Ganguly (editor), Bishnu Chakraborty (art direction) and actress Kanan Devi.

His greatest contribution to Bengali cinema are the films he created with the Uttam-Suchitra pairing, followed by the classic *Saat Paake Bandha* and *Datta*, also with Suchitra Sen but not Uttam Kumar. His earliest films with Uttam-Suchitra, namely *Darpachurna* (1952) and *Grihaprobesh* (1954) carried sparks of the magic he could create but what came later was amazing. He zeroed in on *Shyamali*, which had had a continuous run as a stage play at Star Theatre, Kolkata, with Sabitri Chatterjee as the deaf-mute heroine. Taking a successful stage play and making a film out of it was a considerable market risk. But Kar took the risk and doubled it by choosing a different actress, Kaberi Bose, to play the title role. Uttam Kumar played the hero. The film received a lot of critical acclaim. The success of *Shyamali* (1956) perhaps gave Kar the confidence to pair Suchitra Sen and Uttam Kumar in his next film *Harano Sur*, one of the most outstanding box-office hits in Bengali cinema, the other one being *Saptapadi*, also directed by Kar.

Harano Sur was produced by Uttam Kumar. This is one film that deals with love within a psychological setting. It is the first Bengali film to deal with amnesia, though with a generous dose of cinematic licence with regard to medical authenticity in keeping with the demands of the medium and appeal for the mass audience. In fact, medical precision is discarded at the outset as Roma, the psychiatrist, brings the amnesiac Alok to her father's home and resigns from her hospital job as a mark of protest and also because she has broken the rules of the hospital. The story is presented almost entirely from the perspective of Roma, the heroine, and not Alok, the hero.

Its melodious musical score by Hemanta Mukhopadhyay includes two songs that have become all-time classics in the history of Bengali cinema. One song '*Tumi je amaar*', oozing with romance and shot under a tree shorn of leaves but in full bloom with white flowers, was sung by Geeta Dutt, who mainly sang in Mumbai for her husband Guru Dutt's films. This romantic scene shot under a studio-constructed tree on a set became like a logo of an Uttam-Suchitra film, carried over from *Agnipariksha* and spilling onto other films.

Scripted by Nripendra Krishna Chattopadhyay, an author and also a much-in-demand screenplay writer, having done the scripts for nearly fifty feature films in Bengali, the story is set against the backdrop of a fictitious small town called Palashpur that houses a small psychiatric sanitarium. Roma Banerjee is a psychiatrist in the nursing home. One day, disturbed by shouts and screams from a patient outside, she discovers that Alok Mukherjee, a patient suffering from amnesia following an accident, cannot be controlled by the staff. She takes him under her care and gradually falls in love with him, unwittingly breaking an unwritten medical rule of a doctor not permitted to get emotionally involved with a patient. She also gets married to him and when this raises the nursing home's ire, and she has a severe disagreement with her senior about how to treat the amnesiac, she quits her job and takes Alok with her to Palashpur to reside in her father's house. The father does not impinge on his daughter's way of life though he has reservations about Roma marrying a patient suffering from amnesia.

Even in his amnesiac state, one fine day, a thoroughly bored Alok, who is slowly getting cured, walks out, meets with a small accident, regains his earlier memory but forgets his immediate past, that is, the events in his life that happened during his amnesiac state. Puzzled to find himself in a strange place, he goes to the nearest station, books a ticket to Kolkata, and goes back to his original home, surprising his old mother and his little niece, an orphan. It turns out that he is a famous businessman in Kolkata and is engaged to be married to Lata, a girl from the class he belongs to—thoroughly modern, sophisticated and wealthy.

When Roma discovers that her husband is missing, she is devastated at first but slowly decides to trace him and bring him back to her. From this point on, her medical career takes a backseat and not knowing how and where to trace him, she takes a train to Kolkata, and by chance, finds him. She takes up a job as his little niece's governess and is stationed at his spacious home in the city. Alok, who has lost his memory of his immediate past, including his marriage to Roma, does not recognize her. Roma keeps her medical career aside in her determination to bring about reconciliation in their marriage by making attempts to revive Alok's memory. The initial attempts are doomed to fail because Alok's fiancée, Lata, perceives her as a threat to her own position in Alok's life. She expresses her fears to Alok's old mother. Alok himself is suspicious about Roma's intentions when she attempts to rekindle his lost memory and distances himself from her. Alok's mother throws her out, making way for Alok to suddenly regain his memory, go to Palashpur and call out for Roma. The film ends on this 'happily-ever-after' note.

One of the high points of the film is its music and its two songs, the love song '*Tumi je amaar*' and the other song of lost love '*Aaj dujonar duti poth ogo*'. The first was rendered by Geeta Dutt in her unique voice that, till this day, finds no comparison with other playback voices in cinema. The second song was sung by Hemanta

Mukhopadhyay. '*Tumi je amaar*' became the theme song of the film, the strains of its music filling the air whenever Roma and Alok are together, during the time when Alok does not recognize her at all. But the strains of the song keep haunting him, chasing him to find out what it is that shakes him up when he listens to it, as Roma constantly tries to restore his memory. The song is a metaphor of their relationship and percolates down to the audience who unwittingly get sucked into the tragic story of love, hoping that it ends happily.

Harano Sur is important because though the focus is on love between a young man and an educated, modern woman, it is the woman who is more significant than the man—in love, within marriage, and to the story. Though one might read the second phase of Roma's 'journey' into the Kolkata home of Alok as an anonymous woman who works as governess in the house and appears to be submissive, docile and soft, yet, beneath the surface of femininity and grace lies the mind of a very strong and determined woman. The woman wants to bring around the story to a climax that she desires—she wants her husband's memory to come back because she wants her husband to come back to her. Alok plays a passive second to Roma's primary and active 'first'. Her ideology of living life on her own terms comes across very strongly, phase by phase. She chooses to be a psychiatrist over other professions at a time when there were few women opting for it as a special career within medicine. She rebels against her senior doctor and walks out of the sanitarium after an argument about the appropriate psychiatric methods to cure amnesia and especially the strategies of treatment. She takes the next bold step of marrying the amnesiac, knowing fully well that he might forget her and the marriage once he gets back his memory. She becomes insanely possessive about him. She directs her staff not to post the job applications Alok gives them for posting. She does not realize that while on his way to recovery, Alok is not only alone, and more so because he has nothing to do, but is also frustrated in his very loneliness. Does she not wish that he be completely cured and get back to whatever work it is that he is qualified to do? Or is she scared that if he leads a normal life, he will no longer remain her patient and, therefore, might dispense with his need for her?

Just before Alok wanders away from the Palashpur home, there is a moving scene showing Roma knitting a sweater—clichéd but important, because it is linked to something that happens later on in the film. Alok, all this while, is busy filling up job applications. When she walks over to him, he picks up her knitting and is delighted to find out that it is a sweater for him that she is knitting. This scene takes place right before his second incident of amnesia. The sweater becomes a metaphor, a signifier of the life they were building together, that would no longer remain so close-knit for long.

When Roma shifts to Kolkata, she carries the half-knit sweater along with her. One day, she shows it to Alok who cannot recognize it for what it is. A sad Roma is seen unspooling the knitted wool soon after, and it begins to fall in strands between her deft fingers. Alok's niece, a little girl, surprised, asks her why she is doing this. Roma quietly says, 'To knit a new one,' registering that she still has hope that she will succeed in her mission to make her husband remember her and their love for each other. The film is replete with similar scenes and dialogues that connect to the latter half of the film, assuming a new meaning, almost like a premonition or a foreshadowing of things to happen in the future.

Note that the admission of love, more to herself than to her patient, is by Roma. Alok is in no position even to understand if he has a choice, much less if he can exercise it. The decision to marry her patient is also Roma's alone. She is aggressive in her love in her own way, and Alok is a quiet recipient though he seems happy in this new dimension of their relationship. Eventually, Roma's fight is born of her inner conflict—the subconscious ego tussle between a doctor trying to cure her patient-husband through unconventional strategies beyond the domain of existing psychology, and a woman-in-love disguised as a governess trying to make her husband remember their days together by invoking his lost memories. Roma, the psychiatrist, loses to herself when her husband walks away. Roma, the governess, loses, too, when even the extreme points of desperation she pushes herself to fail to work. Finally, the strains of '*Tumi je amaar*' bring back everything, and the lovers are united.

In the Kolkata phase, she has the same determination, but this time, the purpose is different: she wants to save her marriage with Alok by bringing back his memory. She knits a sweater—obviously for Alok—arranges flowers in vases, tells stories to his little niece, and also gives her the right injection when the girl falls sick. But she is forced to surrender to the whims of destiny when Alok's mother throws her out. Lost and defeated, she goes back to Palashpur. Roma Banerjee is perhaps one of the most multilayered characters Suchitra Sen has played, and that too rather early in her career. Juxtaposed against this multi-dimensional woman who knows what she wants and lives life on her own terms, Alok turns out to be flat, passive, and apart from being dashingly handsome, is one-dimensional. During his amnesia, he is a puppet with the strings held firmly by his puppeteer—Roma. After Alok returns to Kolkata, he becomes the central figure in his ancestral family, adored, respected and admired by the household staff, by his mother and by his little niece. Uttam Kumar excels in expressing his alienation, his distancing himself from many things around him, including his fiancée towards whom his feelings are filled with uncertainty and confusion, heightened by questions and doubts about who this beautiful woman in his house, working as his niece's governess, really is. At the same time, right through the unfolding of the story, he is definitely the weaker character of the two and really does not know what he wants out of love and out of life. To carve him out as a 'hero' figure, Lata and her brother are deliberately fleshed out in negative shades while Alok's mother reacts to gossip and hearsay as normally as any confused mother would.

But the show belongs to Suchitra Sen alone. Even when Alok has 'returned', living his original life as a wealthy and well-regarded businessman in the city, the film is still much more about her than it is about him. She wants to cure Alok because she loves him but also to prove to herself that she can. There is both confidence and a desire to learn. She wants—or perhaps needs—to know that it is her influence and capabilities that have healed him, not just a random blow from a passing motorist. His love is important, but her own assessment of her work is equally important.[10]

In *Harano Sur*, the heroine strides worlds, playing doctor and wife, embodying a perfect balance of resilience and vulnerability, subjectivity and being presented, approached and styled as an object. While her beauty is framed in the soft-focus close-ups that are characteristic of the genre, her powerful presence is embodied through POV shots that structure the gaze of the audience.[11]

Apparently, *Harano Sur* is a domestic melodrama of a subordinate woman (Roma) winning over her boss's heart. It does not have the usual patriarchal chores of subordinating a woman. In fact, the film focuses and revolves around its female protagonist. Roma, as a lady doctor, represents the emergence of educated and enlightened Bengali woman of the post-Independence decade. The familial spheres are significantly excluded in order to develop Roma's affirmative action in rescuing Alok from the asylum. In this sense, this is quite symptomatic of the spirit of the post-Independence period where an emergence of female agency is indicated. However, in the final resolution, the subordinate position is being reworked with the hero regaining his memory. That is, the patriarchal matrix is *remodelled*, even though the female subjectivity is allowed to intervene in this remoulding.[12]

Rajlakshmi O Sreekanto

Sarat Chandra (1876–1938) is one of the greatest littérateurs India has produced. His works have been translated into various languages. He poured into his novels and stories the varied experience he had gathered in different parts of India and Burma. The most remarkable qualities of Sarat Chandra's art are directness and a sense of intimacy. His descriptions of rural life, of human joy and suffering are drawn from first-hand knowledge. He excelled in the depiction of the plight of the downtrodden and the intricate feelings and emotions of women. He was a critique of contemporary society when it did not agree with his own ideas.

Sarat Chandra's works have a sense of timelessness, a universality that makes them both cinema-friendly and topical for film-makers. The director's fascination for this author never seems to cease. This excludes Satyajit Ray who never made any film adapted from Sarat Chandra's works and preferred to stick to Bibhuti Bhushan Bandyopadhyay and Tagore and even a telefilm adapted from a short story by Munshi Premchand. If one were to hazard a guess, it could be perhaps because works like *Pather Panchali*, based on Bandyopadhyay's novel, or *Charulata*, based on Tagore, were full of descriptive, visual details that almost read like a film script as Ray reportedly said many times in interviews specially with reference to *Pather Panchali*. But neither did the other two of the triumvirate—Mrinal Sen and Ritwik Ghatak. Tapan Sinha, a prolific and commercially successful film-maker, also never made a film adapted from the works of Sarat Chandra Chattopadhyay.

The audience never fails to be trapped by the transient hypnosis Sarat Chandra's works engender. The social and domestic ambience in his novels may belong to days long past, but the story interest, the romance of his characters, the fluid and dramatic changes in their inter-relationships hold the reader and the audience in a trance, never mind any question of credibility or logic they might raise. Among novels drawn from his personal experiences are *Sreekanto*, in four parts (1917, 1918, 1927 and 1933), *Charitraheen* (1917), *Biraj Bou* (1914) and *Palli Samaj* (1916). Every single one of these novels has been made into films, some of them more than once, in more than one Indian language. There are fourteen celluloid versions of *Devdas*, written in 1901 but published in serialized form only in

1917. The celluloid versions of *Devdas* cover a span of seventy-four years, from 1928 to 2002.

Rajlakshmi O Sreekanto is one of four parts of *Sreekanto* that features his complex relationship with the beautiful Rajlakshmi. Who is Sreekanto? Is he the author Sarat Chandra's alter ego? Or is he a fictionalized character who portrays, in bits and pieces, slices from the author's own life? He is, perhaps, a metaphorical, idealistic creation like *The Rainmaker* (1956),[13] who represents the dream of every man's wish to break away from worldly ties and step out into the open world in an onward journey, into an exploration of an alternate way of life. Or, perhaps, an endless quest to find out what life and love really mean. Looking back in retrospect at a character created in 1917, placed in a time setting at around 1910, from a vantage point in 1958 when the film was made, one may safely and with some licence take the liberty of labelling him the quintessential escapist who uses his wanderlust as a political strategy to keep away from emotional and social commitments of any kind—love, marriage, children, friends—and avoids getting attached to anyone or anything.

Sreekanto is an aimless wanderer who belongs to a respectable family, is educated, but does not do anything for a living. Dr Satya Bose, a noted doctor in his village, understands him and his beliefs and tries to drill some sense in him, in vain. On invitation from his very rich school friend Mahendra Rao, he joins him and his friends in a hunting expedition into the jungles. Mahendra has all the vices a landlord's son is habituated to, which results in less hunting and more of drinking, and listening to the songs of Pyaribai, a beautiful courtesan settled in Patna. Pyaribai summons Sreekanto to her tent and tells him things about him that surprise him no end. How does she know so much about him? After some hesitation, Pyaribai reveals that she is his childhood mate, Rajlakshmi—Lakshmi to him—the constant victim of his bullying ways. Sreekanto is not happy with the way her life has turned out and he says she could have had a better life had she chosen to live a normal life of marriage and children. She says that not every girl has a choice, and one is often forced into a life, which, under different circumstances, would have been different.

After some intercutting into Sreekanto's adventures such as joining a bunch of wandering sadhus, his foraying into a village emptying out fast because of a smallpox epidemic, the story turns back to another meeting between Pyaribai and Sreekanto when a very sick Sreekanto is brought to her door at Patna and she nurses him back to health. When Sreekanto goes back to Dr Bose's neighbourhood, he is haunted by memories of Lakshmi all the time and they have made him pensive, philosophical and introspective. He again sets out for Patna to meet Lakshmi, and listens as she tells him what brought about her metamorphosis from Rajlakshmi to Pyaribai. It is one of the saddest stories Sreekanto has ever heard.

Before leaving for Burma, he gives her a letter sent by his late mother to her childhood friend Gangajal, promising that her son would marry her daughter Tenpi. But when the mother hears that he does not do anything for a living, she refuses to marry her daughter to him. She informs Lakshmi that he will never marry Tenpi because after meeting his Lakshmi, it would not be possible for him to marry any other woman. Nevertheless, he refuses to stay back and cancel his trip to Burma. He also requests Lakshmi to send Tenpi's parents, who are in dire straits, a sum of Rs 1,000 to help them tide over their problems. He leaves for Burma, promising Lakshmi that he will never marry another woman and will come back some day. Lakshmi knows that neither of these will happen, yet lives in the hope that perhaps, some day, it will. The film ends on this note of hope and hopelessness.

The narrative is generously sprinkled with several adventures of Sreekanto such as his spending the night at the crematorium near the hunting site, against the advice of Mahendra, his friends and Rajlakshmi. Rajlakshmi's servant finds him and brings him back but he goes there again. Everyone is amazed at his courage and his disbelief in ghosts. But as one looks back, one discovers that the drama, the story, its strength and its power rest in the character and life of Rajlakshmi.

Rajlakshmi is shown growing from girlhood to adolescence to adulthood. A pretty little girl portrays the child Rajlakshmi who is a passive witness of things happening around her, to her mother and to her older sister, and can hardly understand what and why, much less do anything about it. Their kulin Brahmin[14] father abandons his wife and two daughters to remarry and is never heard of ever again.[15] They are forced to take shelter in their maternal uncle's home. But he, too, is desperately poor, has four daughters of his own, and is also very sick. His wife forces him to get the sister's two girls married to a very old kulin Brahmin who is a cook by profession, is married, and has children. He is promised a dowry of Rs 101 by the uncle but when the money falls short by Rs 25, the old man leaves in a huff, leaving the two little girls half married. The older sister commits suicide and Rajlakshmi and her mother are thrown out and forced to work as maids in people's homes.

Sen as the adolescent and adult Rajlakshmi and Pyaribai traverses the entire gamut of histrionics an actress can revel in and take up as a challenge. Rajlakshmi is trapped by her poverty on one hand and her beauty on the other. From a beautiful young girl trying desperately to ward off the unscrupulous attentions of evil-minded employers, she is devastated when her poverty forces her to go begging from door to door, and then by the fact that her own mother sells her to a local raja for money. Rajlakshmi runs away and finds shelter in the home of a famous courtesan, Motibai, who takes kindly to her, gets her trained in music by her father and teaches her dancing.

Sen was a very incompetent dancer with two left feet. But the awkward movements she demonstrates during the training suit the character very well. Abandoned by her own father, thrown out by her uncle, half-married to an old Brahmin, sexually harassed by employers and sold off by her own mother, Rajlakshmi's journey is travelled by Suchitra Sen beautifully, tinged with just the right touch of melodrama it demands. She grows convincingly from a sixteen-year-old teenager whose rags cannot hide her natural beauty to the bejewelled, zardozi-wearing courtesan in her mid-twenties still nurturing memories of her first love. At one point, her young foster son tells Sreekanto that she pays for the education of eight destitute girls and also wishes to enter into more philanthropic activities but Brahmins and other elders stop her because of her disrepute and her socially ostracized position.

Beneath the veneer of the zardozi costume of ghagra, chunni and melodious thumris lies the Rajlakshmi who can never forget her first love—Sreekanto. Sen almost plays a dual role within the single character. She dresses up for her mujras and mehfils much less than she slips into the garb of a traditional Bengali housewife with a bindi, bangles and a bunch of keys knotted to the end of her sari. The two personas are distinct in appearance, but there is no difference beneath the 'look'. Gyan Prakash Ghosh's music, both as the background score and in the songs, enriches the tapestry of the film's text. In one scene in the hall where Pyaribai performs, there is no dialogue and the soundtrack is flush with melodies from a harmonium. In another scene, Rajlakshmi, rescued by Motibai, reclines on a bed and wonders, 'I really do not know what I am—am I an unmarried maiden? Or, am I a married woman or am I a widow?'

Pyaribai/Rajlakshmi's interactions with Sreekanto, both now adults, are filled with innuendo, some bit of teasing and intrigue on her part to which Sreekanto is more confused than happy because he really does not recognize her until she tells him who she is. He mistakes her behaviour as part of the seductive manner she is expected to assume as a baiji. This is a telling comment on the sustained value of love of a little girl for a boy who only bullied her and made her cry. The same boy as a grown-up man with his strong secular ideology and adventurous lifestyle does not even remember her existence! She expresses her love by kneeling down to touch his feet, silently asking for his blessings because their relationship is fractured by the differences in their social status. It is also fractured by the strong gender bias that does not forgive a woman for 'falling' from grace but never questions a man who shirks responsibility and, therefore, is guilty of committing the same mistake. They cannot hold each other close or hug or much less, kiss.

Rajlakshmi O Sreekanto is a story of journeys and a running train with the sound of its wheels in friction with the tracks, the engine forging ahead, functions like a metaphor for the journeys. Though Sarat Chandra's four-part magnum opus is understood and read as a series of uncertain, unplanned and strange journeys of adventure by Sreekanto, the protagonist, one discovers that it is perhaps, much more the charting of several journeys of Rajlakshmi whose identity changes by force of circumstances and destiny but who sustains the integrity and honesty of her character, and her love for Sreekanto that she carries within.

Uttam Kumar and Suchitra Sen were paired together in four Sarat Chandra novels—*Rajlakshmi O Sreekanto*, *Chandranath*, *Grihadaha* (1967) and *Kamallata* (1969). Ranked on a grade of one to ten, *Rajlakshmi O Sreekanto* would certainly run away with seven on ten in terms of archival value and audience popularity.

Saptapadi

Tarasankar Bandyopadhyay (1898–1971) was one of the most prolific, creative and versatile authors of post-Tagorean Bengali literature. He wrote sixty-five novels, fifty-three short story collections, four books of essays, four autobiographies and two travelogues. During his lifetime, he received the Rabindra Puraskar, the Sahitya Akademi Award, the Padma Bhushan and the country's highest literary excellence award—the Jnanpeeth.

Tarasankar steeped himself in active politics and social welfare but his writing did not suffer as a result of it. He continued to write editorials, poetry and fiction in a journal called *Purnima*. But his thirst remained unquenched. The light arrived at the end of a dark tunnel quite by accident. Taking rest after a Congress party meeting, Tarasankar chanced upon a tattered and torn copy of *Kali Kolom*, a magazine, and read two short stories by two different writers that left him shaken and fascinated at the same time. The first story was 'Ponoghat Periye' by Premendra Mitra, and the second was a story written by Sailajananda Mukhopadhyay. About the second story, he wrote, 'Strange, how a district like Birbhum can take shape through words held at the point of a pen's nib.'[16]

These two stories gave direction to his writing. He brought new life to writing with his choice of subject—the villages and small hamlets in Bengal peopled by primitive tribes like the Santhals and other lesser known, ignored and marginalized adivasis who lived beyond the periphery of the mainstream, spoke a different language, practised unique lifestyles and followed different ideologies of life. They were also the people who remained marginalized by the literary intellectuals of Bengal. As he said himself, 'It is as if I picked up a golden wand that woke numb men and women up and made them bloom like flowers.'[17]

With his deep, objective and perceptive abilities, Tarasankar saw men and women's potential to commit crime, tackle diseases of the mind and the body, the futile arrogance and the declining value of the zamindars—a class of which he himself was a member—and the ignorance and superstitions that so-called high-caste people were steeped in. Alongside, he wrote about the primitive gypsies, magicians, boatmen, fishermen, idol makers, indigenous decorators, carpenters, ironsmiths, snake charmers, and doms (who cremated the dead). Though it was *Kallol* that triggered the real writer in him, Tarasankar was never a part of the group of writers who identified themselves with *Kallol* and created the *Kallol Jug*—the era of *Kallol*—because he did not believe in revolt and the writers in *Kallol* believed in intellectual and social revolt expressed through their writings.

From within this inner realization were born short stories and novels that became the subject of many films, both Hindi and Bengali. Some of them like *Saptapadi* became box-office hits. Satyajit Ray made two outstanding films based on Tarasankar's fiction. One was *Jalsaghar* (1958), a portrayal of a zamindar who desperately clings to his lost pride by organizing a musical recital he can hardly afford in a state of absolute penury. The other was *Abhijan* (1962) that narrates the story of the contradictions in the character of Narsingh, an arrogant and hot-tempered taxi driver who drives a 1930 Chrysler, and whose permit is taken away by the police. He is forced to take shelter in a small town on the border of Bengal and Bihar. His 'journey' is physical, geographical, metaphorical and ideological because it involves rescuing a young woman, Gulabi, held captive by his new boss, the evil Sukhanram. Tapan Sinha directed *Hansuli Banker Upakatha* (1962). Set in 1941, the story explores life in rural Bengal and goes deep into the realities of the zamindari system that is held responsible for abuse of power, marginalization and oppression of the weak and the poor, and the perpetuation of inequalities, not realizing the changes taking place in social perceptions among the oppressed.

Other notable films based on his works include *Nagini Kanyar Kahini* (1958), the Hindi film *Devar* (1966), adapted from the short novel *Naa, Bedeni* (2011), *Arogya Niketan* (1969), *Kabi* (1949) also made in Hindi as *Kavi* (1954), *Bandini Kamala* (1982), *Ganadevata* (1978), *Bipasha* (1962), Rituparno Ghosh's *Antarmahal* (2005) adapted from his short story 'Protima', and many others. *Saptapadi*, set against the backdrop of the Second World War, is perhaps the biggest hit of them all. It narrates a very cinema-friendly story that found appeal with the mass audience.

The reverend Krishnendu (Uttam Kumar) runs a military hospital in Bankura. A drunken Anglo-Indian woman soldier is brought to him for treatment and he recognizes her as his former love, Rina Brown (Suchitra Sen). The two of them were fellow medical students who initially clashed with each other but fell in love following a stage performance of *Othello* where Krishnendu played Othello to Rina's Desdemona. Rina's father agrees to the match providing Krishnendu converts to Christianity. Rina does not want him to change his religion but Krishnendu is willing to do anything for her. His father, a staunch, orthodox Brahmin (Chhabi Biswas) visits Rina and tells her he will never accept this marriage and pleads with Rina to let Krishnendu, his only son, go.

Rina sacrifices her love even as Krishnendu converts to Christianity. She says she cannot marry him because she has lost respect for a man who can give up his religion so easily! It is an excuse she hides behind and it changes both their lives forever. In response, Krishnendu, now a different man, says, 'I believe in only one religion—the religion of mankind. There is no difference between a temple or a church in that religion.' During an argument with her British father, Rina discovers that she is the illegitimate daughter of her maid (Chhaya Devi) whom her father had impregnated but did not marry. She becomes an alcoholic and joins the army as a nurse with the Red Cross. Back in the present, when Rina realizes the doctor who treated her is Krishnendu, she tries to kill herself. Ultimately, the lovers are united in the midst of war.

Saptapadi has been chosen here for analysis for several reasons: to begin with, the story is adapted from Jnanpeeth award-winning author Tarasankar Bandyopadhyay's novel of the same name; its beautiful storyline of love discovered and lost and united again is structured within a carefully designed screenplay, against the backdrop of atheism versus belief; the small scene from Shakespeare's *Othello* that highlights the racial and caste-centric links to the tragic love story; the wonderful musical score and song picturisations; the brilliant lighting and camerawork by director Ajoy Kar; the touch of conversion from Hinduism to Christianity by the hero; and finally, the magic of romance spelt out graphically on screen by Uttam Kumar and Suchitra Sen.

Saptapadi was released just after Durga Puja, on 20 October 1961. It ran without a break for fifteen long weeks, drawing a full house in each show, bringing back four times the money invested in it. The film was produced by Uttam Kumar and was the twenty-third film in which Suchitra and Uttam were paired as star-crossed lovers. The original story did not have a happy ending. In the celluloid representation, however, for commercial reasons, a happy ending was concocted and according to reports, Bandyopadhyay did not complain.

In an opinion poll by a noted Bengali film fortnightly *Anandalok* from the ABP Group of Publications around a decade ago, asking contemporary actresses to name their dream role, every actress unequivocally and firmly said that they would love to play the character of Rina Brown in *Saptapadi*. If an opinion poll were to be taken today, the response may not be any different. Ajoy Kar, who had already directed Uttam-Suchitra in *Harano Sur*, another unforgettable film and a thumping hit, made the right choice by featuring Uttam Kumar as Krishnendu Mukherjee and Suchitra Sen as Rina Brown in the film. The entire film is focussed on these two characters and the others exist to provide the conflict—Rina's British father and Bengali mother, Krishnendu's strict, religious, Hindu Brahmin father and Rina's Anglo-Indian boyfriend, Clayton. But the characterizations are fleshed out even through the brief cameos.

There is a dramatized recreation of the last scene from William Shakespeare's *Othello,* where the voices of Othello and Desdemona were dubbed by Utpal Dutt and Jennifer Kapoor. Desdemona dies in the play. But Rina rises phoenix-like, saved by Krishnendu and his deep love for her in the film's climax. This intertextuality—use of another text within the main text—a prominent feature of post-modernism, was used when Indians did not even know of the term. This, too, is a high point of the film.

The story carried as many dramatic elements as it possibly could. But these did not even once appear to be forced impositions. These ingredients fit neatly into the commercial mould, yet, Ajoy Kar's treatment, approach and style married to lovely music by Hemanta Mukhopadhyay and brilliant cinematography, also by Ajoy Kar, makes this a classic and perhaps a masterpiece of the time when it was released.

Saptapadi also marked the beginning of a break in the Suchitra-Uttam rapport during the shooting of the film. Halfway through the shoot, Suchitra Sen suddenly announced that she would not work in the film any more. Reports say that the conflict began on the issue of priority of names of actors appearing in the credits. Suchitra Sen wanted her name to appear above Uttam Kumar's. The real reason remains unknown and it might be gauged that Suchitra felt that she was not receiving due scope in films where she was paired with Uttam Kumar. Uttam Kumar, also the producer, persuaded her. The divide widened so much that in the post-*Saptapadi* films, the magic seemed to be on the decline and they stopped working together for several years. When they came back, the magic was still there but its colour, sound and chemistry had somewhat faded.

Suchitra Sen, for the only time in her career, portrayed an Anglo-Indian woman named Rina Brown. The term 'Anglo-Indian' originally referred to British 'colonials' residing in India. The colonial ideology in British India was built on the cultural meanings of two fundamental categories of institutional discrimination in Britain—sex and age. In the imperial mindset, Indian men were just not men enough. To free themselves of this contemptuous image, they had to adopt the values of the dominant culture's view of manliness—aggression, achievement, control, competition and power. Their prolonged stay in the country resulted in the evolution of a race of people born to British fathers and Indian mothers, who called themselves Anglo-Indians. In course of time, Eurasians of every description came to be known as Anglo-Indians. Since they intermarried freely with each other, they were soon indistinguishable, with entire families bearing British, French, Portuguese and Dutch surnames. The common denominator was that they all had one Indian parent. The European half contributed a different facet to this cultural melting pot. The 'Anglo-Indians' shared many of the characteristics that set them apart from their European and Indian parents. They did not fit comfortably either into Indian or in European society and thus, began their lives with an identity crisis they found difficult to either resolve or accept with grace.

Rina Brown is no exception. Her father is British and his British snobbery spills over into the daughter's character who is snobbish, arrogant and bears an attitude that looks down on Bengali-Hindu boys of the medical college where she is studying. Like most Anglo-Indians, she is proud to be of British descent and has no idea of who her mother is. Her snobbery and arrogance are stripped off in one instant when the Hindu boy Krishnendu, whom she is abuses by calling him names, tops the list at the medical finals. The second hit comes when he played Othello to perfection in excellent English diction. Finally, her father points out the elderly ayah who has brought her up as her biological mother. Her world crashes around her. The fact that Mr Brown, despite his nose-in-the-air snobbish attitude towards 'native' Indians, does not object to his daughter's wanting to marry Krishnendu, a Hindu-Bengali Brahmin, reveals to Rina that her father treats her like a native and not like a Briton. He kills the ayah—Rina's mother—in cold blood, and Rina's life changes forever.

For the first time in her entire career, for a major part of the film, Suchitra Sen dresses up like an Anglo-Indian girl, thoroughly westernized, her conversations dotted with English. She wears Western dresses, but after she falls in love with Krishnendu, though he neither objects to her way of dressing nor suggests she change it, Rina switches over to the sari. Years later, she is seen wearing her Red Cross nurse's uniform, a ghost of her former self, drunk, groggy and unaware of her surroundings. Her life is a dramatic story filled with twists and turns not only of destiny, but also circumstantial, over which she helplessly finds she has no control. While Krishnendu, following his conversion to Christianity, copes positively with the tragedy in his love life, Rina cannot. She joins the Red Cross to tend to soldiers injured during the war but along the way, loses herself in a life of alcohol abuse and, through hints she throws across sexual permissiveness. She is forever in an inebriated state but later, with Krishnendu and his nurse's help, she becomes aware of her state of being. That is perhaps a bigger shock for her than when she rejected Krishnendu under false pretences to shield his father.

In this sense, Rina Brown defines a radical departure from the stereotypical image of the ideal Indian woman who lives a virtuous life. She has resigned herself to this life of ruin and destruction, and when hope finally arrives in the shape of Krishnendu's letter from his late father advising him to marry Rina who is a very good girl, she almost does not believe it. The closing shot hints at an open ending—Krishnendu carrying Rina in his arms and walking away from the camera, silhouetted figures captured as if fading away into the horizon. It is a unique perspective on the happily-ever-after theory.

Rina Brown was perhaps one of the most challenging roles of Sen's career, a risk the producers, the director and the entire team, including Suchitra Sen herself, had taken as it was a radical departure from her accepted and popular screen image of a submissive Bengali girl wearing a sari and supporting her hero either as a conventional young woman or as a very modern and sophisticated young woman in love. The risk was well taken because *Saptapadi* turned out to be one of the biggest box-office hits in Bengali cinema for all time. Suchitra Sen lived up to the faith her producer Uttam Kumar and director Ajoy Kar had placed in her.

The song '*Ei path jodi naa shesh hoy*'—shot on a stationary motor cycle, the speed conveyed through back projection, with Sen's hair flying against standing fans in the studio floor on either side—has been immortalized. Clips from the sequence have been used in later films by umpteen Bengali filmmakers. One example is Subroto Sen who used a clip in his maiden film *Ek Je Aachey Kanya* (2001). The heroine in the film lip syncs only to the refrain *lal la la la* and does not lip-sync the main song synced by Krishnendu, yet it enhances and enriches the picturization beautifully, adding to its romantic, lyrical and sensual quality. The songs '*On the merry go round let us ride and roll*' and the well-known devotional song '*Eibar Kali tomai khabo*' are choreographed very well to demonstrate a clash of cultures of the Anglo-Indians (them) versus the Bengalis (us) with, of course, the Bengalis 'winning'. Sen is superb in this scene, beginning with great confidence but gradually losing it with the comic and sarcastic response she meets from her opponent Krishnendu.

Nabaraag (1971)

Nabaraag is one of the most memorable post-Partition representations of women, featuring Suchitra Sen and Uttam Kumar. Director Bijoy Bose was a relatively low-profile film-maker who directed two films starring Suchitra Sen, namely *Nabaraag* and *Fariyaad*. The former paired her with Uttam Kumar whereas the latter featured Utpal Dutt. Both films were released in the same year and though *Nabaraag* is one of the last films featuring the golden couple, it did not do as well at the box office as their other films. Bijoy Bose's contribution to Bengali cinema is commendable especially with reference to films he worked on with Uttam Kumar in the lead. He made films between the 1950s and the '80s. Two of his directorial films *Arogya Niketan* (1969) and *Raja Rammohan* (1965), the latter being a biographical feature on Raja Rammohan Roy, won the National Award for the Best Bengali Feature film. *Bhagini Nivedita* (1962), a biopic on Sister Nivedita, the devoted disciple of Swami Vivekananda, won the President's Gold Medal at the National Awards in 1961. One of his biggest hits in the post Uttam-Suchitra era was *Shaheb* (1981), starring Tapas Pal in the lead. It was later remade in Hindi by Anil Ganguly, starring Anil Kapoor, and though it featured one of the star's best performances, it was not half as successful as the Bengali original.

Based on a story by Ashutosh Mukherjee, *Nabaraag* runs along two parallel lines. One concerns the present that creates a dramatic situation within an affluent family when the son of the couple goes missing and is suspected to have been kidnapped. Who has kidnapped the child, Raja, and why? The parents, Bipul Bagchi and his beautiful wife, Rina, already in conflict over differences about the way Raja is being brought up, are devastated. Bagchi is the owner and proprietor of Bagchi Industries and spoils his son because he considers the boy the sole heir of the huge wealth he has amassed.

Rina, however, thinks differently, but the spoilt Raja does not care about his mother's discipline.

Why is there this difference of opinion between the husband and wife? The second subplot happens in the past. The film goes into a flashback into a village in Bengal, peopled by destitute families who are refugees after the Partition, and are steeped in poverty. A small family comprises a grandfather committed to his Sanskrit chants and prayers and a beautiful teenaged granddaughter called Narayani, who is a naughty, tomboyish girl unaware of the ways of the world, but is forced by her circumstances to take up a job as a housemaid in a wealthy family. Her employers' modern daughter takes her to watch a football match one day. But Narayani, instead of enjoying the game, is very disturbed by the noise and the action. The president of one of the two clubs who are playing the match comes and takes a seat besides her and is amused at this pretty girl's naïveté. Attracted to her beauty and her innocence, Bagchi marries her and brings her to Kolkata. Over time, Narayani becomes Rina—modern, fashionable, sophisticated, confident and arrogant—and Narayani is lost to time.

It is Rina who—worried and anxious about her Raja's future whose whims his father gives in to even if it means bringing great harm to the workers in his father's factory—arranges the abduction of her own son and places him in the hands of Nanda-da, her mentor in the village who runs a school for orphaned, poor and destitute children. When Bagchi learns the truth, he is shocked and looks at Rina's attitude as a great betrayal of trust. Later, wisdom dawns on him, he realizes that it is a mother's deep concern that has driven Rina to take custody of her son and try to bring him up with deeper and long-lasting values.

Nabaraag is a rare film that opens with Suchitra and Uttam already a married couple with a young son, living in Kolkata in affluence, and socializing with the cream of society. This film stands apart from most of Suchitra Sen and Uttam Kumar films in the sense that the character Suchitra plays is not only very complex but also runs along parallel lines that demands her to delineate two roles within one. Narayani becomes Rina and though this 'becoming' is not fleshed out in detail, it brings out the multifaceted potential inherent in Suchitra Sen, the actress, to live up to the demands of two roles within one. The film probably did not do well at the box office because the Uttam-Suchitra pairing had jaded somewhat as both were ageing. The film also lacked the magic of romance their earlier films revelled in so beautifully. But it was a well-directed and well-crafted film.

The way in which the forty-year-old Suchitra Sen slips seamlessly into the sprightly, naughty and teenaged prankster Narayani is incredible. She wears her old rag-of-a-sari anyhow, hitched up to her ankles, her long hair left loose and hanging wildly around her, difficult to rein in. She thrives in this naughty tomboyish role but slips equally beautifully into the dutiful responsibility of working as a maid in an upper-middle-class home. The only person who can somewhat control her is Nanda-da, a generous-minded but poor man who runs a school for poor children. They are recent migrants from East Pakistan and this comes across in Narayani's East Pakistani Bengali dialect. The camera captures her mainly in mid-shots and long shots with a rare close-up of the face, possibly to avoid signs of ageing that might have been revealed in tight close-ups.

Suchitra excels with her body language—confident at home, in the fields, in the village pond, but hesitant and unsure at the football ground, not knowing how to sit on a chair and therefore often lifting up her feet. Yet, she makes it obvious that she does not quite care for the extra attention her employer's relative pays her. The physical backdrop of the village, her old grandfather busy with his pujas and mantras, and the general ambience of the place adds to the credibility of her performance as do the performances of her supporting actors in this phase, namely Bikas Roy as Nanda-da, Bijon Bhattacharya as Narayani's grandfather and the little boy she does not allow to do his homework.

Rina comes across almost as a magical transformation from Narayani. It is difficult to imagine that the two are actually the same woman. She is bejewelled, overly made-up, decked up in very expensive saris or an elegant, expensive nightie when she retires to her bedroom at night, creams away the make-up and prepares to go to bed but hardly, if ever, smiles. Her smiles, reserved for parties and special occasions, are like cut-and-paste toothpaste ads that are fake and shallow. The realization that she is losing her grip over her own child disturbs her constantly but she does not know what to do about it. She mopes and cries when alone, driving the little boy even farther away. The script keeps the reality of the abduction a secret and this adds to the mystery. Suchitra Sen as Rina wears a face that is almost like a mask, caked in heavy make-up, bold eyeliner, etc., and her expressions remain almost frozen in a neck held upright, head held high, with her eyes doing the talking more than the dialogues.

Suchitra Sen looks natural, spontaneous and very young as Narayani while as Rina, as if by design, she appears and even acts like a mask of a woman than a real one. Finally, there is a blending of Narayani and Rina that heightens the exaggerated melodrama of the climax. As Rina, however, Suchitra Sen's incredible beauty, camera friendliness and grace are intact. Though outwardly she remains the sophisticated Rina, officiating at parties and entertaining her husband's clients at his bidding, there is a constant conflict within that places her in a dilemma about what will happen to her son who is learning to value material wealth much more than human life. This conflict comes across very well through Sen's acting.

Two very significantly placed and positioned Tagore songs provide the backdrop for her transformation from Narayani to Rina in principle but not in personality or lifestyle. The first, '*Tui phele eshechish kaare mon mon re amaar*', is sung at a party, by a guest, and functions like an emotional trigger within her that reminds her of the past she has all but forgotten. The second song, '*Ami jene shune beesh korechi paan*', arouses within her moments of self-realization and drive her into what she considers to be the right action.

But the magic one witnessed in films like *Harano Sur*, *Saptapadi* and *Agniparikshа* is absent in *Nabaraag*. Uttam Kumar and Suchitra Sen as Bipul and Rina, respectively, do not look comfortable with each other on screen; this works very well for the demands made by the script for the on-screen husband and wife. The couple's relationship presents an emotional gap between them that is faked for the public domain but comes into its own in the privacy of their home. The earlier juxtaposition of the fashionable, confident and arrogant Bipul against the naïve, very young and rustic Narayani when they come across each other for the first time in the football match disappears when Narayani becomes Rina. But one is left with nagging questions—did Narayani succeed in 'becoming' Rina? Was she happier as Rina than she was as Narayani, with poverty and hunger a constant reality of her life? After the 'rescue' of little Raja—who, with his father's approval, is to be educated at Nanda-da's institution—does the emotional vacuum between Bipul and Rina get bridged? The masculinity of Uttam Kumar as Bipul is beautifully matched with Suchitra Sen's femininity. But one must concede that though Bipul's character has slightly negative shades, it is essentially one-dimensional and flat till the son goes missing, but becomes dynamic when he goes crazy trying to find out who has kidnapped the boy and how he will find him. Narayani/Rina's character, on the other hand, has several layers and dimensions which often merge to create confusion and then to clear it.

Bipul says once, soon after marriage, that he did not want to marry a plastic doll. But that is precisely what Narayani becomes—a plastic doll he did not wish for but unwittingly creates when Narayani becomes Rina. A white teacher is appointed to teach her to dance and speak English with correct enunciation and table manners, too, while Rina herself takes to drinking when depressed. These are contradictions within the script that somewhat weaken the storyline, but Suchitra manages to hold up the values Narayani was brought up with and Rina forgot for a while.

CONCLUSION

Analysing these films featuring Suchitra Sen and Uttam Kumar reveals an interesting aspect: though Uttam Kumar dominated each film with his magnificient screen presence and his exceptional talent which impacted deeply the Bengali-speaking audience, a deeper probe shows that in almost all these films, the character portrayed by Suchitra Sen was more multi-layered and challenging than the character portrayed by Uttam Kumar. It is true that perhaps Uttam Kumar was the more gifted, hard-working and talented between the two. But it is also true that this had to do with the choice of Suchitra Sen mainly for her exquisite beauty, her femininity and glamour. Perhaps this geared the actress towards concentrating more on her screen presence and attracting the audience through her charisma than on character portrayal. Most of the directors who cast them together were confident about the distinct charismatic qualities of the two actors.

Besides, within the patriarchal mode of performance within cinema, it is understandable that it is the hero who, both off-screen and on-screen, gets the maximum attention and scope in terms of the script. This is because the audience is also conditioned by patriarchy and patriarchal values. Uttam Kumar, the hero, is almost worshipped by the audience in general and his fans in particular. Suchitra Sen, the heroine, on the other hand, is a dream to be cherished, nurtured, fantasized about and desired—emotionally and physically aspired for, knowing fully well that she is a dream that will never flesh out in reality. While the women fell in love with Uttam Kumar, they were not jealous of Suchitra Sen but tried to imitate her hairstyle, her saris and her jewellery without really succeeding because Sen had created an exclusive niche persona that did not spur imitations even in real life.

Hindi feature films featuring Raj Kapoor and Nargis in the romantic lead are an illustration in point. So long as Nargis was paired with Raj Kapoor, though her characterizations were well-fleshed out, it was Raj Kapoor who dominated the scenario while back-lighting, effective close-ups and the halo effect enhanced Nargis's beauty and screen image shot in black-and-white. But after she left the RK banner, she finally found her bearings as an actress in films like *Pardesi* (1957), *Miss India* (1957), *Laajwanti* (1958), *Ghar Sansar* (1960) and her two major triumphs *Mother India* (1957) and *Raat Aur Din* (1967), the latter bringing her the Best Actress Award (1968) at the National Awards. Her performance in *Mother India* as a rural woman whose husband abandons her and the family while she is pregnant and already has three children was unbelievably powerful. Her character grows very old during the course of the film. From a newly married bride to a very old dowager, she becomes the most respected person in the village, a role in contrast with every other role she had done in a RK banner film.

Suchitra Sen, like Nargis and Madhubala, was, for a major part of her career, an unwitting victim of her beauty, her grace and her essential femininity that played down her potential capabilities as an actress. With her feminine grace, she perfectly complimented the masculinity of Uttam Kumar and this is another reason for the tremendous success of their screen romance. Uttam Kumar redefined the concept of masculinity that, placed in perspective, merges into the Bengali bhadralok identity that found favour with his audience—both male and female.

These films, chosen from the thirty-two in which they were paired, span nearly two decades of romancing, while covering completely different genres with romance as the common thread running through all. The films offer an insight into the multi-layered romance this celluloid couple brought alive on the screen. They represent different modes of melodrama in different ways. They are neatly packaged for commercial success, yet have stood the test of time. They lead one to think that if these films had national and international exposure at the time they were made, they would also have transcended the borders of culture, geography, language and beliefs. These films speak the universal language of love and romance, keeping away from sexual innuendo, and yet are extremely sensual in the way the romance is orchestrated, choreographed and positioned within the narrative, with the technical support of outstanding black-and-white cinematography, editing, art direction and extremely haunting music so much that audiences across the world will identify with the emotions that come across in these films even today.

3

FROM STAR TO ACTRESS: THE METAMORPHOSIS

INTRODUCTION

This chapter explores how the image of a star, essentially female and beautiful, can impinge upon and restrict the exploration of her potential as an actress. When a star becomes successful on screen more as a partner in a box-office-guaranteed pairing game, there is an unwritten, unarticulated rule that stereotypes the female partner in similar roles with the same hero in a series of films. Film-makers rarely approach the female star in the pair to act in films where the male partner is not featured. Sometimes, if the pair is involved in a relationship, the male partner does not allow the female to act in films he is a not a part of. It may also be the case that the lady herself declines offers from 'outside' with other heroes lest it disturbs the harmony of her relationship with her successfully paired hero. Was Suchitra Sen a victim of this hit pairing that placed her firmly within her glamorous and sophisticated image in films with Uttam Kumar? Or was she really not talented enough to pull the masses solely with her performing skills? Did film-makers bank more on her beauty than try to explore the limits of her histrionic talent? Let us take a closer look.

In his in-depth analysis in *Stars*, Richard Dyer raised questions about and around the concept of stardom focusing on the analysis of stars within representation and ideology. He underscored the relationship between stardom, star image and discourses of individualism.[1]

It would be appropriate—in determining whether Suchitra Sen became famous only because her films with Uttam Kumar became box-office hits and the buzzword in every Bengali family of the time, or, whether she could also attain recognition and affirmation of her talent without Uttam Kumar—to place Suchitra Sen in perspective against three actresses of Hindi cinema whose stardom still raises questions about their beauty versus their talent: Nargis, Madhubala and Meena Kumari. A deeper look into a more successful predecessor of Suchitra Sen within Bengali cinema is Kanan Devi, who rose above her questionable, ghettoized roots and reached beyond her screen charisma when she stepped into directing and producing films, with one of her films going on to win two National Awards. She won the Dadasaheb Phalke Award which, many years later, Suchitra Sen refused because it necessitated her physical presence at the awards ceremony and she did not wish to violate her decision not to disturb her absolute privacy.

Looked at from this perspective, in the matter of beautiful women in the synthetic world of cinema, their beauty often stands in the way of an exploration of their potential talent, much of which might not have come to surface when they are pitted against men who dominate the screenplay, the story and the film as well as the film industry. It is a world that is almost entirely patriarchal. This chapter will focus on some films where Suchitra Sen was chosen for stories with the female protagonist dominating the show. If she had a romantic interest, it was not Uttam Kumar.

The power and command of Suchitra Sen as an actress in films that did not cast her opposite matinee idol Uttam Kumar have been analysed through some significant films like *Deep Jele Jai*, directed by Asit Sen; *Hospital*, directed by Sushil Majumdar; and *Saat*

Paake Bandha and *Datta*, both directed by Ajoy Kar. In the context of the culture at large at the time of her dominance of the Bengali cinema, the screen image of Suchitra Sen, the storylines and her characterization display different layers of gender representation. The stereotyping, if at all it can be called so, of Suchitra Sen in the films in which she paired with Uttam Kumar, was confined to her looks, her appearance and her subdued roles, but there was no stereotyping in terms of characterization.

WHO IS A 'STAR'?

Richard Dyer in his *Stars* proposes that 'A star is an image, not a real person that is constructed (as any other aspect of fiction is) out of a range of materials (e.g., advertising, magazines, etc., as well as films and music).' This perpetuates the idea that icons and celebrities are constructed by institutions for financial gain, and target a specific audience/group of people. Thus, the 'star' persona is a fictional identity that almost subconsciously creates fashion trends, popular phrases for the audience to imitate and imbibe and so on.[2] The persona of the star is, therefore, a fictional identity created, constructed and designed, consciously by the film industry and the media, and subconsciously by the audience. Thus, when an individual attains 'stardom' and becomes a star, like Suchitra Sen, and reigns over the audience and the industry for a long span of time, she can influence her audience and her fans if she so wishes. Even if she does not wish to do so, they can get influenced by the screen image of the star as they see her on screen and through magazines, interviews and so on.

What makes some persons attractive for the mass audience? Two elements are crucial in understanding the rise and success of a star. The first is the concept of authenticity. Stars have to convince the audience one way or another that they are 'real', to show something inherently his or her own in the public appearances we get to see.[3] Christine Gledhill pointed out that to be accepted as authentic, the fragile balance (or, sometimes unbalance) between the person, the persona and the character has to be kept tightly under control.[4] The *persona* is the public domain name she is known by—Suchitra Sen in this case; the *person*—the private individual within her home and family, not known to the public such as Roma Sen or Krishna Sen; and the *character*—such as Rina Brown (*Saptapadi*), Tapasi (*Agnipariksha*), Atasi (*Pathey Holo Deri*) and the umpteen other characters she brought to life on-screen. The balance between the person and the persona is significant in creating a sense of authenticity about a star which, in turn, is almost a mandatory precondition in gaining the love and admiration as well as adulation of a large audience.

The second element is charisma, or, that 'X-factor' a person acquires over time and which turns him/her from an ordinary starlet into a star, with millions of fans waiting for the star's next film. What is charisma? Richard Dyer[5] argues that charisma is not an abstract value but stands for very concrete norms and values as well as tensions in a society. Is Suchitra Sen's star charisma comparable with what Dyer argues about the charisma of Marilyn Monroe? Yes, and no. No, because Suchitra Sen's persona and charisma stand culturally, ethnically and historically distanced from the charisma of Marilyn Monroe, offered as an illustration by Dyer. About Monroe's charisma, Dyer argues: 'Her image has to be situated in the flux of ideas about morality and sexuality that characterized the Fifties in America.' Yes, because Suchitra Sen's charisma can be traced to the existing conventional norms and values that existed in post-colonial West Bengal when she reigned supreme—a situation of ideological flux, morality and sexuality but expressed explicitly and conceptually in Bengali terms. In this context, Sen's star appeal and charisma were initially determined by and with her pairing with Uttam Kumar where, except in rare films like *Saptapadi,* she is given a 'voice' of her own. Her films with Uttam Kumar established her as the biggest star in Bengali cinema, along with Uttam Kumar. There came a time when she wished to act on her own terms without sharing cinematographic and narrative space with Uttam Kumar and also, where the script gave her dominance over whichever male actor she was paired with.

Paul McDonald,[6] for example, summarized Dyer's approach mentioned above as the investigation of how 'cinema circulates the images of individual film performers and how those images may influence the ways in which we think of the identity of ourselves and others'. In drawing attention to new ways of conceptualizing and researching a star 'image',[7] he offered the classic illustration of Marilyn Monroe. Dyer later developed methodological tools to analyse and explore his star theory further, but this study will not go into that methodology. This is because Suchitra Sen, the star, the actress and the image she represented in films, in media and off-screen, existed in a world that socio-politically, a segment of post-colonial India just coming to terms with its political existence, cannot be studied by superimposing an Indian star persona with tools derived from the Hollywood star image. Neither film technology nor the huge variety of media channels that we now have, apart from radio and radiogram, existed at that time.

Professional networking through secretaries, public relations personnel, a fully staffed office, etc., did not exist at that time because the strategies of the film industry were simpler and more straightforward, with less competition and smaller budgets that made such wide, sophisticated and professional networking redundant. Public relations people functioned on their own and were paid by production houses because individual stars did not appoint them.

One needs also to remember that when stars like Nargis, Meena Kumari, Madhubala, Kanan Devi and Suchitra Sen reigned supreme, modern-day advanced innovations in make-up and cosmetics did not exist. Cosmetic lenses, imported make-up equipment, new make-up techniques, body enhancing apparel, false eyelashes, cosmetic surgery to create an artificial pout, or skin-whitening creams, had not been invented or brought in at least in India. These star-actresses made the maximum out of minimum resources. Towards the end of her career, one finds Suchitra Sen using false eyelashes in some films but that came very late. New-wave additions introduced in the 1990s such as stylists, costume designers, hair stylists and personal make-up personnel were unheard of. Many stars preferred to do their own make-up and choose their own costumes. Their only demand was a separate room to themselves in the studios where they shot. Concepts like dieting, zero-figure, body mass index, calorie intake, workouts at gyms, or personal trainers, did not exist in the vocabulary of film stars, male or female, and they had to look out for the maintenance and upkeep of their looks and their bodies themselves.

Suchitra Sen, in particular, almost always wore the sari with a long-sleeved blouse tailored to suit the fashion preferences of her time, or, alternately, created fashion through differently tailored blouses. The body was adequately covered. She made an exception when the character demanded a different style of dressing such as for the Anglo-Indian she played in *Saptapadi* or the courtesan's ghagra-choli-dupatta in zardozi in *Uttar Phalguni*. While her female fans imitated her style in dress, hairstyle and make-up, the men queued outside the theatres to catch a glimpse of their favourite star on the big screen.

Songs were not shot on picturesque foreign locations in those days. Location shooting was often simulated by 'creating' gardens, parks, lakes, etc., within the studio sets. Therefore, the physical 'looks' of a young man or woman were extremely important to step into the film industry. This was especially true for women than for men.

These stars were less visible in public space and since there was no television in those days, the only places where one could see them in flesh-and-blood were at the rare premiere party or at an award function. The only place to find them away from the screen was in the print media and film glossies that published their interviews and embroidered gossipy stories, the authenticity of which was debatable. This created a deep-seated societal ambivalence among their fans and the audience about the complex interplay between the star as an individual agent with a personal life, the star as an individual star image, the hyperactive publicity machine, financially pressurized studio executives and the inquisitive public. As Mary Ann Doane has written, 'The star becomes of interest for her life, but her life mimics that of her films.'[8] Doane adds that the phenomenon of stardom completely exploits and lives upon extra-textuality.

The star in Bengali cinema was defined by the illusory idea of beauty. Somen Ghosh, a film scholar, writes:

> A star, in one sense, is the one who is all-round beauty/handsomeness personified on the one hand and commands mastery in acting on the other. The star spurs the audience to create illusory dreams around him/her. A star fulfils the desire of the audience for a world of fantasy. The star system began in Bengali cinema from the 1930s. The box-office success of several films portraying the same star couple created a box-office screen pairing.[9]

Today, stars and film personalities practically thrive on gossip. Some struggling to find visible space are also known to 'create' gossip when the 'story' does not exist. The studios, the media and the stars themselves are quite vocal about the phenomenon of being a star and a celebrity, and try to sustain this through the brand imaging that the advertising media gives them. 'The current watchword in media commentary appears to be *change*—the prevalent sense that modern celebrity represents a qualitative break with the past. Such claims about modern fame are often made with very broad strokes, but they have made a successful bid for cultural legitimacy and acceptance.'[10] Suchitra Sen and her peers, who were also stars, such as Sabitri Chatterjee, Supriya Choudhury, etc., did not capitalize on their star image by feeding gossip to the media. Sabitri Chatterjee, who is arguably much more gifted as an actress than Sen, could never attain the star charisma that mesmerized fans of Suchitra Sen in film after film.

PLACING SUCHITRA SEN IN PERSPECTIVE

Nargis

In films featuring Raj Kapoor and Nargis, one of the most successful and romantic pairings in the history of Hindi cinema, though Nargis got footage in the script and in the cinematographic space of these films, it was her ethereal beauty that defined the focus. The cameraman had a field day. He captured Nargis in captivating black-and-white with a white halo around her head caught in medium and big close-ups with chiaroscuro light effects to reveal the dreamy romanticism in her eyes, the curve of her lips offering a perfect and symmetrical foil to the somewhat confused and disturbed, sometimes dishevelled and mostly naïve, image that Raj Kapoor presented. In *Aag* (1948), Raj Kapoor took the risk of giving himself an ugly look with half of his face burnt and scarred while Nargis is presented as her beautiful, sophisticated, modern self. If one looks closely, one observes that in most films featuring this legendary couple, the hero's character was multi-layered that evolved over the film, while the leading lady did have her moments but was more a catalytic agent playing her role to bring about a positive change in the man she loves.

It was only when she began to act in films with other leading men such as Balraj Sahni, Pradip Kumar and Sunil Dutt that one got to see what she was capable of in terms of acting. Films such as *Laajwanti* (1958), *Pardesi* (1957), *Adalat* (1958), *Mother India* (1957), *Miss India* (1957) and *Raat Aur Din* (1967) are classic examples of her potential as an actress. These films did not feature Raj Kapoor, and presented different layers of the actress in Nargis that lay hidden behind that veil of beauty, glamour and stardom. Before her pairing with Raj Kapoor began to impact the audience, her roles in *Mela* (1948) and *Jogan* (1950) focused both on her beauty and on her talent. In films that paired her with Raj Kapoor, it was her beauty that was always emphasized and her histrionic skills remained more or less untapped.

Madhubala

Madhubala and Meena Kumari, however, are two great actresses who mesmerized on their own with a screen presence that stood apart, never mind who the hero was. Madhubala, who has been written about extensively in books and articles, drew long queues outside the booking counters of theatres where her films were released. But it was more for her beauty than for her versatility as an outstanding actress. From her first box-office hit *Mahal* (1949), directed by Kamaal Amrohi, through films like *Barsaat Ki Raat* (1960), *Mr. & Mrs. 55* (1955), *Aar Paar* (1954), *Kala Pani* (1958), *Howrah Bridge* (1957), *Gateway of India* (1957), *Insaan Jaag Utha* (1959), *Chalti Ka Naam Gaadi* (1958), till her greatest milestone of all times, *Mughal-e-Azam* (1960), she proved again and again how smoothly she could gravitate from a girl in love with an oil portrait of a young man who is stunned when he steps into the mansion her father looks after in *Mahal* to the cabaret singer in *Howrah Bridge*, or, the intriguing Anarkali in *Mughal-e-Azam* to the naughty and tomboyish runaway in *Gateway of India* and the rain-drenched beauty in *Chalti Ka Naam Gaadi*. Her performances were, unfortunately, always secondary to her beauty and ethereal screen presence. No one denied her talent as an actress but it was her incomparable beauty that stood in the way of recognition of her performance. In *Kala Pani*, she played an impish journalist, in *Barsaat Ki Raat*, she was a qawwali performer, in *Insaan Jaag Utha* she was a construction worker, and with each film, it was as if she cried out to draw attention to her performance and appealed to the audience not to be diverted by her stunning looks.

Meena Kumari

Meena Kumari's story is different because she was not as beautiful as Madhubala and Nargis. Her screen persona came later, and was a consciously constructed image created brick by small brick with heavy make-up, false eyelashes, elaborate costume design and the infrastructural support of the camera, the light arrangement and with the advent of colour, the glamour and the mounting. But on hindsight, one feels that she did not need the support of beauty constructed for the characters she portrayed on screen. This is substantiated by her pre-glamorous films like *Baiju Bawra* (1952), *Dil Apna Aur Preet Parayi* (1960), *Miss Mary* (1957), *Sharda* (1957), *Shararat* (1959), *Aarti* (1962), *Dil Ek Mandir* (1963) and *Main Chup Rahungi* (1962). The 'constructed' beauty image came into play perhaps for the first time in Guru Dutt's classic *Sahib, Bibi Aur Ghulam* (1962) where, as Chhoti Bahu, she effected the perfect blend between screen beauty and acting. This led to films like *Kaajal* (1965), *Benazir* (1964) and *Pakeezah* (1972), the success of which resurrected the almost ruined career of her ex-husband Kamaal Amrohi. She earned the sobriquet of 'tragedy queen', which is victory in itself in an industry that was entirely patriarchal. It did not matter who her hero was, because that ranged from Bharat Bhushan to Dilip Kumar through Ashok Kumar, Kishore Kumar, Raj Kumar, Rajendra Kumar and Raj Kapoor, spanning two generations of marquee names in Hindi cinema. As the audience walked out of a theatre screening a Meena Kumari film, it took away her tragic image and the hero was not as memorable as she was.

Meena Kumari's natural talent for portraying tragic characters helped give extra depth and subtlety to the complex character of Chhoti Bahu, a character far removed from her immediate social environment and also from the roles she played in other films. She won the Filmfare Award for Best Actress for her work in *Baiju Bawra* (1952) and *Parineeta* (1953). She received three nominations for the award in 1962—*Aarti, Main Chup Rahungi* and *Sahib Bibi Aur Ghulam*. The award went to her for *Sahib Bibi Aur Ghulam*. In 1964, she won the Filmfare Best Actress award again for her performance in *Kaajal*. In Vinod Mehta's book, *Meena Kumari*, Mehta quotes from her diaries in his book where she writes:

> This woman is troubling me a great deal. All day long—and a good part of the night—it is nothing else but Chhoti Bahu's helplessness, Chhoti Bahu's sorrows, Chhoti Bahu's smiles, Chhoti Bahu's hopes, Chhoti Bahu's tribulations, Chhoti Bahu's endurance, Chhoto Bahu's, Chhoti Bahu's, Chhoti Bahu's … Oh! I am sick of it.[11]

However, among Nargis, Madhubala and Meena Kumari, the first two were box-office draws because they were both beautiful and photogenic, while Meena Kumari was much less beautiful than they were, and was, therefore, tapped for her talent. This is a sad reality because Nargis and Madhubala were no less talented than Meena Kumari. Nargis's later films without Raj Kapoor stand testimony to this and the greatest proof is her performance in Mehboob Khan's *Mother India*, where the character she portrays spans around four to five decades over the film.

Kanan Devi

The journey from Kanan Bala to Kanan Devi was not just in the change of name, but was a real symbol of Kanan Devi's rise reportedly from the infamous bylanes and ghettos of Kolkata to recognition and respectability, both as star-actress-singer as well as a respectable citizen of the city. The only star and actress who reigned supreme in Bengali cinema before Suchitra Sen was Kanan Bala, who later became Kanan Devi. She began her career during the post-colonial era when the studio system prevailed and actors were employed by studios on a monthly salary. Earlier, males portrayed female roles, followed by Anglo-Indian women who began acting in films. Working in films was considered disrespectful for women, and those from respectable families did not dream of entering films. Women from red-light areas were called to work in films. It is said that Kanan Bala belonged to one such family and her entry into films was preceded by her talent in vocal music.

Her first film as leading lady was *Jore Barat* (1931), one of the first Bengali talkies and she became an overnight star. She dominated Bengali cinema for nearly three decades: first, as a talented singer; second, as a star and an actress shifting base with great success from one studio to another; and finally, as producer and director producing her own films. She was a rage among her women fans who modelled their fashion status by imitating her hairstyles. The way she wore the sari in different films, her tailored blouses, even the way in which she delivered her lines in the style of those days—in a slow and seductive drawl, accompanied by a sing-song tone—were imitated. However, since she was considered as having risen from the dredges, and although her hundreds of fans adored and worshipped her screen image, they were reluctant to bestow upon her the respect she rightly deserved.

Though cinema at that time dealt with patriarchal stories, keeping screen characters of women confined to secondary roles—even the titles of films followed the names of the male protagonists—Kanan Devi created her own space in every film she performed in, for two major reasons: one, her talent for singing, as she acted in leading roles in many musicals, and two, because though she had a dusky complexion off-screen, she was extremely photogenic and the directors and cinematographers of those times took great care to construct her screen image to suit what the audience was looking for. Among some of her best remembered films are *Maa* (1934), *Manmoyee Girls School* (1935), *Mukti* (1937), *Bidyapati/Vidyapati* (1938), *Saathi/Street Singer* (1938), *Sapurey/Sapera* (1939), *Parajay* (1940), *Abhinetri* (1940), *Haar Jeet* (1940), *Parichay* (1941), *Shesh Uttar/Jawab* (1942), *Jogajog* (1943), *Chandrasekhar* (1947), and *Mejdidi/Majhli Didi* (1950).[12]

She is perhaps the most successful Indian star to have played the perfect balancing act between acting and singing, and also exuding a star image for her audience. The studio team and crew began addressing her as 'Madam' when she was at her peak. She refused the role of Parvati in New Theatres' *Devdas* because her dates clashed and P.C. Barua had to seek a new face for the role. She held on to her own in bilingual versions of several of her films because her Hindi diction was functional, though not impeccable. One of her earliest mentors, J.N. Ghosh, who brought her from HMV and Columbia to Megaphone Company, offered her a room to stay within the Megaphone house because she had no proper place to stay where she could train in and practise her music. He also hired an English tutor to teach her to speak and communicate in English. She became the first Bengali star whose name on the billboards assured that the film would be a hit at the box office. Her peak as an actress was after she quit Radha Studios to join New Theatres. She got two great directors to work with—Debaki Kumar Bose and P.C. Barua—and the best among music directors, Rai Chand Boral and Pankaj Mullick.

The most memorable film starring Kanan Devi (with P.C. Barua) was *Mukti* (1937). *Mukti* had a bold storyline. Prasanta, a sculptor and painter, is married to Chitra, a beautiful young girl influenced by the snobbery of the increasingly westernized, urban Kolkata society she comes from. Prasanta, realizing this attraction of his wife to values he considers fake and borrowed, and wishing to free her from an unhappy marriage, fakes his own suicide and escapes to the forests of Assam to begin a new life with the tribals. When Chitra goes to Assam with a long-time admirer on a hunting trip, she learns that Prasanta is still alive. But she is kidnapped on the way and Prasanta dies while trying to rescue her, freeing her from a marriage that never was, and in the process, freeing himself from the all-pervasive conflicts his life was filled with.[13] Kanan Devi fleshed out the character of Chitra as an arrogant woman given to Western values and an attitude that berated her husband because he did not agree either with her ideology or with her lifestyle, yet loved her deeply. Chitra could be considered to be Bengali cinema's first strong brush with a wife who is not the ideal bahu and does not even want to be one. *Mukti* is also a scathing indictment and critique of a married woman wanting to live by her own values and her greed for material affluence. Yet, despite the negative shades given to the leading lady, *Mukti* was an unprecedented success.

Released at Chitra Theatre on 18 September 1937, *Mukti* became an instant hit, turning Pramathesh and Kanan Devi into screen icons overnight. Young women copied the way Kanan did her hair and wore the sari, while men turned Pramathesh's costumes into a contemporary fashion statement. In terms of cinema, there is an element of timelessness about the film and it does not appear dated today. The aesthetic and cinematically appropriate use of Tagore songs enriched the texture of the film, lifting it to a different plane altogether.

The story of *Mukti* was penned by three writers—Sajanikanta Das, Phani Majumdar and Pramathesh Barua himself. The story did not have a title. Pankaj Mullick, who was scoring the music for the film, narrated the story to Rabindranath Tagore when he went to visit him at Santiniketan. *Mukti,* it was decided, would be the film's name. Rabindra Sangeet, the acronym for songs written and set to music by Rabindranath Tagore, had never been used in films till then. Tagore had strong reservations about the use of his songs for films. But Pramathesh aspired to use Tagore songs in his films. He felt *Mukti* could serve as an ideal platform.

Among Tagore's poems was one named 'Shesh Kheya' (The Last Boat). Pankaj Mullick had set the poem to his own musical score, turning it into a soulful number with multi-layered suggestions of a lost love and the loneliness that comes from it. Tagore had heard him sing this number once and had liked it. Pankaj asked permission from Tagore to use the song in *Mukti*. Tagore gave his consent and for the first time, a Tagore creation was used in the music track of an Indian film. *Mukti* had two other Tagore songs and all the songs turned out to become the biggest hits in the history of Bengali cinema. The two songs, *'Aaj shawbar range'*, and *'Taar bidaaye belaar mala khani'*, were melodious numbers rendered by Kanan Devi herself. Mullick himself sang the *'Shesh kheya'* number. Barua wrote the script, directed and also edited the film. *Mukti* has another first to its credit—it was the first film to be shot extensively on location in the forests of Gauripur, featuring Pramathesh's pet elephant, Jung Bahadur, in a major role. The influence of the German expressionist school of film-making on Barua is visible in one of the opening scenes of the film where a series of doors—one leading to the next—opened out to finally reach the room used by the hero Prasanta (Barua), a painter-sculptor, as his studio.[14]

Kanan Devi created her own banner, Shreemati Pictures, in 1949, and produced around a dozen films between 1949 and 1965. Most of these films were adapted from or based on classics by Sarat Chandra Chattopadhyay, the film rights of which she had purchased. The directorial team she had created and named Sabyasachi included her name alongside the names of Ajoy Kar and Binoy Chatterjee. The films did not meet with great commercial success and critics panned them too. Her husband, Haridas Bhattacharya, took on the directorial reins. With the beginning of her production banner, Kanan Devi, having given up her music long ago, graduated to doing character roles in her own films because she was sure that she no longer had the charisma of a leading lady.

Among the productions of Shreemati Pictures, *Andhare Alo* (1957), based on a novel by Sarat Chandra Chattopadhyay, won the All India Certificate of Merit for the Second Best Feature Film at the fifth National Awards. It also won the President's Silver Medal for the Best Feature Film in Bengali. It was the inaugural film at the Karlovy Vary International Film Festival where Kanan Devi and Haridas Bhattacharya were specially invited for the screening. *Rajlakshmi O Sreekanto* was perhaps the biggest hit under her banner because it starred Uttam Kumar and Suchitra Sen in the title roles. The film was directed by Haridas Bhattacharya. *Indranath, Sreekanto O Annadadidi* (1959) was a well-crafted film that featured Kanan Devi in a layered role of Annadadidi, and marked the debut of her son.

Abhaya O Sreekanto (1965), the last film under the Shreemati Pictures banner, though released just before the India-Pakistan war, managed to recover costs and had a reasonably satisfying eleven-week run. There is no denying Kanan Devi's place as one of the most outstanding and versatile creative artistes Indian cinema has ever produced. She wrote an autobiography *Sabare Ami Nomi* (1973) and was bestowed the Dadasaheb Phalke Award for her contribution to Indian cinema in 1977. She also worked as president of the Mahila Shilpi Mahal, an organization that helps aged and needy female artistes of yesteryears.

Arundhati Devi

Arundhati Devi was a contemporary of Suchitra Sen who evolved not only into an actress in her own right but also as producer, director and music composer. She was perhaps the only actress of her time who came from a well-educated and highly respected background. She studied at Tagore's Viswa Bharati and was trained in dance, music and other arts. She was also exceptionally beautiful and exuded class in her very being. She made her debut in *Mahaprashthaner Pathey* (1952) under the New Theatres banner which also had a Hindi version, *Yatrik*, directed by Kartik Chatterjee. Arundhati played the role of Rani, a strong-willed young widow, who develops a soft corner for a young Brahmachari played by Abhi Bhattacharya. It was a box-office hit.

Her oeuvre as an actress was not very extensive in terms of quantity but qualitatively, she did some significant films during the 1950s such as *Shashi Babur Sansar* and *Pushpadhanu*, (both released in 1959), *Indradhanu* (1960) and *Bicharak* (1962), which marked her debut as producer, and she also played the female lead opposite Uttam Kumar. The two most outstanding roles in her career were the title role in *Bhagini Nivedita* (1962), directed by Bijoy Bose, and *Kshudita Pashan* (1960), *Jhinder Bandi* (1961) and *Jotugriha* (1964), all directed by Tapan Sinha. She played a very complex role in the Piyush Bose-directed *Shiulibari* (1962), opposite Uttam Kumar, and also composed its music. She became a director with *Chhuti* (1967), based on a Tagore poem. The film won a Certificate of Merit at the National Film Awards in 1967. Her other directorial film for children—*Padi Pishir Barmi Baksho* (1972) became a super hit. She directed three more films—*Gokul* (1985), *Deepar Prem* (1983) and *Megh-O-Roudra* (1969).

She had her niche audience among Bengali cinema-lovers of her time. She exuded an aura of education, aristocracy, dignity and beauty. But these also turned out to become her limitations because her looks, her body language and her personality typed her into certain roles, and, therefore, did not vest her with the fluidity that aids a versatile actress aspiring for a long run in the industry. Her portrayals were qualified by great restraint, underplaying, low-key emotion, controlled modulation, tone and pitch of voice, besides her way of dressing that befitted a woman of class. Her popularity and charisma among the movie-going Bengali public could not hold a candle to the kind of charisma Suchitra Sen exuded over her entire career. Within her brief career with hardly twenty films in her repertoire, Arundhati Devi proved that she was a versatile performer. If *Bicharak* saw her as a young, qualified girl who plays tennis and is equally deft at playing the piano, who falls in love with her cousin's husband and suffers from deep pangs of guilt for the cousin's death by fire of which she was innocent, in *Jhinder Bandi*, she excelled as a princess caught between a king she is engaged to but does not love and his rakish look-alike imposter. In *Bhagini Nivedita*, she gave an award-worthy performance as Swami Vivekananda's Irish disciple who devoted her entire life to spiritualism, following her mentor.

Sabitri Chatterjee

Sabitri Chatterjee is one of the most outstanding actresses of Bengali cinema, theatre and television. Her career spans nearly six decades. She is a contemporary of Suchitra Sen and had her own slot of audience who loved her for her sense of timing in comedy. Uttam Kumar has gone on record stating that Sabitri was the only female co-star he was a bit diffident about because, according to him, she was the most talented among all the female co-stars he had acted with.

She was equally capable of performing strong roles with dramatic and emotional content, with ease and fluidity.

She played the romantic interest opposite Uttam Kumar in memorable films like *Bosu Poribar* (1952), *Annapurnar Mandir* (1954), *Marutirtha Hinglaj* (1959), *Raja Saja* (1960), *Dui Bhai* (1961), *Manjari Opera* (1970), *Bhranti Bilash* (1963), adapted from Shakespeare's *Comedy of Errors* and later made by Gulzar as *Angoor* (1982), *Momer Alo* (1964), *Nishipadma* (1970), later done in Hindi by Shakti Samanta as *Amar Prem* (1970), *Grihadaha* (1967; she played a cameo in this film while Suchitra was the leading lady), *Dhanni Meye* (1971) and so on. In fact, she acted with Uttam Kumar in more films than he did with Suchitra Sen. She also enacted the title role of Shyamali, a deaf-mute girl, in a play opposite Uttam Kumar which was one of the biggest theatrical hits of the time. Thanks to the industry's casual treatment of prints and negatives of priceless Bengali films, most of her earliest films, including her debut *Paasher Baari* (1952) and a brilliant Mrinal Sen film *Pratinidhi* (1964), in which she was paired with Soumitra Chatterjee, are lost to time.

In *Adarsho Hindu Hotel* (1957) she portrays a maid in a cheap hotel and became famous for her flair for comedy. In *Momer Alo*, she plays a physically and psychologically handicapped dancer who falls in love with her psychiatrist. In *Manjari Opera*, she is the owner and lead actress of a touring theatre group, torn between her love for a man who walks out of his marriage to join her in her touring theatre, and her love for the theatre. In *Marutirtha Hinglaj*, she plays a young girl on a pilgrimage with a group destined to reach a religious site called Hinglaj, now in Pakistan. She is raped and goes insane.

'I have performed a variety of roles not many actresses in Bengal will be able to match. This is no comment directed against them, mind you. I am just mentioning facts. This applies both to the stage and to films,' Sabitri says, adding, 'I never once used glycerine for tears. They come naturally from moments picked out of real life. I am happy that I have fulfilled one of the greatest challenges for any actor—the ability to make people laugh. It is not easy.'

Women in the audience found it easier to identify with Sabitri Chatterjee than they did with Suchitra Sen who was for them an icon, an idol to be worshipped and the woman Uttam Kumar loved in every other film. This is perhaps why Sabitri, in spite of being a better and more talented and versatile actress, could not generate the kind of audience frenzy her peer Sen did. Suchitra's acquisition of the 'mahanayika' tag enabled her to overshadow the 'plain Jane' Sabitri Chatterjee, despite the latter's credentials as a performer. Suchitra managed to create a niche for herself as the star, even if her range of acting appears to be less versatile than Sabitri's.[15]

SUCHITRA SEN WITHOUT UTTAM KUMAR

Suchitra Sen's stardom was determined by her charisma, her tremendous screen appeal and the distance she created between herself and her audience and fans. She very consciously and carefully avoided gossip and scandal through this distance and reportedly counselled younger actors to follow the unwritten rule of 'alienation'. This multiplied her charisma because it added to the intrigue that was Suchitra Sen. Gossip magazines and film glossies did create some gossip but nothing was ever proved. Then, there was her golden pairing with Uttam Kumar that added the invisible tag of 'star' to her name and 'star-actor' to Uttam Kumar's name. In a patriarchal world, this discrepancy was inevitable. But after a point of time, it created problems in the professional relationship between the two. The only gossip that was substantiated to some extent was her unhappy relationship with husband Dibanath Sen, also based almost entirely on hearsay and on the say-so of people close to her.

At a time when Suchitra Sen and Uttam Kumar were ruling the box office, the grapevine went wild with suggestions about Uttam Kumar being the more talented between the two and that Suchitra Sen's star charisma depended both on her mesmerizing screen presence and her playing the foil to the smashing hero Uttam Kumar. During the making of *Saptapadi*, produced by Uttam Kumar, there was a rift between the two. Suchitra reportedly said she would not work with Uttam Kumar any more. She stuck to this for some years but came back in a few other films after around a decade. During this gap in their pairing, Suchitra Sen did roles where the screenplay gave her a dominant position both in the footage and in the story. Her romantic interest was played by different heroes. Even during her pairing with Uttam Kumar, she paired with other heroes but this did not even remotely attain the magic she created with Uttam Kumar.

In charting Suchitra Sen as a performer without the box-office support of her romantic screen partner Uttam Kumar, I have chosen to focus on a few films that throw up the versatility of a star evolving into an actress without having to surrender the star charisma. These films are *Smrittituku Thaak*, *Saat Paake Bandha* and *Datta*. A few other films that explore the journey of Suchitra Sen as a working woman have been dealt with in another chapter.

Smrittituku Thaak

Smrittituku Thaak is one of the two films in which Suchitra Sen has played two roles, the other being *Uttar Phalguni*. *Smrittituku Thaak*, loosely translated as let memories remain, centres around a familiar theme in Gothic melodrama—of fate, destiny and what happens if someone should be so opportunistic as to try and beat the odds laid out for them.

The concept of the double role in Indian cinema dates back to *Lanka Dahan* (1917), a silent film by Dadasaheb Phalke, in which Salunke, the main actor, portrayed both Ram and Sita. But playing the roles of a male and a female is not the conventional double role where the two characters are identical in appearance but often different in demeanour. A double role is often considered a tribute and a challenge to the actor chosen because it is a proof of the confidence that the director places on the said actor.

Double and multiple roles have been the staple of Indian cinema with narratives mainly exploring the stories of identical twins separated at birth. Reincarnation forms another strategy for using double roles within a cinematic narrative and the best example of this is Kamaal Amrohi's classic ghost film *Mahal*. But the twins' theory still wins hands down. Ashis Nandy views double roles in Hindi films as 'both ideal types and representatives of a fragmented self'.[16] The fragments of the divided self are 'only separately manageable' and 'one of the main functions of the Bombay film is to keep them separate'.[17]

The resurgence of films with double roles in the early 1950s and their increased prevalence thereafter points to their close alignment with the logic of the star system.[18] An article in *Filmfare* in 1977 commented, 'Multiple roles have become a status symbol for footage-hogging stars.' But this does not apply to Suchitra Sen because she did not need to hog footage; it came to her naturally from her directors and from the script. Besides, by the time *Smritituku Thaak* was made, she was already an established star-actress. However, one must concede that the commercial value in taking a top star for two roles in the same film adds to the box-office value of the film. There is also the economy in casting a top star in a double role—getting more footage and drama out of the same actor for one film at a lesser price. All said and done, the bottom line of this argument is that the double role is a litmus test for the actor's versatility in portraying two different roles in the same film. This is an additional challenge because the star concerned must make it clear to the audience which of the two characters he/she is playing in a given scene.

A film with two identical characters pitted against each other as twins also adds to the suspense of the drama for the audience that is constantly asking itself: 'Which one of the two is this one?' When these questions are *not* asked, it means that the actor has pulled off a winning feather from his/her cap. When the two characters are framed in the same scene, which is usually shot separately and then joined at the editing table, the differences are obvious, given the differences in their nature, their body language, their way of dressing, speech, demeanour and so on. The two films in which Suchitra Sen played double roles, contrary to popular practice, were not representative of good versus evil, which is usually the case.

In *Uttar Phalguni/Mamta*, she plays the dual role of mother and daughter and neither of them are fleshed out negatively. The same happens in *Smrittituku Thaak*.

Smrittituku Thaak is based on an original story by Malabika Roy, an unknown writer, but the screenplay was penned by a famous littérateur, Premendra Mitra. It is a very cinema-friendly story. It was directed by Yatrik, a group of directors of whom Tarun Majumdar became famous in his own right later on.

The film opens at the spacious, well-decorated and furnished home of a happy couple—Dakshinaranjan Mukherjee and his wife Bibha—whose only lament in life is that they do not have children. At this point, a letter arrives from Bakulpur, written by Abha, Bibha's younger sister. She has just delivered identical female twins, and with many children to look after already and the family being steeped in poverty, she does not know how to bring them up. It dawns on the Mukherjees to take one of the twins as their own, and so they go to Abha's village and bring back one of the twins, Utpola.

As the two babies grow up in different settings, there are intercutting shots without dialogue that express the differences in their upbringing—Utpola being brought up by her aunt, surrounded by toys, parties, picnics and so on while Shovana is kept busy with household chores right through their growth into adulthood. Utpola grows up to become a modern, well-groomed and sophisticated young woman who is a painter and has a studio to herself in her home. Shovana grows up doing household chores and is burdened by looking after the home when the eldest brother moves away with his wife and family and she, along with another brother, is left to tend to the sick mother and younger brothers and sisters. Her brother tries to pull off a match for her with a young doctor who arrives from the city to begin his practice in the village. Jayanta Roy, the doctor, is called to attend to their ailing mother. But before the match can even be proposed, Jayanta suddenly has to leave for the city. He never sees Shovana in person but Shovana sees him from behind the door, or when he falls asleep on an easy chair, and likes him.

Their home is mortgaged, the vessels are sold and they live in dire straits. Shovana cannot get married because they cannot afford dowry, while Utpola has suitors crowding her drawing room which bores her no end. She can sing, paint, play the piano, and her room is filled with symbols of affluence.

On her dying bed, Shovana's mother tells her that she has a twin who has been lucky to be brought up in luxury, and advises her to go to her aunt's house and demand by right from her twin what should also be hers. A very hesitant and timid Shovana sets off for her aunt's home. At the same time, Utpola sets off for Patna to attend a friend's wedding. Utpola suddenly decides to leave Patna a day or two before what she had originally planned. The train she is travelling in meets with an accident and her name appears on the list of four passengers who have died in the crash. She is taken to a nursing home to be tended to and the doctor discovers she has lost her memory.

Her foster parents—she does not know that they are not her real parents—never learn about the accident because, in the meantime, Shovana has arrived at their place and despite her body language, her timid personality, and her quiet nature, they take it for granted that she is Utpola. It never occurs to them that she might be someone else.

The narrative constantly cuts back and forth between Utpola's new life and Shovana's present predicament. She is shocked and confused to discover an unfinished portrait of Jayanta painted by Utpola in her studio and finds out that the two were engaged to be married. Since the family and Jayanta both take her to be Utpola, Shovana is married to Jayanta. For her, it is too precious a prize that has come her way to give up easily. On her urging, Jayanta agrees to shift to a small town and begin his practice there. They have a little boy and their cup of happiness is full. Jayanta asks her to take up painting again, not knowing that this is Shovana who cannot paint and not Utpola who had begun his portrait but could not finish it.

Meanwhile, Utpola's world is full of confusion because Dr Nag keeps telling her to try and remember who she is. She tries but fails to recollect till something dramatic happens. When she regains her memory, she happens to find that Jayanta, along with his family, has come for a short stay in the same town where she lives. The little boy is confused when he meets Utpola while getting into the neighbour's garden and tells his mother and father that he knows another 'mamma'. Shovana is desperate to save her marriage while Utpola does not wish to break up this family which is so content in itself. When Jayanta learns the truth, he prays to Utpola to come back to him but she refuses. The desperate Shovana is driven to the edge trying to save her marriage. Utpola leaves them and goes back to the doctor's home where she has taken shelter, happy that the 'portrait' she had not been able to finish is now complete.

Neepa Majumdar[19] writes that beyond a straightforward display of two radically different characters played by the same actor, double roles often also deliberately complicate the narrative by having the two characters switch identities. Such an exchange of identities is logically written into the very concept of the double role and provides an opportunity for 'metaperformance' or, 'acting persons who are acting'.[20] With the characters switched and only the viewer aware of the switch, there are many occasions for displaying expressive incoherence in doubling them.

Suchitra Sen gave one of her most outstanding performances in the double roles of Utpola and Shovana. The cuts, swipes and editing strategies are contrived to add to the twists in coincidences and in melodrama. The camera closes in on Shovana for the first time on the day her brother has invited Jayanta to lunch at the Bakulpur home saying, 'I have a surprise for you', not elucidating what the surprise is all about. The camera then cuts to Shovana decking herself up in front of a small hand mirror, and we see her in close-up, her face filled with a coy smile. There is a knock on the door. Someone brings a note that says Jayanta had to go away and will not be able to make it. Shovana turns her face away to hide her tears of disappointment.

Then there is a mid-close-up of Shovana intercut with Jayanta journeying to the city, cut to the scene of the river with a boat song on the soundtrack showing Shovana's face—solemn, thoughtful and strong—leaves from the nearby trees tracing shadows on her face which move towards her eyes moist with tears. Though these two characters—Utpola and Shovana—are not influenced by Hollywood and are rooted entirely in their Bengali identity, demonstrating two polar opposites of this identity, the portrayals of the two women by the same actress stand testimony to the star's control over her medium—acting with conviction and credibility without sacrificing her command over histrionics.

As Utpola, she is just that bit more exuberant than needed in order to contrast this woman with the low-key, ready-to-vanish-in-the-wall portrayal of Shovana till she gets married. Once Shovana gets married to Jayanta, Shovana acquires strength from within herself, remembering her mother's last words to her to claim from her twin by right what is hers. Shovana demands to shift to a different town, insists that she will neither paint nor finish the portrait she (Utpola) had started, and will also not stay at the new place they have come to where Jayanta was suddenly summoned by a nursing home. Jayanta is surprised to find that Utpola has changed since her return from Patna after her friend's marriage, but he is a very submissive husband devoted to his wife's commands. Shovana's demands are linked to a deep sense of guilt on the one hand and, on the other, the fear of getting caught at her impersonation of her twin sister. Once she confesses to Jayanta, she feels liberated but sorry because she is sure that Jayanta will go back to Utpola. He tries to but Utpola is 'happy' that 'the picture is now complete' when she sees the three of them—Jayanta, Shovana and the little boy, Raja—standing together much like the portrait of a picture-perfect family.

Suchitra Sen portrays Shovana, who pretends to be Utpola, knowing fully well that she is not, and gives the performance fine nuances of facial expressions that are a blend of fear, confusion, guilt, uncertainty and the rest. Her portrayal of Utpola, following the accident, the shock that she has lost her memory and does not know who she is, where she is from, why she is where she is, and how will she become what she really was, is equally matched by Shovana's performance. As both Utpola and Shovana, Suchitra portrays two Utpolas and two Shovanas, the identities of each having split after the train crash coinciding with Shovana's arrival at Utpola's home. However, the couple of scenes where both Shovana and Utpola are shown together through post-production editing strategies are not handled well either by the script or by the actress.

The range of external signs, gestures, facial expressions, body language, costume, hairstyle, make-up and dialogue delivery that distinguish Shovana from Utpola identifies the double role as a simple binary opposition between the rural Shovana and the very urban, sophisticated and educated Utpola. No moral status attaches itself to either identity. The script never qualifies them as good and evil. They are basically good human beings, one prepared to switch her identity for a better, prosperous and happy life that has been denied to her and the other, Utpola, though strongly tempted by the sight of Raja, and after she discovers whose son he is, to give in to the hope of motherhood and wifehood she has lost out on, controls her temptation even when Jayanta appeals to her to come back to him and begin from where they had left.

Saat Paake Bandha[21]

Directed by Ajoy Kar, *Saat Paake Bandha* was adapted from a novel by Ashutosh Mukherjee. The script, the elaborate screenplay and the dialogues were penned by Nripendra Krishna Chatterjee, who was a noted writer in his own right and was also known for his great screenplays. He was responsible for having authored the screenplays of several hit films starring Uttam Kumar and Suchitra Sen. Some of those films are *Shap Mochan*, *Ekti Raat* (1956), *Harano Sur*, *Indrani*, *Chaoa-Paoa*, and *Uttar Phalguni* which released after he passed away.

This film released after two hits of Suchitra Sen with Uttam Kumar, namely, *Saptapadi* and *Bipasha*. *Saat Paake Bandha* and *Uttar Phalguni* released in the same year, thus consolidating Suchtira Sen's command over the Bengali audience without Uttam Kumar beside her. The following year, her solo film *Sandhya Dweeper Sikha* (1964) flopped because it was an extremely soppy, sentimental film flush with exaggerated melodrama with both the camera and the narrative constantly focused on Suchitra Sen who tried her best to portray a woman against her screen image and failed. The reason for the film's failure lay more on the weak script and story than on her performance, though this was perhaps one of her worst performances ever.

The seeds of dissension in the Uttam-Suchitra professional relationship were already sown during the making of *Saptapadi*. Suchitra Sen wished to do stronger roles in films. She desired storylines that challenged her talent as an actress and where directors did not cast her only because she offered beautiful support to Uttam Kumar which ensured excellent returns at the box office. But after the commercial disaster of *Sandhya Dweeper Sikha*, the romantic pair came together again on screen with films like *Grihadaha*, *Kamallata*, *Nabaraag*, *Alo Amar Alo* and *Haar Mana Haar* (1972.) These films were box-office hits. But during the same period, Suchitra Sen did films with other male stars such as *Megh Kalo* (1970) with Basanta Choudhury, *Fariyaad* with Utpal Dutt, *Sraban Sandhya* (1974) opposite Samar Roy, which found a limited theatrical release several years later, and *Debi Choudhurani* (1974) opposite Ranjit Mullick. None of these films did well and some such as *Fariyaad* and *Debi Choudhurani* were washouts.

Within this scenario, *Saat Paake Bandha* and *Uttar Phalguni* were milestones in the career of Suchitra Sen as an actress who could carry films on her own. *Saat Paake Bandha* is considered to be an all-time great of Bengali cinema. The film bagged for Suchitra Sen the Best Actress Award at the Moscow Film Festival. This was the second international award bestowed upon an Indian actress, the first award having gone to Nargis for her performance in *Mother India* at the Karlovy Vary International Film Festival.

The entire story is narrated mainly in flashback. Archana (Suchitra Sen), the older of the two daughters, with an elder brother, belonging to an affluent family, falls in love with Sukhendu, who teaches at the university. Her father is a professor, too, and though he welcomes her choice, her snobbish, arrogant and rude mother is shocked. The father, a very weak man who is scared of his domineering wife, gathers some courage to back his daughter's choice much to his wife's chagrin. The mother's main grouse is that this is an unequal match and Sukhendu cannot hold a candle to Archana's other suitors. The adamant Archana is married to Sukhendu according to Hindu customs and the two journey to Sukhendu's humble two-storey home where he lives with his widowed aunt who brought him up.

Archana fits herself into this new ambience as best as she can, trying to please her aunt-in-law who comes to adore her. But Archana's snobbish mother refuses to let them be. She looks down on her professor son-in-law because he earns only Rs 400 per month and cannot afford the lifestyle Archana is used to. She sets some labour in front of their home to draw a cable line for a telephone connection they do not have. Sukhendu is angry but does not protest. Instead, he takes out his anger on Archana who is helplessly trapped in the ego clash between her mother and her husband. Archana's mother takes every opportunity to belittle him but he is not the one to take it lying down; he takes it out on his wife. His aunt leaves for Kashi when she feels insulted by the constant slights by Archana's mother. Archana is away when she leaves and she feels genuine hurt when she hears that Sukhendu did not bother to inform her that his aunt had left. She comes back home only to be insulted once again by her husband. She is forced to go back to her parents. This is followed by legal separation on mutual agreement.

Archana drowns herself in studies and spends most of her time in the library because she wants to forget her pain and avoid her brother and mother who pester her to marry a good-for-nothing rich boy, the scion of an aristocratic family who spends his entire time at Archana's parental home. Disgusted with their persistent interference in her personal life, Archana suggests her mother shift her attention to her younger sister's marriage. As the marriage mantras are being chanted, Archana, standing in the distance, watching pensively, suddenly recalls her own marriage and rushes back to her old home to go back to Sukhendu. But he has left his job, his country and no one knows where he is. She takes up a job in a school in the suburbs and narrates her story.

In real life, the institution of marriage has undergone a metamorphosis. The pressures are not totally new but they were comparatively invisible till recent times. The education of women, industrialization, urbanization and widespread dissemination of information about the evils of patriarchy and injustices towards women have resulted in lesser tolerance among wives. After marriage, women are caught in a web of contradictions and ambiguities. They are expected to distance themselves from their natal kin at marriage, for that has been the social custom in Bengali families and for reasons connected with the power to be wielded over them by their husbands. Yet, they are discouraged, by those same considerations of power and authority, from forging intimate bonds with their husbands. In spite of their attempts to become 'one' with their husbands' families, the latter do not quite accept them as their own and the sense of alienation sustains.[22]

Films, both from within the mainstream and outside, have handled the theme of schisms in marriage with aesthetic sensitivity, technical finesse and, most importantly, strong social relevance. The aesthetics have sometimes been compromised for the sake of the social statement the film has made. Sometimes, the aesthetic stress may have tended to overshadow the social statement. But the fact remains that the portrayal of a problematic marriage offers greater scope to a film-maker to play with the form, the content, the technique and the aesthetics of the film, not to talk of the background score, the histrionic credits, etc. Sometimes, a popular film on divorce or separation may have fallen flat on its face because the script shied away from carrying the marital argument beyond a particular point. Sometimes, the director may have been too immature to handle a subject like marital discord and could not carry it through. Often, the script turned out to be too weak to hold the cinematic narrative through. Then, there have been instances of gross miscasting.

Mainstream cinema's exploration of changes, subtle and visible, in the institution of marriage, has been more lip service than a genuine movement to make a political statement on the man-woman relationship sanctioned by religion, or law, or both. A closer, insightful look at *Saat Paake Bandha* throws up the irony of the title that demonstrates that never mind if the marriage is an arrangement between families or where the partners have made the decision to marry, many Indian marriages are ruined due to men and women's minds functioning under the influence of patriarchy.

In the irony inherent in its title, *Saat Paake Bandha* suggests the eternal character of a Bengali Hindu marriage. It is an insightful critique of patriarchy that men and women are both conditioned to. Archana's mother is patriarchal within a capitalist mindset, and is convinced that her daughters should marry into aristocracy and affluence, never mind if the groom-to-be does nothing for a living and practically spends all his time in their home. She has a bias against a son-in-law who is happy as a professor, earning Rs 400 per month, and who has no aspirations of 'sending his thesis for evaluation to London'. He is not going to become the principal of his college and rebukes Archana for her mother's lies.

As the marriage begins to disintegrate, Archana realizes that she is helplessly trapped between loyalty to her husband and his family and her inability to stop her mother from interfering in her married life. When, in a moving scene, she asks why Sukhendu is accusing her of what her mother has done, he says, 'To me, the two of you are the same.' She is speechless for a moment and then lashes out at him for not supporting her in her grave crisis. He then says, 'It is no use "acting" like husband and wife like this.' Archana is quiet for a few moments and then says, 'Mutual separation should be resorted to.' Sukhendu's response is, 'Will that create a scene?' and she says, 'It will be done as you desire,' realizing that Sukhendu is more troubled by the possibilities of a scandal than by the separation itself!

Juxtaposed against Archana, Sukhendu is not only arrogant, rude and lacking in social decorum, he is also a coward and an escapist ever-willing to make his wife the scapegoat of his anger. Instead of standing by her in her moment of crisis, he backs out and becomes party to her humiliation. He takes two private tuitions after his lectures are over to keep away from home as much as possible. He does not respond to Archana's telephone call from her mother's home. He makes no attempts to mend fences in the library when she purposely leaves her purse behind to wait and see if he picks it up and gives it directly to her. He does not even gather the courage to keep his colleagues and superiors in college informed about the break-up of his marriage with Archana. When his senior congratulates him for Archana's excellent results at the master's examination, he remains quiet. He lacks the minimum courtesy of congratulating her. Finally, he runs away from his job, from the city and the country to some unknown destination, leaving Archana to bear the brunt of his cowardice. Only once during the entire film does he try to placate Archana: when she returns from her brother's birthday party feeling very angry and doubly insulted because he stayed away and because her parents derided her for the 'expensive pen' she had bought as a birthday gift.

Suchitra Sen as Archana could easily have slipped into the role of a martyr portraying the soppy, sentimental and sobbing woman who has been wronged both by her paternal family and by her husband. But, with the power of her performance, she turns celluloid martyrdom on its head and finally decides to write her own destiny. Maybe, her action is triggered by her circumstances, and her taking up a job is the last option left to her to keep away from her mother's and brother's intrusion into her life. But it is a decision she decides to stick to, and when her male colleague expresses his liking for her, she explains her beliefs and her practice to him with a dignity that has always been a part of her character. In retrospect, the viewer sometimes wonders what made this woman of great dignity, beauty, grace and charm fall for an arrogant and proud man like Sukhendu.

The brief honeymoon in Kashi, Lucknow, Delhi and Rajasthan forms the only segment where we find Archana and Sukhendu enjoying themselves like any normal newly married couple.

Saat Paake Bandha is a rare film for its time where most films ended on a 'happily-ever-after' note and leaving a film with an open and sad climax was a big box-office risk. Another unique feature of the film is that the entire story unfolds from Archana's perspective—the perspective of a woman. She is the storyteller, the voiceover, the anchor and the central character. The first seventeen minutes of this 125-minute film are dominated by Archana alone—coming to be interviewed for her teaching job, getting the job, moving to her quarters with the old family retinue Dasu-da as her only emotional baggage, making friends with a little boy who wants to study, befriending the drawing teacher who is also her male colleague's older sister—before the film moves into flashback.

The show belongs to Suchitra Sen, though she has the solid backing of a talented cast that stands by her. Her father, the weak-willed professor who lacks the courage to stand up to his wife and silently witnesses the disintegration of his favourite daughter's life, shows that though he is a man, he is a very weak link whose silence is a contributor to his daughter's tragedy. Her mother appears to be a harridan and a nagging persona. Sukhendu, admirably played by Soumitra Chatterjee, with his disrespectful repartee, only adds to the mother's bias against low-salaried men who cannot afford a telephone in the house! Her brother is a good-for-nothing who is forever planning to go into business with his equally useless but rich friend and is eager to hitch him to Archana for his own benefit. He cannot respond to her when she accuses him of trying to exploit her through the rich friend.

Her younger sister is the only one who understands her and empathizes with her, but cannot do anything because she lacks both the power and the voice. Sukhendu's aunt is good-natured and kind, but withdraws and leaves when she finds she cannot handle the situation any more, leaving the kind and generous daughter-in-law to fend for herself. All the men in the film are paper-thin figures overshadowed and overpowered by the women, mainly by Archana. Suchitra Sen masterfully brings this across through her restraint, her low-key acting and the dignity with which she holds herself even when she is insulted and accused by Sukhendu's colleague of having spoilt his life. The colleague, however, hardly knows the other side of the story.

The scenes capturing Archana when she virtually drowns herself in academics are shot in panning shots superimposing hand-written notes on Archana's face which turns this way and that, perhaps trying to catch a glimpse of Sukhendu in the library. This might seem repetitive but it is not when one considers that he was and still is the only man in her life, and the books, thesis and notes are only an escape route for her while she lives in the hope that some day, they will be together. This, however, does not happen. The expression on Archana's face, slightly blurred by the superimposition of the notes on her face and vice versa, is filled with anxiety, hope, desperation and a strange angst and that convinces us that the Best Actress Award was well-deserved.

This is preceded by another telling scene in the library where Archana has gone to make notes for her master's that she had left halfway to get married. She sees Sukhendu at another table. They glance at each other but do not talk. She purposely leaves her small purse behind to see if Sukhendu will make a move to pick it up and bring it back to her. But he does not. He picks up the purse alright but hands it over to the library clerk at the counter, pointing out to the lady who left it behind. The clerk comes and gives it to Archana. She takes it quietly, along with the message that Sukhendu will not approach her.

This is a modern story of a modern husband and wife who marry out of love. There is no dowry issue. There is no physical or sexual assault. There are no demanding and cruel in-laws to deal with. There is no direct attack to her person in any way. There is no alcoholic or womanizing husband who tortures her. The violence is silent, invisible and, therefore, very strong. She is not out to make a career. She is content in mundane household chores like any middle-class housewife—handing the handkerchief to her husband before he steps out, making him his morning cup of tea, laying out his clothes, sharing the chores with her aunt-in-law are things she is happy doing. Yet, the marriage, like a large sheet of fragile glass, disintegrates into fragments so small that one can no longer pick them up and put them together. The fine nuances of just one look cast at her mother, or, her brother, breaking into silent sobbing at her father's shoulder, surprised and pained when she hears the silent click at the other end of the phone when Sukhendu disconnects without answering, trying to make small efforts to reach out are glimpses of the director's ability to create collages of silence and the actress' command over her craft, using silence more eloquently than dialogue would have made possible. Her grasp over every scene shows how an actress can portray her tragedy through tiny movements without surrendering to the temptation of turning herself into a martyr or wallowing in self-pity.

The last shot shows her reclining in an easy chair in her quarters, as her voiceover talks about the long wait her life has been reduced to. The titles in the opening scene come up against the visual of the leafless braches of a tree, a metaphor for the emptiness in Archana's life. Interestingly, the film was remade in Hindi as *Kora Kaagaz* (1974). It starred another actor par excellence in the lead role, Jaya Bhaduri, but despite the soul-stirring number '*Mera jeevan kora kaagaz*', the film lacks the edge of the original, and a sloppy 'happy ending' dictated by commercial constraints mars whatever merits it possesses.

Datta

Datta, which means 'betrothed', authored by Sarat Chandra Chattopadhyay, was published serially in the noted literary journal in Bengal, Bharatbarsha, from Poush of the Bengali year 1324 to Bhadra of the Bengali year 1325. It appeared in book form on 2 September

1918. *Datta* was translated into Marathi by Pravakar Vase as *Bijaya* in 1919. Sarat Chandra Chattopadhyay wrote a dramatized version of the novel and titled it *Bijoya,* published in 1934. The Gujarati translation of the novel was done by Krishna Prasad Shastri in 1921, under the title *Sreemati Vijoya,* while T.K. Rama Menon translated it into Malayalam in 1937 and titled it *Narendrababu.*

Film versions of the novel were also made in different periods of time. *Vagdanam*, a Telugu film made by Acharya Atreya, came in in 1961. Ajoy Kar made *Datta* starring Suchitra Sen in 1976, a couple of years before she stopped acting for good. In 1991, a Hindi telefilm called *Bijaya* was made with Sumita Sengupta in the title role. Though rooted in rural Bengal, *Datta* plays around the theme of love so beautifully that it remains timeless and universal.

Datta is basically a love story set in a village in Bengal that is controlled and owned by the erstwhile zamindar Bonomali Bandopadhyay who leaves his village to the care of his friend-turned-manager Rashbihari Das when he converts to the Brahmo[23] faith. His adult and educated daughter, Bijoya, returns to the village, contrary to the belief of the village elders who had felt that she would not return. She finds that her home, her entire zamindari and her subjects are in the control of Rashbihari Das and his crude son Bilash Bihari. Stories of Rashbihari and his son Bilash Bihari's exploitation and inhuman treatment of her subjects reach her, and she slowly but steadily begins to take control of her small 'kingdom'.

Among the people the diabolic Rashbihari continues to mistreat and exploit is Naren Mukherjee, the only son of the recently deceased Jagadish Mukherjee, from the neighbouring village, who was a close friend of Bijoya's father. Jagadish Mukherjee died an unnatural death having left a huge burden of debt he could not repay his friend Bonomali. Rashbihari is determined to appropriate Naren's home and the land around it because the loan has not been repaid, and Naren is in no position to do so. Naren is a doctor who has done his MRCP in London, and has come to perform the last rites of his father. He is more of a researcher and a social activist than a professional doctor. Naren treats the poor villagers for free, teaches the unlettered peasants the alphabet and productive methods of farming when he is not trying to invent medicines for certain chronic diseases the villagers suffer from. Naren visits Bijoya when he learns that the landlady has arrived but does not reveal his identity. The two begin to get close, with Bijoya remaining unaware that the man she is growing to like with every passing day is Naren.

We learn that Rashbihari was originally a peasant but through his underhand dealings as the manager of Bijoya's estate, he has appropriated a lot of land in his name in the same village. Rashbihari and his son Bilash Bihari do not like this strange man, Naren, befriending Bijoya, and they do not recognize him initially. Because of his impractical approach to life and money, Naren is deep in debt. All his works are social and philanthropic so he has no income. This gives Bilash Bihari the opportunity to appropriate Naren's ancestral home with the help of his goons. But he is physically overpowered by Naren who fights back only to save his school. He surrenders the keys of his home to Bilash Bihari and leaves. His financial debts are actually owed to Bijoya but as the greedy father and son have taken charge of her property, they throw their weight around as if Naren is indebted to them.

Against the backdrop of these rural frictions over ancestral property, loan repayment, the construction of a Brahmo temple, the cancellation and then restoration of the annual Durga Puja organized in Naren's uncle's house, grows a beautiful, low-key and subtle love story between Bijoya and Naren. But the thorn in the flesh is Rashbihari's declaration of getting Bijoya married to his son. After some misunderstandings, the two accept that they are doomed to part because Bijoya's marriage to Bilash Bihari is fixed. Then, Bijoya learns from a saddened Naren that her father had originally promised his daughter Bijoya's hand to Jagannath's son Naren. He says he found this by accident while thumbing through bundles of letters between his father and hers, and her father had written about this in one of them. Bonomali had also written off the so-called debt and declared in the letter that Jagadish should hold back his property as dowry from his close friend for his son's marriage to Bijoya. Naren is a pure Brahmin but is an agnostic and an atheist. Bijoya is Brahmo but that does not come in the way of their love, unstated but understood and finally acknowledged by both Bijoya and Naren.

Bijoya is stunned but it is too late because there is only one day left for her wedding. But Dayal Babu, the learned scholar of the village who does the accounts in Bijoya's home, organizes a quick wedding at his home, complete with all Hindu rituals and rites for an unsuspecting Bijoya, and the story ends 'happily-ever-after'.

Datta is as much Bijoya's story as it is Naren's. But as the title of the story is a giveaway to Bijoya, the 'betrothed', she somewhat dominates the scene and evolves along with the story while Naren remains the same in the end as he was when the film began—good-natured, straight-talking, naïve, strong, kind-hearted and generous. Suchitra Sen was forty-five when the film was made, almost towards the end of her career.

Hers is a solid, author-backed role right from the opening frame of the film where the soundtrack heralds an approaching horse-drawn carriage, followed by visuals closing in on Sen's face—beautiful, dignified and regal. Bilash Bihari, who is in the carriage with her, pales beside her. From this point on, till the last scene that shows Naren and Bijoya right in the midst of their marriage ritual, Suchitra Sen holds the film in total command. Soumitra Chatterjee complements her very well with his simple, straight-forward performance, his easy repartee, unsuspecting of the impact he is making on this beautiful woman.

Suchitra Sen brings Bijoya to life and invests her with more power and force than Sarat Chandra depicted in the original novel. This comes across in almost every scene where she is framed with Rashbihari or his son Bilash Bihari, or both. When they reach home for the first time after Bijoya's return to her village, and Rashbihari summons the servants to bring some sherbet for her and arrange for the hand fan, she turns around, smiles and says, 'This is my house.' This is the first nail in the coffin of Rashbihari's plans to appropriate her estate. It sets off a chain of events that makes it obvious that Bijoya is aware of her rights of ownership, her responsibilities as the zamindar towards her subjects, and her control over her life.

Another example in continuity of the same scene shows Rashbihari suggesting that she keep her jewellery and cash for safe-keeping at his home, and she quietly says that there is a safe in her bedroom and she will keep them there. Rashbihari's face falls. When Naren approaches her without revealing his identity to her to request her not to stop the annual Durga Puja celebrations, Bilash Bihari insists that doing so will contravene his father's strict instructions but she takes her decision and allows the celebrations to be held as usual. She is not bothered about the fact that Rashbihari had suggested the stopping of Durga Puja because the noise and the chaos would disturb her; he also wanted to appease her Brahmo mindset that does not believe in idol worship. However, Bijoya visits the pandal and even talks to the idol-maker who has come all the way from Kumartuli in Kolkata to create the figure of the Goddess.

In the novel, Bijoya is about eighteen years of age. The forty-five-year-old Suchitra Sen does the slightly flirtatious and teasing act beautifully in the microscope scene with Naren. She smiles naughtily and teases him about the uselessness of the microscope so that he tries to teach her, and draws her close asking her to shut one eye and peep through the lens with the other. She is not interested in learning to use the microscope but is joyous just being in his physical proximity. 'Everything is hazy,' she says, ostensibly referring to what she sees under the microscope but actually suggesting what she feels about him at that moment. Her slight tremor, her self-conscious behaviour, her awareness that she finds Naren very attractive, are brought across through nuanced shades of facial expressions, her expressive eyes, her teasing ways all of which confuse the naïve Naren about what is happening and why. The subtle eroticism that comes across in this scene lingers.

The microscope functions as an 'agency' in the ups and downs in the evolving love between Naren and Bijoya. Naren wishes to sell the microscope to be able to gather funds to go to Burma. Bijoya offers to buy it and this sets off a chain of interactions between the two that both brings them together as well as sets them apart several times. Bijoya's behaviour reveals that her attraction towards Naren is something she is conscious of and happy about. But Naren, though he too is attracted, is not very aware of his growing feelings for her. The awareness comes later in another poignant scene when, seeing her come out to meet him in the living room, he says, 'Great! You are looking beautiful. I used to paint when I was in London and had painters seen you today, they would have wanted to paint you.' She stands speechless at this open admiration from the man she is falling in love with.

The Tagore song '*More bina othe kon shure baaji, kon nobo chanchal chhande*', lip-synced first by Bijoya when she feels the first stirrings of love within her, becomes a leitmotif, a signature tune whenever she and Naren are shown together, like a romantic interlude that reminds us that these two are destined for each other. In another scene, when the dallying with the microscope is over, Bijoya comes momentarily out of the room to find two angry men, Rashbihari and Bilash Bihari, waiting for her. Rashbihari asks the servant to tell Naren to leave. But Bijoya stops him and tells the older man, 'Can't we talk tomorrow? I need to discuss some things with him. He has to go a long way.' He goes to the room where Naren is waiting and asks him to come back tomorrow. Naren observes her silent tears, turns her face towards him, holds her chin up and asks, 'You are crying!' She is visibly disturbed. She leaves the room to get the money for the microscope but when she returns, he has already left.

During her high fever, in the presence of Rashbihari and his son who come to visit, followed by Naren, Bijoya, in her delirious state, addresses Naren informally and desperately requests him not to leave her. She is not aware of her condition and Naren is both worried and embarrassed. Yet, she comes into her own when she finds Rashbihari insulting Naren about his medical knowledge and implores him to leave and not tolerate the insults. It is a very poignant and emotionally loaded scene where Suchitra, as a sick, delirious and very much in love Bijoya, clearly dominates and leaves an impact.

When she is introduced to Nalini, Dayal Babu's niece who has come to visit her uncle during the summer vacations, Bijoya finds herself immediately suspecting something between Nalini and Naren, a natural trait for any woman in love when she sees another young woman beside the man she is in love with, even though she is engaged to another man. She learns that Nalini is engaged to someone, and, like all women in love, she wrongly assumes that the man Nalini is engaged to is none other than Naren. This suspicion is traced back to Naren and Nalini's friendly relationship, modern by the social standards of those days. Besides, by then, her own marriage fixed with Bilash Bihari is just two days away. Naren, however, is more forthright about his envy of Bilash Bihari. He admits this quite openly to Bijoya, not aware of the impact he is making on her. These small slices of images create a beautiful collage of a love story that stands the test of time and place.

With her subtle expressions and modalities of performance within the confines of convention, Suchitra Sen effectively recreates the period of the story. With the aid of her costumes, her hairdos, her make-up (minus the plucked eyebrows that break the rhythm of authenticity), the kind of saris and the way she drapes herself in them, and the long-sleeved and frilled blouses, Sen fleshes out Bijoya as if she has walked out of the pages of the novel and has pushed the edges of the character beyond the written word. It may be noted that though Bijoya is an unmarried young woman, she believes in keeping herself decked up in ornate jewellery around her neck, dangling earrings in her ears, bangles on her slender wrists that not only enhance her physical beauty but also befit her position and status as the owner and administrator of the village. This contradicts the prescribed dressing for a Hindu woman after she is married. The following paragraph will explain this more lucidly.

Symbols of binding and confinement show up in customs and manners, specifically in those linked to the wife. A proper wife wears a chignon or braid because loose hair implies lack of sexual restraint.[24] The jewellery she wears symbolizes her married status which she has to abandon the moment she becomes a widow. Nose rings and forehead ornaments tied back into chignoned hair (in some parts of the country) symbolize a woman's attachment to her husband and his family. The sari is almost mandatory because, wrapped round the body, it carefully conceals her sexuality. The jewellery a married Hindu woman wears represents control in marriage and good fortune, primarily expressed through children. The wedding sari, mainly red in most of the regions, is the colour of auspiciousness and is also linked to menstrual blood, the blood of childbirth in various ritual and mythic contexts.[25] The bride so adorned is often compared to the Goddess, who, when united with her husband, is the source of worldly prosperity and fertility. The same notions of auspiciousness are attached to the vermillion that married women (in the northern, north-eastern and eastern parts of India) wear in the parting of their hair, or the bindis they sport on their foreheads. The confinement of women to a female sphere with its various symbolisms of binding, then, is generally seen as controlling and channeling power towards approved ends.[26]

What does this practice of remaining dressed up signify for Bijoya? It is a sign that despite her very submissive appearance and feminine grace, she is her own woman and takes almost all the decisions about her subjects, her village and even tries her best to take decisions about her life that get thwarted by the efforts of Rashbihari and his ill-mannered son. In one scene, when Bilash Bihari, finding Dayal Babu in Bijoya's room, rebukes him for remaining absent from work (though he knows Dayal had fever), as some very important work is pending, an angry Bijoya lashes out to him and says, 'Why did you not do it yourself then? Are you not being paid a salary of Rs 200 every month? If you cannot do your work, I am sacking you right now.' A repentant and humiliated Bilash Bihari is roundly rebuked by his father for spoiling his chances of gaining ownership of Bijoya's estate once he gets married to her.

Datta is a very cinema-friendly novel. The characters are either black (Rashbihari and Bilash Bihari) or pristine white (Bijoya, Naren, Dayal Babu, Nalini and the household staff) and any shades of grey are conspicuous by their absence. This made it is easy for director Ajoy Kar, cinematographer Bishu Chakraborty, music composer Hemanta Mukhopadhyay and editor Dulal Dutta to ensure aesthetic beauty, social statement and box-office returns for the film, especially with the powerful performance of Suchitra Sen in the title role where she tries her best to rise above the star charisma created by Suchitra Sen to 'become' Bijoya. Though it is nearly impossible for the audience to see beyond Suchitra Sen, the fact remains that she, as an actress with a long track record of cinema behind her, tried her best to reach out and succeeded to a large extent.

CONCLUSION

Neepa Majumdar writes: 'Star personae in Indian cinema are constructed rather like melodramatic character types partly because of their repeated association with certain roles and, in the case of female stars, because of the severely limited options for roles—either as a romantic heroine or as wife and mother. An example of the convergence of star and melodramatic personalities is to be found in the negative iconicity of the notion of the female star concentrated in visual signifiers such as cigarettes, hair length and clothing styles.'[27]

Majumdar's paper was on star-actress Nargis in her double role in *Anhonee* (1951), directed by K.A. Abbas. The above argument, however, does not apply to Suchitra Sen when she began acting without Uttam Kumar. This is underscored by almost all the films she acted in, both Hindi and Bengali, without Uttam Kumar as her romantic hero. These films, with three major ones discussed in detail earlier in this chapter, and some more in another chapter, show Suchitra Sen cast against the grain. She is not only placed centrally in the script and in the cinematographic space, but is also fleshed out in multiple layers where the characters are rarely one-dimensional and the stories, though elaborated from the original stories with enhanced melodrama, showcase her confidence and her histrionic versatility. In other words, this central character demanded command over histrionics much more than stereotypical roles did. The sole exception in this list of classics is Bimal Roy's *Devdas* where she played Parvati pitted against the towering personality of Dilip Kumar with Vyjayanthimala portraying Chandramukhi who was also one of the reigning stars of Hindi cinema at the time. This list does not include mainstream Hindi films like *Champakali* (1957), *Sarhad* (1960) and *Bambai Ka Babu* (1960). Hrishikesh Mukherjee's *Musafir* (1957) is also excluded because this was a three-story film which few have seen.

According to Bhaskar Sarkar, 'The characters that Sen played exuded a poise that was essentially iconographic. In this respect, Sen's characterizations were rather similar: they were all smart, active, gorgeous creatures who nevertheless remained curiously frozen through the narratives, rarely posing a serious challenge to the status quo.'[28] But this is not true of many of her films. Her 'characterizations' were not similar but her portrayals of the characterizations were. Not all the characters she portrayed were 'smart' nor did they all remain 'curiously frozen through the narratives'. Rina Brown of *Saptapadi* did not remain 'frozen through the narrative' not did Indrani in *Indrani*. In *Sadanander Mela*, though Sheela is the only child of a millionaire, she decides to stay in a hostel and lead life on her own terms. The metamorphosis she manages in her father does not come from remaining 'frozen through the narrative'. Her character is perhaps the most dynamic in this film.

According to Smita Mitra, 'Her star text was calibrated very carefully along the grids of sensual beauty and glamour. In effect, it was this combination that led to a sense of unease that is seen in the numerous reader's letters and responses in the film magazines of that time. She eventually became a recluse after her retirement from the industry in 1978 and after scattered brief public appearances has not been seen in public.'[29]

Suchitra Sen played a working woman in many of her films: towards the end of her career she gained pan-Indian recognition with Gulzar's *Aandhi,* where she essayed the role of a politician who prioritizes a career over family. © Subhash Chheda

Though she made only fleeting appearances in Hindi films, she starred opposite the biggest names of the era: (top) with Dilip Kumar in *Devdas*, (middle) in *Bambai Ka Babu*, (bottom) with Dev Anand in *Bambai Ka Babu*.

Stills from *Hospital*, the only Bengali film in which she starred opposite Ashok Kumar. They would star together again in *Mamta*, the Hindi remake of *Uttar Phalguni*. © Subhash Chheda

Still from *Hospital* © Subhash Chheda

With Uttam Kumar in *Shilpi* © Subhash Chheda

The face that launched a thousand dreams and heartbreaks: (below) Collage downloaded from the net which appeared as cover of a woman's magazine following Sen's demise

UTTAR FALGUNI

A STORMY DRAMA FROM FILMYUG
GULZAR'S
Aandhi
J OM PRAKASH R.D.BURMAN

অগ্নি পরীক্ষা

Some cult films Suchitra Sen starred in: (facing page, top left) *Uttar Phalguni*; (facing page, top right) *Aandhi*; with Uttam Kumar she formed arguably the most successful on-screen pairing in Indian cinema which boasted some memorable music: (facing page, bottom) *Agnipariksha*, the film that made them a household name; (top) *Kamallata*; (middle) *Shap Mochan*; (bottom) *Indrani* © S.M.M. Ausaja

In *Uttar Phalguni*, one of her most memorable roles © Subhash Chheda

4

WORKING WOMEN, BENGALI CINEMA AND SUCHITRA SEN

BACKGROUND

The history of cinema across the world, including India, has proved time and again that the woman has remained trapped in a 'denial of identity'. This is a reflection of the anonymity bestowed on her in real life within and by a patriarchal society. Universally speaking, cinema's image of a woman, either as a patriarchal construct or as a socio-historically differentiated product, is almost always made subservient to voyeuristic and fetishistic impulses; this is done mostly at the expense of realism or creative and aesthetic expression. If handled by unskilled people, often for commercial considerations, the results could be negative or amateurish or both. Rather than attacking this 'denial of identity' to woman—in real life and in cinema—it becomes necessary under these circumstances to target the dominant construction of the celluloid woman's identity as *total, non-contradictory, homogenous and unchanging*.

It may be noted, however, that the notion of 'identity' is itself neither stable, nor permanent. It is a continuous process of construction and reconstruction that functions as a warning to any student of cinema trying to establish final, rigid and achieved models of representation. The very notion of 'process' suggests flux, discontinuities, digressions and progressions rather than fixed and rigid positions. It suggests that a range of positions of identification may exist within any text; and that, within the social situation of their viewing, sections of a given audience may shift subject positions as they get involved with the film. Vijay Anand's *Guide* (1965), for example, offers multiple perspectives within the same character—that of Rosie, the wife-turned-lover-turned-danseuse, though she is not the central character in the film. Chhoti Bahu in Guru Dutt's *Sahib, Bibi Aur Ghulam* offers similar fluidities in the same character as it evolves over the narrative space of the film. At times, these perspectives are revealed on repeated viewings of the same film over a span of time. Sometimes, they unfold to the discerning viewer at the first viewing itself.

Many Indian film-makers have focused on and often tried to counter the constricted roles women are either coerced into or forced to play in Indian society. Many of them have, in the past, tried to, as many still are in the present, constantly explore spaces of negotiation between the conditioned roles women have to perform and the options that could open up new windows of thought, lifestyle and perspective. Through their films, they have tried to draw women out of their enforced isolation, raising questions about their status of self-denial and martyrdom, either in the audience, or within the characters in the films, or both.

Time has shown that across the world, paid employment of women does not necessarily lead to the economic independence of women, much less to equality between men and women. Structural changes in the economy have caused the displacement of many women into occupational sectors that are gender-specific and offer low-wage and low-benefit employment opportunities. The shift into a knowledge-based economy has meant that women with basic education and minimal skills will be least likely to access work that can effectively and permanently take them and their families out of poverty.

Men find these occupations less attractive and leave the field open to women.

One example is teaching as a profession. Earlier, when teaching was less paid than most other mainstream occupations, it was crowded by women. The crowding of women in teaching functioned like a vicious circle because it brought down the wages even further. Interestingly, when teachers' wages began to rise, men began to enter the profession. The male-female ratio in teaching which was tilted against men is now more democratic and egalitarian. The downward pressure on wages in occupations invaded by women would not happen if women stopped flocking a few occupations and were trained for an entire range of economic activities open to men, writes Esther Boserup.[1]

Article 14 of the Indian Constitution states that all persons, male and female, are equal before the law and shall get equal protection before the law. Article 15 states that there shall be no discrimination against any person on grounds of sex. Article 16 guarantees equality of opportunity in matters of public employment irrespective of sex. But reality shows that these constitutional rights are more in theory than in practice. The Hindu Code, passed as a separate set of Acts between 1950 and 1955, rewrote for Hindus the laws of marriage and divorce, and marriage and adoption. Adult suffrage added women to electoral roles and political parties pledged their commitment to women's issues. The Medical Termination of Pregnancy Act enacted in 1971 sought to legalize abortions provided they are carried out under conditions specified in the Act. But illegal abortions have not stopped at all because of unmarried pregnancies and the fear of social stigma they carry.

The main difference between women's struggles during the freedom movement and today is that earlier the struggle was for the democratic and political rights of women. This included the right to education and employment and the right to own property. In other words, earlier feminists fought for legal reforms to gain legal equality in society.[2] Today, women have moved beyond the framework of legal reforms to work towards their emancipation. This includes the fight against women's subordination to men within the home, against their exploitation by the family, against their continuing low status at work, in society and within cultural and religious practices. Feminism also challenges the notions of femininity and masculinity as mutually exclusive and biologically determined categories. Feminism may be a foreign term but the concept of feminism is universal, standing for a transformational process. It is a foreign term but not a foreign ideology. Feminism and feminist struggles arose in Asia when women developed a consciousness about democratic rights and about the injustice of depriving half the population of its basic rights.

A woman has always been misled by the imposed ideal of womanhood. Be it her gentle manners and natural tenderness, or her lack of physical strength, she has found herself hidden behind illusions, fenced in from all sides and forced away from the real world into the seclusion of a helpless and dispossessed life. It is the unfair system that fostered the absurd notion that she has no place in the world of work outside her home. The man is the maker of that world, and a woman's duty is to make him a home.[3]

Women in general are challenged by the elements of exclusion, devaluation and misogyny in their personal interactions and institutional experiences. Ideas and images of femininity in the media, science and politics, education, health, social and employment systems dictate parameters for 'normal' females. When women begin to question the 'truth', 'universality' and 'normality' of these assumptions and images, insisting that their authentic experiences and equality of rights be taken into account, their behaviour, both assertive and atypical for their assigned sex role, serves as a processing mechanism vis-à-vis the reality with which they must cope, a paradoxical reality embodying potential for change.

They then no longer observe the rules that sustain feminine 'normality'. Making their own rules is often equated with breaking the prescribed ones. This is frequently opposed by demonstrations of force or coercion—direct or indirect, active or passive, creating power struggles that sometimes become difficult to cope with. Such oppositions are basically an attempt to maintain the existing dichotomy between male and female power, the cultural meanings and values that describe the mechanism locking women into subordinate positions through the imposition of a gender-specific catalogue of structures.

Within Bengali cinema, traditional gender roles and a renewed emphasis on the value of the home contributed to what might be called a 'domestic revival' in the mid-1950s. Suchitra Sen was a product of this time and was a living celluloid evidence of sexist gender representation in the films that saw her rise to the top. But looked at in retrospect, if one were to look closely enough, one could perhaps be able to discover finer arguments within the narrative and the characterization of the leading lady that supported a woman's right to choose the way she wanted to lead her life. If she sacrificed her terms for her love for a man such as in *Harano Sur*, that too was her choice. If she refused to abort her unborn child because she was not married in *Hospital*, she did that, too, and led the life of a single mother, supporting herself and her son with her earnings as a qualified doctor. Therefore, even within the framework of a strongly patriarchal ideology, the films of Suchitra Sen were not degrading to women and by and large, beneath the surface, tried not to reinforce patriarchal values. The dignified persona of Suchitra Sen, on screen and off it, helped uphold the dignity of a woman even when she was a courtesan in *Uttar Phalguni*.

Any film about a woman in equal partnership with the man she loves—be it her husband or her lover—in strength, intelligence and independence, would not have been accepted by the audience in the 1950s through the '60s and '70s in Bengali or Indian cinema. In spite of the optimistic image, it would not have reached the audience because it would have seemed foreign, and somewhat unacceptable at the time. Looked at from this point, it becomes interesting to read some significant films of Suchitra Sen against the grain, trying to show that she is as independent and as modern as today's women are, though she fits into the moral and socially acceptable framework for women at the time. Her arrival in Bengali cinema predates the time-space paradigm of feminist readings of Indian cinema. Yet, her films taken together form a focal point.

WORKING WOMEN

The term 'working women' specifically refers to women whose work is economically productive and involves exchange value in cash or kind or both. In this sense, the term would apply to the courtesan in *Uttar Phalguni* as much as it would apply to the single mother who works to bring up her child in *Hospital*. 'Working women' would refer to the widest range of economic and productive activities from a nurse in a psychiatric ward in *Deep Jele Jai*, to a sex worker in *Mondo Meyer Upakhyan* (2002) or a saleswoman as in Satyajit Ray's *Mahanagar* (1963).

There are at least three terms, namely female participation in labour market, labour force and workforce, which are used interchangeably while analysing women's participation in economic activities. These terms are indeed related, but denote different dimensions. While labour force includes all types of employment status, labour market participation excludes unpaid family workers who do not enter the market.[4] Similarly, labour force consists of both employed and unemployed, whereas workforce captures only those who are employed. Given the primary intent of the present research, women's participation in the workforce—that is, paid work—is the preferred focus of this research, and integral to it.

Confining our attention primarily to paid work and relating it to aspects of empowerment does not imply that unpaid work—subsistence-related economic activities, domestic maintenance work and caring labour—performed by women is unimportant and unrelated to their empowerment. Though these kinds of unpaid work do not fetch a direct income, they are no less productive than paid work, since the latter are parasitic on the former.[5] These unpaid activities propel, on a daily and intergenerational basis, the labour force that performs the paid activities.[6]

Notwithstanding the significance of unpaid work, paid work is associated often with certain characteristics, mainly immediate economic rewards and hence associated decline in economic dependency together with social recognition and standing, which are considered to be critical inputs to women's empowerment and well-being. Paid work has, therefore, attained some prominence in the policy discourses on gender and development in the South Asian region, where social norms, religious practices and legal entitlements restrict or deny women's access to, and their claims on familial, economic resources.[7]

SUCHITRA SEN AS A WORKING WOMAN

Before embarking on an analysis of Sen's representation on screen as a working woman, one may point out that Suchitra Sen was a working woman right through her adult life that spanned nearly three long decades. One does not quite know at first hand whether there was some intercutting between her real life as a working woman and her screen roles as working women. One is, however, aware that she slowly became a single working mother to her daughter along the way during her career after her separation from her husband and after his demise. She was independent in the sense that she made her own decisions about her career choices and on how she would bring up her only child Moon Moon Sen. But this very 'independence' also vested her with the financial, emotional and social responsibility of running her family alone, all by herself. According to her close family members, including her daughter, she was against her daughter joining films. Her emphasis was on a strong and solid foundation in education which she herself did not get but ensured that her daughter did. But when her daughter joined films after she was married and became a mother, Sen could do nothing about it and refrained from interfering.

Sen has portrayed the working woman in several films opposite Uttam Kumar. Notable ones among them are *Indrani, Harano Sur, Saptapadi, Sabar Uparey, Haar Mana Haar,* etc. But in most films where she was paired with Uttam Kumar, the 'working woman' identity was almost rendered invisible in the narrative except in two major films, *Indrani* and *Harano Sur*.

I have chosen four films that depict Suchitra Sen in the role of a strong working woman without the celluloid support of Uttam Kumar. Two films with Uttam Kumar in which she plays the heroine in a hero-centric film are discussed here to demonstrate how, even when given secondary significance and space, she left her mark with her portrayal of the character she played. One is *Sabar Uparey* and the other is *Indrani*. Both were great hits and are remembered among outstanding films pairing Suchitra with Uttam Kumar but it is the glamour and beauty of Suchitra Sen that left a deeper mark on the audience than either the character she portrayed or her performance. This is precisely why these two films have been chosen. Two other important films namely *Harano Sur* and *Saptapadi* that also show Suchitra Sen as a working woman pitched opposite Uttam Kumar are not included here because they are discussed in a separate chapter that explores and analyses the magical chemistry of this great pair.

The films in which she played a single working woman chosen here include *Deep Jele Jai, Hospital, Uttar Phalguni/Mamta* and *Aandhi*. These films do not necessarily back feminist readings of the texts because the female protagonist is not a slogan-raising, flag-hoisting feminist by any stretch of imagination. However, she is a working woman, and the protagonist's working life is presented in different manifestations in these four films.

It is not accidental that she was repeatedly cast as a dedicated professional woman in many of the films—doctor, teacher, nurse—committed to her work and attempting to create a balance between the demands of love and romance and work. So if she is the mahanayika, that stature is hers not because she compromised on her values and morals, but because she had the conviction to reach the top without resorting to easily available publicity stunts and negotiating her position and status. The contours of this model of stardom successfully deployed a certain image of this modern young woman/star who performs and enacts both tradition and individuated desires.[8]

Sabar Uparey

Sabar Uparey was directed by the Agradoot group. It was based on A.J. Cronin's *Beyond This Place* (1953) which was also made into a Hindi film *Kala Paani* (1958) under the Navketan Films banner, and was directed by Raj Khosla. It starred Dev Anand, Madhubala and Nalini Jaywant in key roles. However, the credits of the Bengali film do not acknowledge the original writer, and Nitai Bhattacharya is credited with the story and the script.

This is a Suchitra-Uttam film that is actually focused on a father-son relationship. The son is determined to prove his father's innocence in the murder case of Hemangini, a woman of dubious reputation, when Shankar, the son, was a small boy. The father is imprisoned for life and has lost both his mind and memory. Shankar and his mother migrate from Krishnanagar to Patna after the father's sentence. Shankar (Uttam Kumar) returns to the small town of Krishnanagar after twelve years to search for evidence that will prove his father's innocence. When everyone shuns him either for his past or because the real culprit is a very powerful man, he meets this sympathetic young woman, Rita, who lends him a shoulder to cry on and stretches out a hand to hold, though she herself, a refugee, is in no better position. In one scene, she refers to herself as *nigrihita* which means 'a tormented and tortured woman'. Though this seems to be tinged with the aura of a budding romance, if probed deeper, one realizes that her empathy for a young man ostracized by society for his 'tainted' father springs from her own sordid past. Their respective private tragedies become a bridge to bond the two individuals in a deeper relationship.

Suchitra Sen as Rita Das enters the scene after more than twenty minutes into this 125-minute film. We learn that she works as a teacher in a school, though one never actually sees her going to work. She also moonlights in a forty-year-old local newspaper in Krishnanagar. She lives independently in a flat with two other female flat-mates. When Shankar is thrown out of the guest house where he has taken shelter and is wandering aimlessly and hungrily across the streets, Rita finds him. She brings him back with her to her flat and offers him shelter in the living room. This is a sign of great courage for a single working woman in the 1950s in Bengal. Does this unusual courage come from the torture she had already suffered while fleeing her village in East Pakistan in 1947? Or is it a sign of her love for him? Perhaps it is both.

This unusual courage does not compromise on the inherent femininity in the character of Rita who is soft-spoken, non-interfering and a woman of few words. The character is fleshed out by Suchitra Sen in a way that one can see through that grace, that low-profile reticence, to catch a glimpse of the fiercely moral, emotional and determined young woman who uses her tragic past as a source of strength to draw from instead of being sucked into a cauldron of self-pity and victimhood. She never tries to curry sympathy for her past tribulations and mentions it only once almost casually as a frame of reference and not as an incident that scarred her life. The camera captures her mostly in medium long shots and long shots, in full portraits, unlike the huge close-ups her screen image is famous for. She is presented in soft focus, mainly to enhance her submissive character and also, perhaps, to underscore her secondary status in the bigger plot.

Rita, as presented and portrayed by Suchitra Sen, is a fine blend of a mother-substitute and a lover without whose support it would never have been possible for Shankar to succeed in his struggle to establish the truth. When Shankar is arrested for disturbing public peace, Rita takes up the challenge and asks her famous journalist brother to bail Shankar out. She also nurses him back to health when he collapses while walking out of court. Thanks to the journalist brother, the media creates enough pressure for the old case to be reopened. A special committee is formed and Shankar is asked to defend his father. Rita is beside him even when everyone discards him as a 'lost' case.

Sabar Uparey, however, is mostly remembered for the subtle romance between the struggling lovers and for the superb performance of Uttam Kumar and Chhabi Biswas as his wronged father. The other actors were also established names in Bengali cinema—Pahari Sanyal, Nitish Mukherjee, etc. It was a hero-centric film where Rita is merely a complement. But this film stands out as a solid example of how Sen could bring out the best and do justice to her character even when the hero has been given prominence and has the author-backed role.

The quality of the 'working woman', as seen through Rita, is subtle yet significant. Having no family to fall back on or seek support from, she garners independence for herself from her tragic past on one hand and her 'working' present on the other. Though the 'working' element remains in the background, it is an important feature of her character and for the relationship between Rita and Shankar. Looking back, placing the two romantic leads in perspective, Rita's character could be read as the stronger one between the two. She offers moral support without expecting anything in return from the man she has fallen in love with.

Indrani

Indrani, directed by Niren Lahiri and based on a story by Achintya Kumar Sengupta, is a regular Uttam-Suchitra love story with some twists that diverted from the syrupy on-screen romance the audience was accustomed to watching in any Uttam-Suchitra film. While in college, the beautiful Indrani falls in love with Sudarshan who fails to make it big in life. The two get married and, initially, Indrani has no compunctions about a husband who is jobless. But slowly, as she grows to become the assistant headmistress of a small-town school where they have settled after marriage, the parameters of their relationship begin to change predictably. Indrani, a strong and patient woman who is very much in love with Sudarshan, gradually loses her patience with him though there is still deep love between them.

Indrani was much ahead of its time. It is one of the first films of the 1950s to explore the ramifications of a husband-wife relationship where the wife is successful and the husband is a failure and is not even interested in making something out of his life. He holds a first-class master's degree in psychology and is working for his PhD but does not take it seriously. Misunderstandings crop up between the two. Indrani slowly becomes weary of her husband's lackadaisical attitude towards working for a living while Sudarshan develops a complex about his wife's success. There comes a point when he cannot take it anymore and leaves home. Though Indrani is devastated, she is confident that he will come back; he does not.

But from this point onwards, the script almost dispenses with Indrani altogether to concentrate on how Sudarshan reconstructs his life with the help of an old man who takes a liking to him. He comes to a remote village and helps the villagers to cut through rocks to draw water and also completes his PhD in the meantime. Fifteen villages now have a steady source of water supply and Sudarshan becomes a household name. Indrani sees a newspaper article on his work, quits her job at once, and comes to his village to work with him. He rejects her help but something catastrophic happens, and the pair lives 'happily-ever-after'.

Suchitra Sen as Indrani plays out the different dimensions of her character quite lucidly. Her father used to bring out a paper that rebelled against women's education. When his wife delivers a girl child, he is devastated and the paper shuts down. But he educates her all the same and sends her off to Kolkata for further studies. From a young girl coming for further studies to a hostel in Kolkata, to falling in love with her roommate's handsome cousin, through marrying him against the express wishes of his family and her father, to comment caustically about how the same family that accepted her as 'friend' could not accept her as 'daughter-in-law', to being an extremely supportive partner to her husband, Indrani knows her own mind. It is she who proposes marriage to Sudarshan and pushes him to marry her. It is she who informs her parents and walks out when her father rejects her. Indrani is a very courageous character for the time and the social setting the film is placed in.

One fails to understand why the script suddenly develops cold feet and plays to the patriarchal gallery to paint Indrani with negative colours and turn Sudarshan into an ideal human being in every sense. The other question that remains with us after the film is over is: does Indrani come back because she still loves Sudarshan and cannot live without him? Or, does she search him out because he is now famous, highly educated and successful? It could be the latter because the script does not give us the opportunity to find out what happens to Indrani after Sudarshan leaves her. In this sense, *Indrani* is unfair both to the character the film is named after as well as to Suchitra Sen whose talents are completely wasted in the second half.

There are some beautiful moments of togetherness in the film. One is in the small cabin in a restaurant where Indrani and Sudarshan have a teasing exchange. Another is during the song sequence '*Neerh chhoto khoti nei akash to boro*', in which Sudarshan begins to sing and a smiling Indrani joins him. It is sad that though the film is named after her character and though she does justice to the character as well as adds to the film through her ethereal beauty and glamour, at the end of it all, she is given short shrift by the director and the script.

Deep Jele Jai

Deep Jele Jai is based on a Bengali story 'Nurse Mitra' authored by Ashutosh Mukherjee. This was later made in Hindi as *Khamoshi* (1969), produced by Hemant Kumar under his production banner and directed by Asit Sen, who also directed the Bengali version. However, the mainstream Hindi audience did not respond as positively to

Khamoshi as they did to *Deep Jele Jai*. The musical score for both films, composed by Hemant Kumar, was a big hit and remains popular till this day. When comparisons were drawn between the Bengali and Hindi versions, Waheeda Rehman, who portrayed Radha (originally enacted by Suchitra Sen), fared unfavourably because her weeping-and-laughing scene towards the tragic climax had to be dubbed while Sen did the scene 'live' or in sync-sound. Critics who had not seen the Bengali version begged to differ. They opined that what really made this film stand out was the black-and-white cinematography by Kamal Bose, who won the Filmfare Award for Best Cinematography. *Khamoshi* 'is considered Waheeda Rehman's finest acting feat, as she carries the entire film through her powerful yet understated acting, she received a Filmfare nomination for it,' writes Nitin Bali. Gulzar's memorable lyrics are another milestone of this film.

Asit Sen (1922–2001) was one of the most outstanding directors of his time in Bengali cinema when the schism between mainstream and art cinema practically did not exist in the sense of form and content. He joined films as a camera assistant to D.K. Mehta before assisting his uncle, noted cameraman Ramananda Sengupta, on *Purbaraag* (1947). He then joined Gandhiji's entourage for a month, shooting an independent documentary on 16mm covering Gandhiji's tour of Noakhali and Patna. He made his directorial debut with the Assamese film *Biplabi* (1948). *Biplabi* tells the story of an Indian radical who sacrifices his life for his country. The film remained a standard work in the genre of films depicting the struggle for freedom. Ironically, Sen failed to get his name in the credits following a dispute with the producers over its ending!

He was deeply influenced by the works of Alfred Hitchcock and Danny Kaye. His first Bengali film *Chalachal* (1956) was a thumping box-office hit. It starred Arundhati Devi. The director-actress chemistry worked with his next film *Panchatapa* (1957). Sen will remain linked to two landmark Suchitra Sen starrers: *Deep Jele Jai* and *Uttar Phalguni*. The Hindi remake of *Uttar Phalguni*, *Mamta*, was also a big hit.

A technically accomplished director, Asit Sen did not use flashy technique to tell his stories. He maintained that if you have to resort to technical gimmickry to prop up your film, it means you have nothing of substance to say. To him, film-making was about sharing emotions, sharing pain. Much of Asit Sen's style as a film-maker was in the vein of Bimal Roy in its simultaneous assimilation of romantic Bengali literature, Hollywood and neo-realism. Bimal Roy produced two of his films in Hindi—*Parivar* (1956), his first Hindi film, and *Apradhi Kaun* (1957). He directed Rajesh Khanna in two films, his two most well-known Hindi films—*Khamoshi* and *Safar* (1970). He won the Filmfare Award for *Safar*, which was a remake of *Chalachal*. After *Safar*, none of his films could strike gold at the box office. *Bairaag* (1976) was a total disaster. His last film was *Pratigya*, in 1985.

Ashutosh Mukherjee (1920–1989) was a very popular author of novels and short stories in contemporary Bengali literature through the 1950s into the 1980s, and is known to be the most cinema-friendly author of his time. 'Nurse Mitra', on which the film *Deep Jele Jai* is based, was his first published story in *Basumati*, a noted literary magazine in Bengali. His first novel *Swaha* was also published in *Basumati* and was later published as a book under the title *Ruper Hate Bikikini*. He joined *Jugantar*, a leading Bengali daily in 1955 and became the head of the Sunday special of the newspaper. Many of his novels have been made into films, both in Hindi and in Bengali. Among the Bengali films are *Panchatapa, Chalachal, Nagar Darpane* (1975), *Alor Thikana* (1974), *Kaal Tumi Aleya* (1976), *Saat Paake Bandha* (1963), *Ami Shey O Sokha* (1975), Among Hindi films made on his novels are *Khamoshi* (1969), *Safar* (1970), *Kora Kaagaz* (1974) and *Bemisal* (1982). He shared very good writer-director chemistry with film-maker Asit Sen who made many a film based on Mukherjee's stories. Many of his novels have been translated in different Indian languages.

In *Deep Jele Jai*, Radha Mitra (Suchitra Sen) is a London-trained psychiatric nurse who works in a mental hospital in Kolkata. She is dedicated to her work and is a favourite of the chief medical officer, the Colonel (Pahari Sanyal), for her ability to cure a patient of any kind of depressive state linked to a love affair gone sour. He tells her to pretend to fall in love with the patient till he begins to depend on her emotionally and morally. The film opens with a patient being discharged from the mental home after a complete cure.

This patient is soon replaced by a new admission. The Colonel assigns the case to Radha. She refuses to accept the case papers, saying, 'I cannot act,' because she is just a nurse. Circumstances force her to take the case of Tapas (Basanta Choudhury), suffering from deep depression that has driven him over the edge and made him prone to extremely violent behaviour. With Radha's kind and patient supervision, Tapas begins to depend on her. When Radha persuades his girlfriend Sulekha (Kajari Guha) to approach him, he turns violent and tries to throttle her. Radha saves him in the nick of time from being administered electric shock. This makes Tapas even more dependent on Radha.

But Radha is no longer the fresh, optimistic and efficient psychiatric nurse she once was. This playacting with Tapas has taken a heavy toll on her. She requests the Colonel to keep Tapas away from her before he leaves the nursing home, now cured. But Tapas is desperate to meet her one last time to ask her whether she was really putting on an act or whether she is in love with him. Radha does not open the door. A saddened Tapas goes away. In the end, we find Radha reduced to a ghost of her balanced self, a mental patient in the same nursing home. 'Why did I not realize that there was a woman behind that nurse's uniform?' the Colonel keeps asking himself as he stokes his pipe with tobacco, and the chief matron (Chandrabati Devi) wipes off a tear when she calls out Radha's number. Some of her former colleagues escort her to the same cabin Tapas has just vacated.

We see Radha reading her diary with a voiceover mentioning Debashish, the patient who has just gone back, cured, to his girlfriend, prepared to marry her. Cut to a roll call of the inmates with a nurse calling out numbers, a telling suggestion of human beings reduced to simple numbers without name, face or identity.

One patient (Anil Chatterjee) approaches Radha and laments that his son had to go without food even that day. It sets the ambience within the nursing home. One patient takes a cheque book out of his pocket and writes out cheques to everyone. Another sits quietly at a table in front of a chessboard. A fourth keeps writing postcards. In the women's wing, a giggling young woman imagines the approaching doctor to be her lover. The climax rounds up the beginning—a roll call by the matron calling out numbers of women patients. At the end of the queue, we see a distraught, mentally imbalanced Radha, not able to walk, her hair dishevelled, her sari trailing any which way, deep black circles under her eyes, and she being escorted by two colleagues.

The Colonel is a ruthless scientist who is more interested in the subject of his 'research' than in the mental health of his paramedical staff. Radha points this out in one scene. He narrates an anecdote of his war backdrop to cite what commitment means to a war-time nurse. Chandrabati Devi as the matron almost without any dialogue fleshes out the seriousness in a few scenes. Basanta Chowdhury is uneven: good when he is sane but unconvincing when he is not. Kajari Guha as Tapas's girlfriend is artificial and crude, perhaps by design. Anil Chatterjee has a wonderful song sequence when he wants a peg and Radha pours water from a jug into his empty bottle and he drinks and sings in his 'tipsy' state! The song carries references to the legendary Devdas-Parvati story. Tulsi Chakraborty is brilliant in a well-fleshed-out cameo as Tapas's sympathetic friend from the mess he stayed in. The character offers an insight into the social reality that existed in the late 1950s where even mess colleagues bonded with warmth and concern.

One of the most outstanding features of the film is its musical score by Hemanta Mukherjee. The theme song '*Ei raat tomar amar*' on the soundtrack is said to have created copyright issues for Mukherjee as it is alleged to have been inspired by a Western music theme. But over time, it has survived most competitions with its haunting, eerie effect together with brilliant cinematography. Bijoy Bose's art direction and Tarun Dutta's editing offer a firm complement to the rest. There are repeated references to Tagore through his collection of poems, *Sanchayita*, that Radha falls back on and even gifts to a patient on his wedding.

Deep Jele Jai was made when cinema was mostly shot in black-and-white. Jyoti Laha and Anil Gupta's cinematography reveals a beautiful encapsulation of this technical mode that generates an ideal balancing act between Suchitra Sen's magnificent close-ups and the shot-breaks that span everything from very slow panning shots to silhouetted shots to shots taken in semi-darkness, to long-angle shots and even an overhead crane shot in the opening frame of the film. Some shots show Suchitra Sen in backlight with the halo her screen image was famous for. There is one moving scene where she imagines herself with a bindi, in a coloured sari and jewellery. *Deep Jele Jai* has survived the onslaughts of time, technology and evolution to remain one of the best films directed by Asit Sen, marking Suchitra Sen in one of her unforgettable performances in a heroine-oriented film.

The film stands out because the main grouse of nurses in India—responsibility without power—comes across lucidly and movingly in the film. The Colonel forces Radha to take on the responsibility of being a personal nurse to Tapas, the new patient who steps in place of the earlier one, Debashish, with whom she 'fell in love' during the treatment. She tries to persuade the Colonel not to burden her with difficult cases but he insists. An experienced war-time doctor, he misses out on the stress she is under. He does not even try to find out why she is refusing the case. This is emotional blackmail that takes advantage of her dedication to her profession and her patient.

The film uncovers the sad truth of how a woman totally dedicated to her profession can, wittingly or unwittingly, be stripped of her right to a normal life filled with love for a man, marriage and a happy family life. Radha never thinks about a normal family life till she falls in love first with Debashish and then with Tapas. The woman in her is suppressed under the duty-bound nurse Radha who conditions herself to believe that for her, the patient comes first. The self-conditioning is so extreme that she breaks under pressure and becomes a patient herself in the same hospital where she has cured many. Her love is genuine, not 'manufactured' or 'manipulated' for professional reasons. She is not an actress, as she keeps insisting. But no one is listening.

Despite not having a romantic hero in the lead, the film was a box-office hit. It is perhaps one major film with a female protagonist that does not offer a feminist slant on the film, the story or the character. There is an undertone of truth in a psychiatric nurse getting emotionally involved with her patient/patients that is shown in *Deep Jele Jai*. 'A Comparative Study of the Perceptions of British Mental Health Nurses and Psychiatrists of their Work Environment'[9] by Janie Dallender, Peter Nolan, Joaquim Soares, Sarah Thomsen and Bengt Arnetz proves this. This study was undertaken in the West Midlands in England. The aim was to ascertain the extent to which the environment in which mental health professionals' work impacts on their personal mental and physical well-being. Seventy-four psychiatrists and 301 mental health nurses responded to a postal questionnaire. Analysis of data indicated that significant differences exist between nurses and psychiatrists in their physical working environment, their sources of support with a work-related problem, and the effects of their work on their own mental and physical health. The main recommendation derived from this study was to improve communication between mental health professionals and their managers by giving more structured feedback and guidance about one's work performance. This may help alleviate the mental strain many mental health professionals experience in their work.

Deep Jele Jai marks a milestone performance in Suchitra Sen's career. It takes full advantage of her camera-friendly, sensuous beauty as much as she gives to it her best in histrionics. If she seems a little melodramatic in a few fractional moments, it is due to the demands of the script, the time and the fact that this is a mainstream film. She brings out the two dimensions of her character extremely well. One needs her to depict a woman silently pining for love, knowing that for her the story will always be a tragic one. The other shows her as an efficient, low-profile but warm nurse who has a kind word for every patient.

She lives out her mentor, the Colonel's belief that it is rapport between the curing and the to-be-cured that carries the magic of cure in every mental case. In order to fulfil her mission, she can be diabolic at times. She literally blackmails Tapas's girlfriend with her old love letters sent to him to force her to come and visit him at the mental home at once. She threatens Sulekha's two boyfriends when they warn her about complaining to the police. It is the delicate play of hide-and-seek between 'acting' and 'not acting', between 'pretending' to fall in love as a therapeutic measure and 'actually' falling in love in real life somewhere along the way that enriches the humane realism in Radha's character. Sen's unforgettable performance, the chiaroscuro cinematography, the haunting musical score and small touches like the diaphanous white curtains in Radha's room swaying in the breeze as she sits on an easy chair, refusing to respond to Tapas crying out to her, banging on her closed door, captured in a top-angle long shot, enhance the film immeasurably.

Radha's is a slow and steady regression into a depressive mental state. Her regression is due to the very radical and unorthodox form of treatment that has no basis in psychiatry or in the treatment of mental illness her doctor-mentor adopts. He uses her wrongly as 'agency' to attain his 'objective'. He does not think even once what the consequences of such an action might be on her mental state. In this lies a moral lesson for all psychiatrists everywhere.

Hospital

There are several reasons for choosing *Hospital*. Firstly, it is the only film in which Suchitra Sen was cast opposite Ashok Kumar, who, by then, was one of the most established and talented actors of Hindi cinema and rarely did Bengali films; secondly, it was directed by Sushil Majumdar, a very successful mainstream film-maker in Bengali cinema; thirdly, it is based on a novel of the same name by Nihar Ranjan Gupta, a contemporary author of the time who commanded a mass readership; and finally, the film explores, through its female protagonist, a woman burdened with the dual responsibility of motherhood and work. In the initial stages of the film, Sharbari, who practises medicine, places work as the focus of her life. Once she becomes pregnant, her profession is relegated to second place and personal factors take preference. Work from then on becomes a necessity and motherhood, a priority, responsibility and an emotional crutch she refuses to compromise with.

Sushil Majumdar was one of the most successful film-makers of his time. He made around thirty-two mainstream films that were mostly drawn from Bengali literature. He debuted as director in 1932 with the film *Ekoda*. His last film was *Basanti Purnima* (1973). He was also a very good actor and one of his best-known roles was in Satyajit Ray's *Chiriakhana* (1967).

The 1950s and '60s were Majumdar's best years. His film *Moner Mayur* (1954), starring Uttam Kumar and Bharati Devi in the lead, was one of the best-known box-office hits of its time. It is a tender, romantic entertainer, setting the signature stamp for its director who was known for choosing cinema-friendly stories with a strong cast and very good music. In 1959, he had two releases, *Shubharatri*, starring Suchitra Sen and Basanta Choudhury, and *Pushpadhanu*, starring Uttam Kumar and Arundhati Devi.

But his most successful film in the latter part of his career was *Lal Pathar*. A Hindi remake followed in 1971, but could not repeat the success of the original Bengali version. It is a dramatic story of love, betrayal, passion, jealousy, obsession and loss of mental balance. Starring Uttam Kumar, Supriya Debi, Nirmal Kumar and others, the film's climax was shot against the historical backdrop of Fatehpur Sikri. The entire film revolves around the complex character of Kumar Bahadur who traps the two women in his life—his mistress, Madhuri, and his wife, Sumita—in different ways so that they have no way out of the web. Sumita dies accidentally in a sudden shot fired from her husband's gun. Kumar Bahadur loses his mental balance. Madhuri is forced to continue to replay a scene from history to try and appease the guilt Kumar Bahadur suffers from as he keeps searching for that stone stained with his wife's blood (*lal pathar*) at Fatehpur Sikri till his hair turns white and Madhuri is bent with age.

Nihar Ranjan Gupta was a famous novelist and short story writer. He developed his writing abilities alongside being a highly qualified dermatologist. His creation of the detective Kiriti Roy led to his immense popularity among readers across generations. In addition to writing detective novels, some of which have gone into volumes, he also wrote dramatic novels with twists and turns that made them extremely cinema-friendly and which crossed genres, ranging from family dramas, relationships, romance and intrigue. Some of his novels also treaded the fragile world of ghosts. Film-makers found in his stories the ingredients of hits. As a consequence, many of his novels have been turned into films, both in Hindi and Bengali. Among famous Hindi films based on his work are *Do Anjaane* (1976), *Mamta, Mere Lal* (1966), *Dosti* (1964), *Badsha* (1963) and *Meri Surat Teri Ankhen* (1963). Bengali films based on his works that became all-time hits are *Lalu Bhulu* (1959), *Raater Rajanigandha* (1963), *Maya Mriga* (1960), *Hospital, Uttar Phalguni, Kalankini Kankabati* (1981) and *Kajallata* (1975).

Hospital is basically a love story that goes sour, thus triggering the main narrative. Sarbari and Saibal, both doctors, are in love and are planning to get married. While on an outing into the rivers, they are forced to stay the night at a bungalow as they cannot get back home. Sarbari gets pregnant. She is quite happy. But she is shocked when she finds Saibal accepting responsibility for the pregnancy but asking her at the same time to get rid of the unborn baby. She informs Saibal that she will in no case abort the baby she is carrying, and adds that she will never ever ask him to assume the responsibility of being the child's father. Saibal is afraid of the social stigma that will ensue if the baby is born too soon after the marriage. An adamant Sarbari takes the medical chief's help to get a job in a nursing home out of Kolkata and moves there. All attempts by Saibal to trace her whereabouts come to naught.

Once she learns that she is pregnant, she is completely focused on the child she is bearing. The story of *Hospital* can be split into two halves. The first half deals with the love affair between Sarbari (Suchitra Sen) and Saibal (Ashok Kumar), both students of medicine. But when Sarbari becomes pregnant, Saibal has to leave on a medical assignment and both part ways. But the woman turns out to be a gritty young lady, far ahead of her time. She becomes a doctor and also takes on the responsibility of being a single, unwed mother of a small son. Saibal comes back into her life. But does she take him back? The charisma of Suchitra Sen in a film without her 'hit' partner Uttam Kumar proved that she was much more than sheer glamour. She held on to her own despite the tough competition offered by none other than the great actor Ashok Kumar.

Sarbari's child is born in another hospital somewhere else and is brought up by her and that, too, in surroundings that are unfamiliar. The little fellow does not even know that every child has a father. The school refuses to admit a child whose mother cannot tell the name of the father. It is an uphill job for Sarbari but she is adamant about not revealing the name of the father even to the doctor who has helped her greatly and has arranged for her to have the baby in an unknown place. At one point, Sarbari holds forth on how in a patriarchal society such as the one we live in, it is always the woman who has to bear the responsibility as well as the stigma of a pregnancy out of wedlock.

The desperate Saibal tries to find out where she is. Finally, he goes to UK for higher studies while his little son grows up with the affection of a mother, not knowing where he is or what the mother and son are up to. The film becomes extremely melodramatic when Sarbari is diagnosed as suffering from terminal cancer and her son's life is at stake if the mother passes away leaving him alone in the big, bad and ugly world. The kind-hearted doctor tries to find out who the child's father is, while a deeply repentant Saibal, back from UK, also makes it his mission to find out where his lady love is. By the time he finally discovers her and finds out he has a son, it is almost too late to save her. Defying all advise to the contrary, Saibal decides to operate on her himself and she is saved from certain death.

Though Sarbari is fleshed out as a gritty young lady, far ahead of her time, it is the beauty and glamour of Suchitra Sen the star that overshadows the real character. The film is one of many melodramas that Sen did against the backdrop of the medical profession. Some of the others are *Sagarika*, *Harano Sur*, *Deep Jele Jai* and *Saptapadi*. Sen looks as luminous as ever—with a face made for close-ups—and gives her trademark 'woman suffering with great dignity' performance. But her star persona shot with effective backlighting proves to be the undoing of the actress in her when one looks at the film after all these years.

Hospital does not do justice to the working woman in post-colonial Bengali cinema. The film repeatedly stresses on Sarbari's medical expertise but this is not elaborated at any point in the film. It does not even make a passing reference to her work as a doctor except that she falls back on the profession to remain financially independent. Not a single case she treats is depicted throughout the film. Ironically, her positioning as a patient is emphasized when she falls sick. Being a doctor herself, she completely ignores taking medical advice or consultation though she knows that she is a single mother and if she dies, her son will become an orphan.

If Sarbari was not a doctor in the film and was instead a typist or a stenographer, it would have made little difference to the script. Her father's complete rejection of his daughter, an only child who takes such good care of him, when he learns that she is pregnant is a reflection of the way single mothers were treated by their own families. He comes around but only when he comes to know that his daughter is dying. The 'working' motif attached to Sarbari does not change the portrayal of the romantic element in the celluloid woman in any way. She behaves almost exactly the way one expects a woman in love to behave. Her strength lies much more in her determination to run away from the man she loves than it does on her focus on becoming a good doctor.

However, at the time when the film was made, it must have taken a character like Sarbari tremendous courage to stick to her principles and run away from her lover rather than bend to his diktats, especially considering she is part of the medical profession where abortion is a way out. This also reflects the courage Suchitra Sen had as an actress, to take the commercial risk of portraying an unwed single mother who refuses to abort her unborn child though the future seems dark.

Hospital offers neither a sociological reading of the text nor a Marxist reading of Sarbari's working life except that her earnings are necessary for her own needs and for the upbringing of her son. Sarbari's character is portrayed by Sen with a marked, melodramatic emphasis on the character's martyrdom rather than on the courage of being a single mother, highly educated and working at a time when this was considered almost social blasphemy. Sarbari's father's sudden turnabout where he changes from an affectionate and progressive father who encourages and funds his daughter's medical education to a feudal, cruel and unfeeling masochist reflects the double standards of patriarchy that still sustain in large segments of Indian society.

Uttar Phalguni/Mamta

This is a double version film shot separately with a different star cast for the two versions, Bengali and Hindi, with a three-year gap between the two. The director Asit Sen and Suchitra Sen herself in the dual role of mother and daughter are the two common threads that bind the two versions together. The Bengali version was called *Uttar Phalguni*, while the Hindi title was *Mamta*. The film was produced by Uttam Kumar who kept away from acting in the film because with Suchitra essaying a double role, the script would be dominated by her. As an actor, he was perhaps reluctant to play second fiddle to the actress he had successfully romanced in many films. But as producer, he had the sharp business sense to realize that with Suchitra Sen in an author-backed double role—she would pull audiences into the theatres—it was best for him to stay away from acting in the same film. The Hindi version, however, was produced by Charu Chitra. Among all her Hindi films, *Mamta* is Suchitra Sen's biggest commercial success. The original story was written by the popular author Nihar Ranjan Gupta while the screenplay for the Bengali version was by Nripendra Chatterjee who was also a noted author in his own right.

Debjani, a beautiful young woman, is the motherless daughter of a man steeped in debt under a dubious man named Rakhal Bhattacharya. Debjani is in love with Manish, as aspiring lawyer poised to go to London for his bar-at-law course for three years. During his absence, Debjani's father persuades her to marry Rakhal in lieu of the Rs 10,000 her father owes him. She remembers Manish telling her to approach his mother if in a crisis during his absence. Manish's mother, however, insults her and throws her out of the house. Debjani is forced to marry Rakhal who turns out to be an alcoholic, a gambler, a womanizer and also a husband who does not think twice before trying to pimp his own wife! A shocked and disgusted Debjani, pregnant by then, runs away.

When she tries to jump off a running train, Meena Bai, a veteran courtesan travelling in the same coach, rescues her and takes her to her kotha in Lucknow. She takes care of Debjani like a mother would, and organizes singing and dancing lessons for her. Debjani becomes the famous Pannabai, a household name among connoisseurs of courtesans' music. When Manish returns and finds her in her new environment, though she tries to escape his attention, she refuses his attempts to rescue her from this life. She requests him to take her daughter, Suparna, then a small girl, under his care. She implores him to save the child from the evil eyes of the husband who comes often to blackmail Debjani and threatens to take away the daughter. By then, however, Debjani has already persuaded the reluctant head of a missionary boarding school to admit her daughter. The blackmailing husband is confused about his missing daughter but is determined to find her whereabouts and use this knowledge to continue blackmailing Pannabai. Meanwhile, Suparna grows up to be a fine young woman, who is pursuing the study of law.

One morning, when Suparna is walking within the court corridors with Manish, her 'uncle', and Indranil, her beloved, Rakhal happens to see her and recognizes her because she looks exactly like her mother. This time, when he approaches Pannabai again and threatens to disclose her identity to their daughter, Pannabai takes out her gun and shoots him, emptying all the bullets into him.

Manish takes up the defence of Pannabai though the sick Pannabai does not seek justice or freedom. She is already suffering from a serious heart ailment and is not concerned about getting cured. So, she responds with silence. Meanwhile, the snobbish Suparna is not happy about the way her uncle is refusing to be involved in financially important cases, but is rather focused on this particular one. She consults with Indranil to find out what the case is all about and is shocked to learn that her uncle, a bachelor by choice, is completely dedicated to saving a courtesan who has killed her own husband. This is an interesting presentation of two opposite perspectives of the same issue. While Manish's sympathy is triggered by his love for Pannabai, his knowledge about the tragedy of her life and his undying love for her, Suparna, the modern, aggressive and educated bar-at-law, full of attitude, is disgusted about a wife who is also known as a courtesan/prostitute, who has killed her own husband and that her uncle is trying to save her from the gallows.

Pressured by Suparna, Manish breaks his promise made to Pannabai to not reveal her identity to her daughter. He tells Suparna about the woman he is saving, her relationship with Suparna and the sacrifices she has made to give her daughter a respectable life and to save her from the kind of life her mother has led. Suparna takes the case from her uncle and arrives at court the next morning. When she begins to argue her case, offering the jury the story of Pannabai's life and the circumstances that led her to kill her husband, the visibly sick Pannabai keeps looking at her with wonder, amazed that her daughter has turned out to be the woman of her dreams. But by the time the daughter's arguments end with her admission that the woman in the box is her own mother and that she is proud to be her daughter, Pannabai has a heart attack and dies on her daughter's lap, after hearing her address her as 'ma' for the first and last time since Suparna became an adult.

Uttar Phalguni/Mamta is one of two films in which Suchitra Sen played a double role, the other being *Smrittituku Thaak*. In *Uttar Phalguni/Mamta*, she plays both mother and daughter. But there is a third dimension. The mother's character is structured dually: first as Debjani, and then as the famous courtesan, Pannabai. Once Debjani becomes Pannabai, she refuses to be identified with Debjani even when Manish addresses her by that name because she insists that Debjani 'is dead' and it is Pannabai who lives on. As Debjani, Suchitra Sen presents the image of a beautiful young woman, very much in love with Manish, dreaming of marrying him when he returns from England.

The transformation from Debjani to Pannabai is brought across through effective editing and song-bridges with Meena Bai giving her lessons in song and dance. In the beginning, Debjani is diffident, shy and lacks confidence in picking up the finer nuances of the trade. But slowly, she masters the two performing arts of singing and dancing, and becomes a famous kothewali with rich, feudal clients thronging Meena Bai's kotha to hear her sing and watch her dance. Her daughter, Suparna, is born within this new world. Pannabai spends her free time concentrating on bringing up her daughter. A doctor comes in regularly to check the little girl. Pannabai, along with Meena Bai, takes her to the zoo, to various gardens and to other interesting places to give her as normal a childhood as possible.

Suchitra Sen was not a good dancer but this deficiency was compensated for by the beautiful music. The juxtaposition of the mother image and the courtesan image within the same time-space paradigm is convincing. In a touching moment in the film, Pannabai tells Manish that his love towards Suparna is selfless; that it expects nothing in return. But as mother, her love for her daughter is very selfish because it is through her daughter that she seeks liberation. This is one of the core messages in the film—how a mother almost encrypted into the script of a courtesan's life has, somewhere at the back of her mind, a desire for salvation, never mind if it is vicariously achieved through her daughter. The Debjani in Pannabai peeps from behind the façade and the make-up and the heavy jewellery. Debjani is not dead. She lives on wearing a different face—Pannabai.

The daughter, Suparna, portrayed by Suchitra Sen again, is the dramatic opposite of her mother. The only way to recognize her as the daughter of Pannabai is that she is the split image of her mother. She is a modern, educated woman who returns after finishing her bar-at-law in UK to take up practice as junior to the 'uncle' who adopted her. While in England, she has fallen in love with a senior, Indranil, who stays over for one year to wait for her to finish her course. Indranil comes to India and joins Manish's law firm. Suparna does not know that her mother is alive, let alone that she is a courtesan, now in retirement. She is ignorant of the fact that her mother has financed her education through her earnings as a courtesan/prostitute. She has no knowledge that this 'uncle' Manish, who brought her up and educated her, is the man who still loves her mother but could not marry her due to circumstances beyond their control. Suchitra Sen does justice to the 'three' characters by changing her body language, her way of delivering her lines, her smiles, gestures, carefully enough to see that the personas do not blur or get out of focus or confuse the audience. The lines between Debjani and Pannabai are deliberately blurred in the beginning and merge to become Pannabai towards the end, reinforcing her insistence that 'Debjani is dead, this is Pannabai'.

There is a melodramatic romanticization of the kothewali in the character of Debjani-turned-Pannabai which is a staple stereotype of Indian mainstream cinema. Note that Pannabai is a courtesan or kothewali and not a prostitute. This means that she does not mandatorily have to sell sexual favours in exchange for cash or kind. Her clients are not permitted to directly proposition her for sexual favours and whether she surrenders to indirect demands is entirely her choice or the choice of her mentor in the house. Her clientele visit her to entertain themselves with her music and with the varieties of wine she can serve them, apart from the vicarious titillating pleasure the men appear to enjoy from their visits. There is also a false sense of 'male prestige' attached to a man from a feudal family whose regular visits to a given kotha to listen to a particular courtesan or kothewali reflects his aristocracy, his affluence and his taste for good music and dance.

This romanticization comes in all shapes, sizes and colours beginning with the genre of the Hindi/Urdu courtesan film like Kamaal Amrohi's *Pakeezah* or Girish Karnad's *Utsav* (1983), working its way through 'modern' interpretations like B.R. Chopra's *Tawaif* (1985), Sagar Sarhadi's *Bazaar* (1982) and Muzaffar Ali's *Umrao Jaan* (1981). Place this against Yash Chopra's *Deewar* (1973), where Anita is a prostitute, or B.R. Ishara's *Chetna* (1970), where Radha is a sex worker who has entered the flesh trade tempted by greed. She finds she does not like it when she falls in love and gets married.

Indian cinema's representation of the kothewali is merged into the prostitute identity. In real life, however, the common thread that binds the kothewali and the prostitute is their marginalization by mainstream society that considers them as belonging to an ostracized society because of the social stigma attached to these professions. Indian film-makers have either deliberately or due to ignorance often clubbed the two professions. Film-makers have mostly been unable to distinguish between the hierarchy of respect and dignity that existed in the courtesan's life but was completely absent in case of the prostitute, who is confined in a world defined by extreme social stigma, her clients visiting her clandestinely because that in no way adds to the social status of the client.

Interestingly, however, unlike other mainstream films that place the practice of the courtesan and/or prostitute subservient to the romantic angle, in *Uttar Phalguni/Mamta*, it is the other way round. Pannabai's work as courtesan is not rendered subservient to the romantic angle but predominates and also determines her function as a single mother, a rarity in Indian films of the time. Suchitra Sen expresses this dichotomy between the courtesan-mother duality extremely well. Whenever she is away from entertaining her clients, she devotes her entire attention on the little Suparna; Meena Bai, now old, becomes a grandmother-like figure for Suparna and a mother for Pannabai.

The courtesan/prostitute films open up possibilities of reading, or re-reading, from a woman's, if not from a feminist's, point of view. Cinema as an audio-visual medium of mass appeal which inspires, influences and motivates the audience also has another use for prostitution within its framework: titillation. For this, it is more the technique than the art of cinema that is called upon to play its role and prove its creativity, skills and expertise—sound, camera, action, editing, direction.[10] But Asit Sen, the director of *Uttar Phalguni/ Mamta*, does not fall back on the sensual and titillating aspect of the courtesan's lifestyle. Pannabai is never shown revealing skin, cleavage or any part of her body. This sustains the dignity her character is bestowed with right till the end when she is placed in the box of the accused.

In an interesting postscript, Suchitra Sen was once reportedly chosen to play the lead in a film version of the life and loves of Noti Binodini, the famous stage actress and singer who ruled the Bengali stage. Binodini Dasi (1863-1941) became a phenomenal star of the Bengali stage during the era of the famous Girish Ghosh. But like many of her peers in theatre, she was forced to depend on patrons and protectors as her benefactors. Even her mentor and guru Girish Ghosh persuaded her to become the mistress of a rich Marwari businessman, Gurmukh Rai, when the theatre fell upon bad days and the owner wanted to pull down the shutters. As a way of expressing her gratitude to her guru on one hand and to save the theatre on the other, she agreed. The businessman kept his promise of building a theatre house for the company. His only condition was that the theatre house should be called B-Theatre. But his wish was sacrificed in favour of the name Star Theatre because a theatre named after a fallen woman would draw neither audience nor prestige. Ironically, this theatre was bulldozed many years later for widening Beadon Street, where it stood. The Star Theatre that exists today is a different one.

Binodini became more famous than the others because she charted a great stage history by packing in around ninety characters across eighty plays within the short span of twelve years. In *Meghnad Badh*, authored by Michael Madhusudan Dutta, she played six roles. Her performance in the title role in *Chaitanya Leela* became so spiritually enriched that intellectuals like Bankim Chandra Chattopadhyay, Edwin Arnold, author of *Light of Asia*, theosophist Col Olcott and Ramakrishna Paramahansa (who blessed her after a show he attended) were amongst her audience.

Even a poster of the said film with Suchitra Sen dressed up like Binodini was printed and published, but the film never got made. So *Mamta/Uttar Phalguni* and *Rajlakshmi O Sreekanto*, are the only films that present Suchitra Sen as an ostracized woman in public space.

The difference of approach, treatment and style by Asit Sen and his entire team in the two films—*Uttar Phalguni* in black-and-white and *Mamta* in colour—reflects the respective complex relationship between physics, technology, culture, economics and audiences. These were precisely balanced in both films and the results are obvious in the commercial success of the two films and also in the reassertion of Suchitra Sen as a star actress who could carry the burden of an important film with dual characters alone, without the support of the conventional hero. The three important men—Rakhal and Manish in the life of Debjani and Pannabai, and Indranil in Suparna's life—are not heroes or villains in the conventional, stereotypical sense. They are more like pillars of support, negatively and positively, in the history, transitions and evolution of the life of the 'three' characters. Though *Mamta/Uttar Phalguni* is very much reflective of patriarchy's victimization of women, it is a powerful, woman-centric film even when it places the central character as victim. But Debjani/Pannabai rises above her victimization to take control not only of her own life but more importantly, of her daughter's life, though she has voluntarily kept away from any direct contact with her during her growing-up years. In this sense, Pannabai remains an absent and almost non-existent person in the life of her own daughter.

Under the guidance of Asit Sen, Suchitra manipulates her expressions differently in the two films through her emotional response mainly as Debjani/Pannabai because the portrayal of Suparna did not demand much change in strategy in the two versions. For both versions, credit goes to Asit Sen who masterfully controlled the visual frames with the help of his cinematographers (Anil Gupta and Jyoti Laha) who used slow dissolves effectively as transitions between and among scenes. The scenes showing Pannabai shooting Rakhal cuts to a close shot of the bars of a jail cell appearing before her. Even before the first shot fades out, the camera tracks back from the bars and moves to show her with Manish in her cell. In other words, the technical mastery most certainly added to Suchitra Sen's performance as Debjani, as Pannabai and as Suparna.

If there are strong elements of melodrama in the performance of Pannabai, these are mere reflections of what is written in the script and what the director has decided; it is not the actor's fault. The film, with special reference to the Hindi version *Mamta*, throws up an image of heightened melodrama with lavishly mounted sets, glittering zardozi costumes, heavily made-up face with bold eyeliner, glitter and eyeshadow, and upwardly curled eyebrows that make Sen look much older than she would have looked with more subtle make-up. But looking back, one can presume that this was done by design because the Hindi audience would expect more colour and glamour than the Bengali audience which is culturally attuned to black-and-white films starring Suchitra Sen with or without Uttam Kumar. If this was done by design—to make *Uttar Phalguni* in black-

and-white and *Mamta* in colour—the concept worked very well indeed because the films in both versions were very big commercial hits at the box office.

Colour in cinema is not just a technological advance over black-and-white even if it was conceived initially as a technological advance in cinematography that was expected to add to the commercial value of the film by drawing more audience into theatres. But with time, as colour became the norm and black-and-white slowly began to fade out till raw stock was so short in supply that a film-maker could hardly afford it, film-makers and technicians realized that the ten shades between the two extremes of black-and-white offered a greater horizon of challenge both to the cinematographer and the post-production crew than colour did. There is very little research done on the impact of colour as against the impact of black-and-white in cinema but in common understanding, colour and black-and-white have their distinct effects in terms of aesthetics, drama and adding glamour to the screen, respectively.

The distinct impact of black-and-white and of colour in the same film with the same actor featuring in both versions, directed by the same director, and based on the same story, comes across lucidly in the case of *Uttar Phalguni* and *Mamta*. The code for narrative and ideological expression comes out differently in *Uttar Phalguni* than it does in *Mamta*. *Uttar Phalguni*'s black-and-white focuses more on the story, its unfolding on screen, on the major characters, and on their interaction. *Mamta*'s colour concentrates more on the mise en scène, on the physical beauty of Pannabai, and on the material universe constructed around her. The story emerges out of these surroundings and adds more melodrama to the film as it unfolds within the darkened interiors of a theatre.

Uttar Phalguni is more intense in its drama and characterization for the precise absence of colour that dilutes the intensity of the drama in *Mamta*. When the two films were made—*Uttar Phalguni* in 1963 and *Mamta* in 1966—the Hindi cinema audience was accustomed to watching colour films and perhaps would not have accepted *Mamta* so warmly had it been made in black-and-white. In Bengal, however, it was still the era of black-and-white, and colour was a rarity. But the difference this made to the final films in the two versions is dramatic. The aesthetics differs because at that time, colour in cinema was more flat and glamorous, and cinematographers were just getting used to the new technology and were yet to incorporate innovations in light and shade and use of lighting in colour to enhance different moods, ambiences and locales. So, aesthetically, even today, *Uttar Phalguni* is a richer film than *Mamta* and this applies to the performance of Suchitra Sen in all the three roles in the two films. She is louder even as Suparna in *Mamta* than she is in *Uttar Phalguni*. The auteur signature of Asit Sen remains the same in both the versions.

In recent times we have seen black-and-white films changed to colour as production and marketing strategies, perhaps to accommodate the change in audience taste. From the black-and-white *Mughal-e-Azam* to the coloured version, it has not made much difference to the final film because it is based on historical fiction where glamour, high production values and lavish mounting are demanded by the script in order to enhance the drama and the history structured into the film. *Uttar Phalguni* is based on a more contemporary and 'modern' story where aesthetic qualities are distinctly clear in the black-and-white version while *Mamta* plays more to the gallery of Hindi viewers three years after the Bengali version was made.

Why must one discuss the music of a film in a book devoted to the contribution of a star actress? Music and songs in many films help and enrich the performance of the actor in a given film and both *Uttar Phalguni* and *Mamta* are classic examples of this truth. Had the music, the soundtrack and the lyrics not been what they turned out to be in the final film, one wonders whether Suchitra Sen's performance would have been as rich and as near-perfect as it is. Sound in Indian cinema has a specific rhythm which is unique unto itself. The sound design of an entire film is composed of speech, music, songs, noise and silence.

Songs play an extremely significant role in Indian cinema, which is a reflection and, perhaps, an exaggeration of the actual social and cultural lives of Indians. In cinema, songs come in different manifestations and guises: theme songs repeated over the narrative space of films, songs lip-synced by the characters in the film in solo or in duets, or even chorus songs, songs sung to dance numbers, mood songs on the soundtrack and so on. Sometimes, the same song is repeated in varying tempos to signify the changing mood of the character and the changed situation in the story/script.

Most importantly, there are purely sound-centric and sound-based songs in Indian films where the lyrics of a song are peppered with actual sounds such as the sound of quickened heartbeats as in '*Dhak dhak karne laga*' from *Beta* (1992), the sound of thundering rain in '*Lapaka jhapaka tu aare bhadarava*' from *Boot Polish* (1954), the sound of the spinning wheel in '*Chappa chappa charkha chale*' from *Maachis* (1996), the sound of dancing bells in '*Jhanak jhanak payal baaje*' from *Jhanak Jhanak Payal Baaje* (1955), the ambience of night in '*Jhoom jhoom dhalti raat*' in *Kohraa* (1964), the sound of lapping waves on the shores in '*Chhai chhapa chhai, chhapapa chhai*' in *Hu Tu Tu* (1999), a song to match the beat and rhythm of a running train in a hilly terrain in '*Chal chhaiyyan chhaiyan*' in *Dil Se* (1998), the sound of the nightingale in '*Kuhu kuhu bole koyeliyaan*' in *Rani Roopmati* (1957) and so on, offering a rich texture and a never-ending panorama of sounds within songs, making for a unique blend of sound, music and words. Usually combined with colourful visuals and harmoniously choreographed dances, these songs add both to the market value of the film at the box office and to the final audio-visual effect the film leaves behind.[11]

In all these respects, *Uttar Phalguni* and *Mamta* offer a model lesson in how important a role music and songs can play not only to the current and future value of the film but also to the performance of the lead characters.

There is a difference between the Bengali and Hindi versions of the film in terms of the musical score, the lyrics and the songs.

The music is rich, memorable and melodious in both versions but there are cultural differences between the two determined by the language in which the films were made. In the Bengali film, the music was composed by Robin Chatterjee. The songs and the music were used tellingly as editorial strategy, as expressing time-leaps in the life of Pannabai and then Suparna, as denoting mood swings and narrative progression. Pannabai being skilled in music more than in dance, the songs serve a definite purpose in the narrative. Three classical pieces in the Bengali film deserve mention. The first is when Pannabai is established as a very good courtesan. The second appears in a flashback sequence where Debjani is being trained by Meena Bai and she slowly metamorphoses into Pannabai. The third mixes sound with music to enrich the aesthetics of three shots and also adds to the given mood of the scene. In the first of these three shots, the music director uses the melodious sound of church bells and mixes it with the sound of thunder and blowing wind, symbolically, with the camera capturing a singing Pannabai in slow dissolves juxtaposed against Suparna and Manish in her missionary residential school. The second blend of sound and music shows Pannabai singing against a backdrop of dark monsoon clouds, moving on to a leafless tree in the last of these shots as a time-leap conveys Suparna growing up and Pannabai slowly greying and getting older. This also suggests the radical differences in the evolution of the two women—the mother and the daughter—the latter growing up in a conducive and productive environment created through the sacrifices of the former. The pace and tempo of the classical piece becomes slower towards the end and the camera moves to show a greying Pannabai suffering from a heart ailment.[12]

The music of *Mamta,* however, composed by Roshan on lyrics penned by Majrooh Sultanpuri, two giants of Hindi film music, has greater archival value than the music of the Bengali film. The reason for this is not the narrower audience reach of *Uttar Phalguni,* the Bengali version, but because of the immortal quality of the music and lyrics of *Mamta*. The first line of each song immediately brings alive the film and the positioning of the song. The music complements as well as enhances Suchitra Sen's performance in the film and offers solid support to the narrative progression of the text. The music and lyrics of *Mamta* are milestones in the careers of Majrooh and Roshan - numbers like '*Rahe naa rahe hum*', '*Chhupa lo dil mein pyar mera*', the immortal ghazal sung by Lata Mangeshkar '*Rehte they kabhi jin-ke dil mein*', alongside her other number '*Vikal more manwa unn bin hai*'. The romantic duet belted out by Mohammad Rafi and Asha Bhosle, '*Baharon mein akele na phiro*', also adds to the drama of the scene elaborating the relationship between the lovers.

There are four chief areas of discourse of the courtesan's life in literature and in cinema: the courtesan as *subject*, or the agency-issue as it is called; the courtesan as *object*, analogous to a slave, who has been coerced into the profession, and is therefore, a *victim* whether of an organized trade, or, of specific agents of force and oppression, or widespread economic circumstances; the courtesan and her sexuality; and the courtesan as a *working woman* like any other, in an essentially capitalist, but democratic state. As the above analysis reveals, for the most part, both *Uttar Phalguni* and *Mamta* have focussed on the *victim* identity of the courtesan Pannabai rather than on her agency. At the same time, the agency role has been segmented into the courtesan-as-mother whose only dream in life is to save her daughter from a similar fate through proper education and upbringing in an education-friendly environment. The narrative and cinematographic space avoids any focus on the sexuality of Pannabai, and therefore, does not use her as an object of titillation. The 'working woman' identity gets somewhat blurred by the drama of her life as she does not *choose* to be a working woman but is circumstantially forced to become one. But for Suparna, the time-leap and her upbringing map out a strong evidence of the impact of environment and time on the shaping of a modern woman. Her economic identity, which makes her a bar-at-law, is influenced by her uncle who is also a barrister and by her personal choice.

However, even in Suparna's case, the representation of the working woman in Bengali cinema during the time reflects the dominant politics of patriarchy that existed, and still exists, in Indian social, political and filial life. It should be appropriate to assume that the politics of representation of Suchitra Sen as a working woman in some of her films is more a matter of culture than of nature. Thus, the working women in *Hospital, Deep Jele Jai, Sabar Uparey, Indrani, Harano Sur, Saptapadi, Uttar Phalguni/Mamta* are very distanced and distinct from the career woman in *Aandhi*. Yet, it is also true that the working women in both these genres are celluloid reflections of women who continue to be shaped by the historically specific, unstable, plastic and malleable character of the sexual identity of their respective cultures, and patriarchal implications. Suchitra Sen excelled in both these kinds of films and if she appears loud in some films over others, it is the script that demands her loudness, as in *Mamta*, and in some moments in *Saptapadi*.

Aandhi

This film brings together two stalwarts of film and literature in India: Gulzar and Kamleshwar.

Gulzar—poet, lyricist, dialogue-writer and director—has written stories for more than fifty films, and songs for many more. His directorial roster has films on the pathos of living and on the triumph of human survival from *Mere Apne* (1971) to *Hu Tu Tu* (1999). He has also made television serials like *Mirza Ghalib* and *Kirdaar* besides creating biographical documentaries of outstanding merit. He has composed several volumes of poetry and used to publish a book for children every year to celebrate his daughter Bosky's birthday when she was growing up. His love for classical and contemporary Bengali literature comes across clearly in his choice of source for many of his films. *Khushboo*, for instance, is adapted from a famous Sarat Chandra classic (*Pandit Moshai*) whereas *Kitaab* and *Namkeen* are inspired by Samaresh Basu's novels *Pathik* and *Akal Basanta* respectively.

But like in *Ijaazat* (1987), he often takes just a single thread of the original story and merges it with some of his own creative thread to weave it into a rich tapestry of human relationships based on love and its many-hued splendour. He won the Dadasaheb Phalke Award in 2013 for his contribution to Indian cinema.

His films, with their soft lyricism, melodious music and a mellow undercurrent of pain and rhythm, are his evocation to love in all its myriad manifestations. Even in his penultimate film *Maachis*, this very sensitive director unspools a tale of love against the backdrop *and* in the midst of terrorism. Therefore, what could have evolved into a strong political film, changes tracks to turn into a tragic statement of love falling an unwitting victim to terrorism in Punjab.

'I express myself through poetry, literature and films. Film expresses itself through photography, architecture, acting, music, other than my own medium of expression. This helps me extend my contact with other forms of art and thus enrich my knowledge, my persona and my contacts with people. I find cinema the most fulfilling of all arts in terms of creative effort,' he elaborates.

Kamleshwar was among the pioneers of Hindi's Nayee Kahani movement in the 1950s. He edited *Sarika*, the premier literary magazine of the era. His film scripts *Mausam* (1975) and *Chhoti Si Baat* (1975), to name just a couple, deftly blended the thin line between art and commerce. After he moved to Mumbai in the 1970s, Kamleshwar started writing scripts and dialogues for Hindi films. In the next decade or so, he worked for over seventy-five feature films which include films like Gulzar's *Aandhi*, based on his novel *Kaali Aandhi*, *Mausam*, Basu Chatterjee's *Rajnigandha* (1974), *Chhoti Si Baat* (1975), *Rang Birangi* (1983) and Ravi Chopra's thriller, *The Burning Train* (1980). Reminiscing about his works, Gulzar says, 'In *Kitne Pakistan*, there is a description where a handkerchief falls off the bridge; I used to tell him that I could write a complete short story on this one line only.' He was bestowed the Sahitya Akademi Award for his novel *Kitne Pakistan*, which was translated into English as *Partitions*. He was also bestowed the Padma Bhushan in 2005.

He is credited as the writer of *Aandhi*, though some stories say that Gulzar had asked him to write a script after he did not care for Sachin Bhowmick's script on the subject of a woman political leader. It is said that he wrote his novel *Kaali Aandhi* based on his experiences of writing *Aandhi*. Kamleshwar said that his characterization of the politician was inspired by Maharani Gayatri Devi of Jaipur, and not on Indira Gandhi. This underscores the difference in interpretation of a celluloid character when time and contemporary political scenarios play their role in influencing audience reception. He once said that he had observed Maharani Gayatri Devi during one of her election campaigns and the idea of the story came to him at that time.

Aarti Devi, an electoral candidate from the ruling party at the Centre, arrives at a small town to campaign for the forthcoming elections. She is placed in a good hotel in town only to discover that the manager of the hotel, JK, is her estranged husband. They had fallen in love twelve years ago and eventually married each other despite objections from her powerful politician father who aspired to pass on his political mantle to his daughter. Slowly, egged on by her father who often takes her away from her filial duties, and tempted by the fame and glory of a political career, she is pulled towards her political career and dislikes being 'suffocated' within the four walls of her home, her husband and their daughter. The husband makes it clear that she needs to concentrate on the home front more and take care of the little girl. As a kind of political compromise, with the help of her father, she appoints her husband 'president' of some board as a means to appease him, without his permission. But this very independent and proud man will have nothing of it. They separate and three years into the marriage, she goes back to her father while her husband takes the responsibility of the little girl and shifts base to a different hotel in a different city.

The two meet after nine years in this small town and they realize, with pain, that embers of the fire of love that once made their union so sweet, are still burning slowly but surely. They begin to have night-time rendezvous at an ancient archeological site. A press photographer leaks some photographs of the couple and sells them off to the chief political opponent Chander Sen and all hell breaks loose. In a pre-electoral speech, Chander Sen publicly floats the scandal to the huge audience gathered in the open. Though her workers ask her to leave, she sticks to her guns and refuses to run away. Aarti Devi walks up to the podium and announces that the man she is being linked to in a very negative way is her husband. She also announces that she would be quitting politics. But she wins the elections and her husband advises her to go along and concentrate on her political career. 'Your quitting what you began will not translate to my win,' he says quietly, promising that he will send their daughter to her when she comes on holiday from Shimla, where she lives and studies in a boarding school. The film closes on this open-ended note, as she gets into the helicopter that will take her to Delhi. Her husband clicks the door shut and walks into the distant field. Will they meet again? No one knows.

The film tellingly depicts the changing shades of a husband-wife relationship. With the narrative telescoping between the past and the present, the story zeroes in on a politically ambitious wife who drifts away from her hotelier husband, driven by her political father to do so. It is interesting to note that it is not the woman who aspires for a political career; it is her father who wishes to pass on his mantle to his only child. Nine years later, when the couple meets in a small town where the wife has come on a political campaign, the fire of love is rekindled, leading to a scandal. She wins the election when she publicly announces her relationship with the man. Gulzar leaves the film open-ended, with the husband spurring her on to go to Delhi, for higher aspirations, opening up possibilities of a reunion in the future.

Aandhi was banned a few weeks following its release in 1975. It is reported that Indira Gandhi felt that the protagonist's character, played by Suchitra Sen, bore similarities to her and there was a scene showing the protagonist stubbing out a cigarette in an ashtray to suggest that she was a smoker. It had to wait for nearly two years before it got cleared. The ban drew more attention to it. But after Indira Gandhi's party was defeated in 1977 by the Janata Party, the ban on the film was lifted and it was premiered on the state-run television channel.

The media, quite low-key and subtle at that time compared to its blatant fearlessness and sensationalism today, hyped the Indira Gandhi angle. There were some whispers, some not-so-hushed allegations, that the film was based on the life of Indira Gandhi. A poster in a south Indian daily declared, 'See your Prime Minister on screen'. An advertisement in a Delhi daily called the film 'the story of a great woman political leader in post-Independence India'. The prime minister herself had not seen the film but felt compelled to ask two of her staff members to watch it before deciding whether it was fit for continued public screening or not. The staff members gave the film a clean chit and I.K. Gujral, who was the information and broadcasting minister when the film was shot, liked what he saw.

About *Aandhi*, in an interview with V. Gangadhar, Gulzar said, '*Aandhi* was supposed to be based on the life on Indira Gandhi but this is not true. I looked at it as the first film on a modern Indian politician. We wanted a model and Indira Gandhi and to a lesser extent Tarakeshwari Sinha fitted the bill. But *Aandhi* had nothing to do with Mrs Gandhi's personal life. In that sense, *Maachis* was a more topically political film which I would not have been able to make some years before I actually made it.'[13]

However, some of the parallels in the film are too close to pass suspicion. Indira Gandhi's marriage to Feroze Gandhi ended in separation because she was politically and ideologically closer to her father than to her husband. Her father, one of the biggest political leaders in India, much more famous, popular and powerful than Feroze Gandhi, was grooming her for a full-fledged career in politics and she enjoyed it. The only difference between Aarti and Indira Gandhi is that her two sons were with her and not with their father. Feroze Gandhi was as fiercely independent as Aarti's husband in *Aandhi*.

The film is a realistic portrayal of Sanjeev Kumar as the husband and Suchitra Sen as the wife, where the actress imitated the body language, gestures, manner of speech and dress of Indira Gandhi. Suchitra Sen's outstanding performance, among her best and most memorable roles, gave more grist to the Indira Gandhi mill. She wears beautiful white saris that span the entire traditional handicrafts of India from Gadhwals to Patolas through Benarasi silks to Jamdanis and pure silks. She wears long-sleeved, high-necked blouses, carries herself in an erect posture defined by the dignity the character demands. She does not deck herself with jewellery either. Her facial expressions are controlled and even when her meeting with her husband after nine years fills her with cheer, she expresses this happiness with a slight smile. She is controlled even in her anger as we see in the scene where a stone strikes the side of her head and she begins to bleed. In her public speech, too, she is in full control of the audience, the opposition on the dais, and the scenario. One does not hear her raise her voice in a single scene. The way she pours tea out of the teapot is touched with sophistication. Her fumbling in the kitchen in one scene spells out her complete lack of skill in that area.

The love scenes between Aarti and her husband, both before and after marriage, and again when they meet after nine long years, are realized by emotionally moving performances by both Suchitra Sen and Sanjeev Kumar. The editing between the past and the present and back to the past is seamless and smooth, sustaining the rhythm of time and at the same time, the state of flux in their relationship. Their first meeting is dramatically conceived by Gulzar and that is the only time when we see Aarti dressed to her teeth in a rich, purple, sequined sari with lots of jewels. She arrives at the reception desk of a hotel, drunk out of her wits, demanding a room from the assistant manager, with whom she subsequently falls in love. Gulzar constructs the discovery of Aarti by Sanjeev Kumar in the washroom with great restraint, expressed only in dialogue and in Aarti trying to cover herself with the bed sheet, clearly embarrassed and shy, which does not suit the brashness of her drunken stupor, but brings out how her position as a leading politician's daughter can render her vulnerable to outsiders with dubious motives, political or otherwise.

The budding romance between the two, leading to marriage, is expressed through two beautiful songs with lyrics by Gulzar and music by Rahul Dev Burman. The lyrics and the enchanting, hauntingly effective musical score enrich the emotional texture of the film. These songs have been archived in the memory of the Indian audience forever. The pre-marriage romance is expressed through '*Is mode se jaate hain*', sung by Kishore Kumar and Lata Mangeshkar, and '*Tum aa gaye ho, noor aa gaya hai*', also a duet. When they reunite and go wandering at nights, the song '*Tere bina zindagi se koi shikwa toh nahin*' brings out the inner pain of the couple desperately wanting to cling to each other but not being able to do so for circumstances beyond their control. This song was shot against the ruins of the Martand sun temple near Anantnag that dates back to the seventh and eighth centuries. The locations for the song sequences were chosen with great care to fit into the mood and the situation the leading pair was placed in.

Looking back at the history of Indian cinema, an interesting reality that comes across is that *Aandhi* is, till date, perhaps the only Hindi film from mainstream as well as offbeat cinema that features the dilemma of a top woman political leader, who, by suggestion towards the end of the film, might one day become the prime minister of the country. The protagonist is caught between her political aspirations and the emotional pull towards her family. Suchitra Sen has not done another role like this in her entire career, and with this film, she created a benchmark for other actresses. In this sense, *Aandhi* is a unique film.

Historically speaking, Indian women have been contesting elections from the pre-Independence era. In the 1930s, the powerful motivation of Jawaharlal Nehru made the United Provinces a showcase for women's active participation in politics. The legislative council and the legislative assembly had sixteen women members. The most prominent among them were Begum Aizaz Rasul, the deputy speaker of the legislative council, and Vijaya Lakshmi Pandit, who held a Cabinet post. But one must note that both these women came from highly politicized, elite families who had no first-hand knowledge of the political situation and were not in touch with the masses. After the first general elections in 1937, almost every province had a sprinkling of women legislators. Every election from 1967 to 1984 in the post-Independence era was dominated by the towering personality of Indira Gandhi. Till 1984, among the twenty-eight women members of the Lok Sabha, two-thirds came from well-known political families and had no independent base of their own. One finds that the family legacy has now percolated down to regional politics also in quite a big way. Not all political candidates, women or men, are elite or Western educated, like Rabri Devi, but the filial connection is too obvious to be brushed aside.

One unique aspect of high-profile women in Indian politics is their political family background. Women not necessarily from elitist backgrounds, such as Ahilya Rangnekar, were from politically conscious family backgrounds. Few women like Mrinal Gore and now Mamata Banerjee and Mayawati came directly from the grassroots. Many contemporary women politicians such as Sonia Gandhi and Rabri Devi are the direct outcome of their close relationships with politically important men. In journalese, we often call this 'wife-cracy', 'widow-cracy' or 'daughter-cracy'. All these women have successfully extracted emotional mileage from these relationships.

The strange contradiction that exists in the scheme of filial politics that brings the woman from her inner domain to be a part of the public sphere is that, though family stability is an essential prerequisite of a woman's political success, once she attains a certain position, the very stability of the family that formed her support structure begins to collapse. Families, by and large, appear extremely supportive of their women joining the 'political battlefield'. But they feel threatened when the same women assume larger-than-life proportions by virtue of their fame and power earned through electoral triumph and personal grit. The very entry of a married woman into politics involves a renegotiation of duties and responsibilities among family members, even in countries as culturally disparate as Australia and Malaysia.

This comes across lucidly in *Aandhi* through the interactions among the dramatis personae. In what sense, then, is Aarti Devi a 'working woman'? She has a political career carefully and diplomatically built brick-by-brick by her influential, industrialist and politician father who hopes to use his daughter's education and talent to further his own 'business interests'. 'Please do not use me as your business interest,' says Aarti to her father when he argues with her against marrying an ordinary man after having studied at Oxford[14] for five years.

Politics is a career she has been cleverly coerced into. Slowly, over time, especially when the duties of being a homemaker, wife and mother begin to wear her out, she falls in line with her father's reasoning. The unease and discomfort she is feeling inside comes out in the open when she tells her husband that she feels suffocated in the environment and the only reason she has not moved out till then is to protect her famous father from carrying the ignominy of a daughter whose marriage has failed. The husband is shocked. This marks the logical end of the marriage, though they never seek a legal annulment. Her husband forces her to choose between home and career, and as an argument heats up between them, she chooses to leave home, husband and daughter to become a political leader. The script does not spell out her position within the party or even the party which carries the symbol of a pigeon-in-flight, but the people she is surrounded by suggests her importance.

The script is also silent about whether during the nine long years she was away she bothered to find out about her daughter. It is suggested through her own observations that, after a point, she did not.

When she finds herself suddenly confronted by her past, she is both happy and sad. Happy because she discovers that people she was close to, the faithful family loyal Binda (A.K. Hangal), for example, remembers that she loved kheer. She is happy that someone has placed sandalwood incense and a surahi for water in her room, knowing her liking for these things. 'Someone here seems to know what I like,' she says more than once. The receptionist brings her a bouquet of yellow roses, her favourite. She is sad to discover that all these years, she had been missing these soft, emotional touches and did not even know it. She is sad that their daughter is now ten years old and she has never seen her for nine long years. All this is brought out in a restrained, low-key performance by Suchitra Sen.

However, once she discovers where she is staying and who she is surrounded by, her remarkable confidence displayed through body language, posture, gait and speech is dented. One can discern a touch of uncertainty, anxiety and guilty angst in her feelings. These finer nuances of facial expression captured in mid-close-ups and mid-long shots, contrary to the use of huge close-ups Suchitra Sen's Bengali films are known for, add both depth and perspective to her performance. The streaks of grey in her long hair lend an air of class and dignity, enriching the performance and demonstrating how an actress's 'look' created for a given character goes a long way in impacting the performance. This is a significant quality at a time when 'looks' were not as significant as they are today.

Her husband is the ideal picture of balance and stability. He understands and respects her need to keep their relationship a secret. Once, when he comes out and addresses her by her first name and her political advisor is surprised, he tries to save the situation though it is too late. He really begins to enjoy her company, especially the night-time outings in the architectural site that gives her a bad cold. Small touches like his removing his coat to cover her when she has forgotten to carry her shawl, or, gently pulling her head to his shoulder to rest on bring out that their love is not really lost; it has simply taken a backseat all these years. In the beginning of the song sequence, '*Tere bina zindagi se*', the husband and wife are distanced and divided by the pillars of the ruins. Gradually, they skirt the pillars and get close to each other, touching and embracing in a manner that a mellow couple would. Extending the same logic, when Aarti Devi comes out in the open on the public platform to tell the audience who the secret man in her life really is, he walks slowly from the audience up to the podium and lends support by pulling her to himself. Looking back, all this is a bit melodramatic from the cinematic and aesthetic points of view, but at the same time, one is tempted to ask: could it have been any different? Aarti goes back to her career without any hint that she might be united with her husband in the future. Do the schisms remain, or have they faded away after the reunion, or is it too late for both of them to mend bridges? No one knows. So, at the end of the story, Aarti Devi remains a working woman with a career she looks forward to.

Though gender is a social construct, it is the one that constitutes women both through the impositions of power and the identifications of the psyche. In cinema, these constructions are covertly and overtly shaped, controlled and dictated to by patriarchal norms, institutional power, producers' dictates, commercial backings and so on. The films chosen in the present study are no exception. The films in which Suchitra Sen has performed the role of a working woman were a precursor of the future, where today we see some bold representations of the working woman in Bengali cinema.

5

THE CONCEPT OF WILFUL SOCIAL SECLUSION AND SOCIAL ANXIETY DISORDER

INTRODUCTION

After Suchitra Sen retreated voluntarily from films, from public space and from mainstream life and went into complete social seclusion, she consciously redesigned her persona, keeping herself away from the limelight, from interviews, from functions, film premieres and so on. Suchitra Sen is a unique example of moving from high-powered visibility, fame, success and affluence into oblivion, of creating an 'invisible' persona, as if trying to wipe herself away from history. On hindsight, it seems to have been a calculated move on her part. However, this very self-designed invisibility added more grist to the media mill and her fans, film-makers, co-artistes were as intrigued by her seclusion as they were by her glamour and stardom.

The prima donna of Bengali cinema, who passed away in January 2014, has raised questions and debates about why some celebrities live in social seclusion. Suchitra Sen disappeared from public space after her last film *Pronoy Pasha* flopped miserably. She looked terrible in this very shoddily made film. She came out of this seclusion twice:

once, when Uttam Kumar passed away and once when she came to get photographed for her voter's identity card.

For thirty-five years, she refused to attend telephone calls, give interviews, attend public functions or meet friends. Some call it 'social anxiety disorder', while others call it 'agoraphobia'. But few have tried to diagnose the psychological causes that led her to shut herself away.

ON *PRONOY PASHA*

This film is important because it marks a turning point in the life and career of Suchitra Sen. It was a commercial failure and marked the end of her career as an actress. Not much information is available on this film which made Suchitra Sen sign off from her long reign as the top star-actress of Bengali cinema. Why did this film fail to win over the hearts of the audience even with an established director like Mangal Chakraborty at the helm, Soumitra Chatterjee cast opposite her as her manipulative husband, Ajitesh Bandopadhyay in a character role and music by the legendary Hemanta Mukherjee? It is notable that two films that featured her opposite Soumitra Chatterjee, namely *Datta*, based on Sarat Chandra Chattopadhyay's novel, and *Saat Paake Bandha*, based on a novel by Ashutosh Mukherjee, that fetched her the Best Actress Award at the Moscow Film Festival, were big hits at the box office and also among critics and connoisseurs of Bengali cinema. Yet, *Pronoy Pasha* was a miserable flop. Why?

Mangal Chakraborty was a noted director in Bengali cinema known for some very successful films with Uttam Kumar such as *Tasher Ghar* (1957), *Shikar* (1958), *Sonar Harin* (1959), *Teen Adhyay* (1967), *Ami She O Shokha* (1975) and *Anandomela* (1976). He also acted in and wrote the scripts of many films. Towards the end of his directorial career, he chose to make *Pronoy Pasha* which was 'inspired' by the Hollywood film *A Kiss Before Dying* (1956), based on Ira Levin's novel of the same name (1953).

Pronoy Pasha, however, was such an inferior film that no one seems to have noticed the similarities. Interestingly, the Bollywood remake of the same story, *Baazigar* (1993), that marked the directorial debut of Abbas-Mustan, was a super hit that firmly established the lead pair Shah Rukh Khan and Kajol. If one takes Suchitra Sen's entire body of work in Bengali cinema, *Pronoy Pasha* is easily her worst film ever. At forty-seven, she was well past her prime as leading lady, especially in a story that was essentially centred on the character she played. She was overly made-up but looked tired and ill at many places and, sometimes, did not seem interested in her role or in the film. She did not fit the role of a much younger woman and looked much older that Chatterjee, who played her husband. Soumitra Chatterjee was no different. He looked visibly ill-at-ease in his negative role of a diabolic, manipulating, cold-blooded, suave and sophisticated criminal who tries to kill his wife and marry her younger sister to appropriate their huge inheritance. But his wife does not die and returns to rescue her sister from certain death. The cinematography of the film, the editing, and worst of all, the sound, are all so badly put together that it is difficult to understand what is going on. It was not only bad for Suchitra Sen, the actress and the star, but for Bengali cinema, too, featuring two top actors of the industry. Even Hemanta Mukhopadhyay's musical score got drowned in this insipid and incoherent film.

The disaster this film turned out to be must have been a very big shock for Suchitra Sen. Though her earlier films like *Fariyaad*, in which she did what is now known as 'item number', also did not show her in a good light, it was much better compared to *Pronoy Pasha*.

AFTER *PRONOY PASHA*

Though she had withdrawn herself completely from public life, producers wanted her to sign films. Directors waited for one sign from her to say 'yes' to a role. But she remained away from the public eye. No one knows what instigated this strange decision, because she did not ever give anyone the chance to find out. Her mind turned to spiritualism and she took deeksha from Swami Bireshwaranandaji, then president of the Ramakrishna Math and Ramakrishna Mission.[1] She also developed a close bonding with Bharat Maharaj. She looked up to him as a father figure and when he passed away, she was so heartbroken that she could not talk properly even to her own family. She began to pay regular visits to the Ramakrishna Math at Belur, a few kilometres away from Kolkata, and to the Dakshineswar temple in the northern extremes of Kolkata. Suchitra Sen also visited another branch of the Ramakrishna Mission at Aantpur in Hooghly district. Aantpur is famous because it is where Naren, one of Sri Ramakrishna's closest disciples, took sanyas. Ramakrishna Paramahansa gave him the name Swami Vivekananda. Suchitra felt a strange attraction towards this place. She would often go down to Aantpur, an hour's drive from the city, to spend the day in this natural ambience like any ordinary woman. She would sit at the feet of the sanyasis and listen to their recitation and chants from religious books. Then, she would sit on the floor along with them and partake of the prasad after the recital.

Gauri Chatterjee, in her personalized obituary to Suchitra Sen, following her demise, writes:

> So it was almost inevitable that Mrs Sen would have to walk away from the film world after her latest release bombed in 1978. She was then 47, too old to be a romantic heroine, and she didn't know, or wanted to know, anything else. She never made another film, never involved herself in anything related to films, never engaged in public life at all. She even refused the Dadasaheb Phalke award in 2005 because it would mean personally having to go up to receive the award from the President. Giving, in the process, a fresh lease of life to the myth and magic of Suchitra Sen. But actually, in her canny, hard-fought battle for privacy, Mrs Sen established

> a model for superstardom that turns everything we know about celebrity on its head. She was so successful at silence that she accomplished a quiet revolution in mythmaking that must have today's fame-seekers seething. In a celeb-hungry age when any two-bit wannabe starlet gets more than her 15 minutes of fame, the real money is in mystique—the gold standard of any cultural economy. And nobody sits on a bigger stockpile of mystique than a recluse.[2]

Once, during this period of seclusion, noted author Kana Bosu-Misra called her up at her residence. 'They are telecasting *Deep Jele Jai* on the small screen right now,' she informed. 'What a brilliant performance you have given in the film,' she added. The voice at the other end of the line kept quiet for a few moments, and then said, 'That is the actress Suchitra Sen, that is not me at all. The Suchitra Sen on screen and this Suchitra Sen talking to you over the telephone are two different people. I did all that once upon a time for my bread and butter. I do not reflect on those days any longer. Today, my entire world is filled with thoughts of Thakur (Ramakrishna).'

Another anecdote states that once, a close friend of hers informed her about a newspaper report that Ramakrishna Paramahansa was said to have been reborn in the home of a rickshaw puller in Konnagar, a small town some kilometres away from the city. The minute she heard this, she took this director friend along and, at the unearthly hour of three in the night, they drove to Konnagar to see the newborn. She spent a few hours at the modest home of the rickshaw puller and then came home, finally at peace with herself. Having learnt that Ramakrishna was fond of jalebis, Suchitra Sen offered jalebis to Thakur Ramakrishna during her daily puja. After the puja was over, she touched the jalebi to her forehead and then put a bit into her mouth.

Once, Suchitra Sen requested singer Sandhya Mukherjee, whose playback played a significant role in her films, to come along with her to the Belur Math. Sandhya Mukerjee says, 'She had learnt from

Bharat Maharaj that he was a fan of my songs, specially the bhajans I had recorded. Suchitra called me up and asked me to go along to meet Bharat Maharaj because he wanted to see me. I agreed at once. I asked her if I could take my husband along. She said "yes". All along the drive to Belur Math, we had a long chat, about our respective families, household matters and such mundane things. Neither her films nor my songs were a part of our conversation that day.'

Only twice did Suchitra Sen emerge from her cocoon of fiercely guarded private space. One of these was on 24 July 1980, when Uttam Kumar's body lay in state, awaiting cremation. She stepped out of her car, approached Uttam Kumar's body, garlanded it with flowers, stared at his peaceful face for a few moments, and then quickly stepped back inside her car to go home. In 1982, during the Filmotsav in Kolkata, Suchitra Sen would sometimes come to watch an occasional film at the festival venue. She tried to remain incognito through her signature go-go sunglasses. But these, too, were part of her persona and people knew who was wearing them. She also stood by the bedside of her deeksha guru Bharat Maharaj when he passed away. His death seemed to shatter her completely for some time.

SOME SOCIAL RECLUSES FROM THE WORLD OF FILMS

How can someone, whose job is to be in the media spotlight, shy away from social interaction and visibility? It happens. No one is immune to anxiety disorder. Many celebrities feel extreme anxiety. Interestingly, though, their staying away from the limelight does not help their fans forget them. The public is always eager to find out why they are refusing to meet people, how they are leading their lives in total seclusion, etc.

Suchitra Sen finds herself in good company. Littérateur Emily Bronte, poet Emily Dickenson, who wrote 1,800 poems but less than a dozen were published during her lifetime, Canadian pianist Glen Gould, one-time millionaire, film director and producer Howard Hughes, and Greta Garbo, who, after starring in twenty-eight films, retired to New York in 1941 and died of natural causes at the age of eighty-four. Like Sen, she refused to be interviewed, to attend award shows, or to face the paparazzi.

Noted actress Shashikala disappeared from public view. She surfaced after years of oblivion. She walked out of Bollywood twice, to embrace a life of abandonment the first time, and of selfless service as an active participant in Mother Teresa's Missionaries of Charity the second time. Would one call this a case of 'social phobia'? No one knows.

In an interview in 1996, Shashikala said, 'There was this deep frustration in spite of the fame, the money and the happiness. One morning, I just walked out of the house in search of peace. I wandered around like a mad woman and came back after two months. But this no-peace condition turned me into a mental case. I withdrew from films and family, donned saffron and went in search of peace from one ashram to another in Rameshwar, Dwarka, Bhuvaneshwar, Benares for five years, searching for peace. Finally, I did a meditation course at Goenka-ji's ashram at Igatpuri and felt better. I was unable to cope with the reality that my fans were identifying me with the negative roles I played. It hurt. After the Igatpuri experience, I was cured and there was no confusion anymore. I came back to Bombay and to films.' But during this interview, she remained adamant about not giving photographs of herself from films, from real life, old photographs, new photographs, family portraits, single photos, nothing. She staunchly refused to even show her albums.

Hollywood star Kim Basinger, famous for the Bond girl role in *Never Say Never Again* and other noted films, is one rare star who talked in public about her social anxiety disorder. She confessed that her fears began over reading out loud in class. It was so extreme that teachers felt she was having a nervous breakdown. While accepting the Oscar for her role in *LA Confidential*, she struggled with her speech, though she had rehearsed it for days together. 'When I came to Hollywood, I could wear a bikini, but I was in misery because people were looking at me. So I wore baggy clothes and watched other girls get the big parts and awards. I used to go home and play the piano and scream at night to let out my frustrations. This led to my agoraphobia,' she said in a HBO film *Panic: A Film about Coping*.

WAS SUCHITRA SEN A PATIENT OF SOCIAL ANXIETY DISORDER?

Social Anxiety Disorder (SAD) is said to be a result of a combination of genetic and psychosocial factors. It is believed that genetics account for roughly 30 to 40 per cent of cases. For some people, a traumatic social event may correspond with the onset of the disorder. Taking the core of this definition, one could ask whether the commercial disaster of her last film *Pronoy Pasha* was so traumatic for an actress of her calibre that she could not cope with this failure. The interesting fact is that in the case of Suchitra Sen, it was probably not seen as a 'disorder' but as wilful withdrawal from public space. The issue of diagnosis and treatment did not seem to take place ever.

The other possibility is that she turned into a social recluse. A recluse is someone who chooses to live away from mainstream society. People become recluses for a variety of reasons. Among these are religious beliefs, survivalist goals, mental illness, or desire for privacy. There are many types of recluses as there are reasons for people to retire from society. Celebrities too become reclusive either from the public eye or from society in general or both.

The difference between normal shyness and SAD is the severity and persistence of the symptoms that SAD patients experience, which are both emotional and physical.[3] Some of the emotional symptoms are intense fear of situations when you do not know other people; fear of situations where you will be judged; anxiety about being embarrassed or humiliated; fear that others will notice your anxiety; and fear and dread of upcoming events weeks in advance. Examples of physical symptoms are blushing, profuse sweating, tremor in hands, tension in muscles, and racing pulse rate. The anxiety and discomfort become so extreme that they interfere with daily functioning. SAD is one of the most common mental disorders; a certain percentage of the general population experiences its symptoms at some point of their lives. With proper treatment, symptoms can be managed and the quality of life can generally improve.

Without treatment, this disorder can negatively interfere with the person's normal daily routine, including school, work, social activities, and relationships. Celebrities live in pomp and show all the time. Some of them cannot cope with it. They are so alienated from their own self as well as their kith and kin that they find themselves alone at crucial stages of their lives and once trapped, they cannot come out.

However, one must add that SAD is a mental disease that was little known of, read or written about when Suchitra Sen withdrew from public space and sustained her intense privacy within the four walls of her home. But within her home, she kept herself busy by watering her plants, performing puja, feeding crows that gathered around her balcony in the mornings, and giving instructions to her household staff. Her weekly spiritual sojourns to Belur Math also slowly faded away after the demise of her guru and mentor Bharat Maharaj.

Without medical evidence or any documents to support the theory of whether she really became a patient of SAD, it would be wrong to conclude with any degree of certainty about what exactly kept her away from public and social life. Her everyday behaviour, as recorded from her routine lifestyle post her exit from films, did not indicate any of the physical and emotional symptoms of SAD listed above. Therefore, it would probably be safe to conclude that Sen did not really suffer from Social Anxiety Disorder but voluntarily withdrew from public life without explaining to anyone why she did so. This remains one more mystery in the last phase of Suchitra Sen's life.

COMMENTS ON HER SELF-ENFORCED EXILE FROM PUBLIC SPACE

'I respect and take pride in my mother not only because she entered films when very little technical know-how was available to play tricks with her looks and with her performance, but also because long before the hoo-haa about women's liberation began, she stood for the triumphant woman who won over her male peers,' says Moon Moon Sen. 'She brought respectability to her profession at a time when there was little of it to pass around. I respect her because she has defined herself as a legend in her lifetime—something even Uttam Kumar could not boast of.' The proud daughter adds that Suchitra Sen was a woman who held herself with dignity throughout her long career spanning several decades. 'She has proved that she was a true sophisticate, in the manner in which she gave up her career when she did, proving her unwillingness to be greedy and thus keep the magic intact.'

Moon Moon adds, 'But she wasn't always like this. Late nights and partying were her forte and she was a party animal. She loved music, friends and laughter. She had her own circle of friends. She took my daughters out for movies and lunches. She later distanced herself for personal reasons, reasons I have never questioned.' Asked to pick five of her favourites from her mother's oeuvre, Moon Moon promptly ticks off *Sandhya Dweeper Sikha*, *Aandhi*, *Mamta*, *Saptapadi* and *Saat Paake Bandha*. 'I am a bit scared of my daughters joining films. My mother, strangely, had no such qualms so far as the grandchildren are concerned. She never commented even on their partying all night. She allowed them complete freedom and would not entertain any complaints against them. She adored them and even tried cooking for us at times though she is a terrible cook!'

Summing up, the proud daughter says, 'My mother spared us the humiliation of watching her being walked all over the screen by youngsters less talented and less able than she was. She lived life without excess, always uninvolved, always exclusive, always dignified. I hate the way everyone keeps harping on her desire to hold on to her privacy. I respected it totally and I wish others did too. In fact, there are very few things about my mother that I did not admire. She remains my greatest pillar of strength. Without my mother, I would have turned out to be a completely different person. She instilled in me the importance of keeping a marriage stable and I imbibed it from her. My mother and I are perhaps the only two female stars in films to have begun acting *after* we had mothered our children.'

COMPARISONS WITH GRETA GARBO

For many years after Suchitra Sen withdrew from public life and from cinema, comparisons have been drawn with Greta Garbo about this by critics, friends, family, industry people, the media and so on. Are these comparisons viable? The common thread running between the two star-actresses of two different times is that their very withdrawal/disappearance from the screen and from public life kept them alive in the memory of their fans, their audience, their directors and colleagues. It is possible that if they had continued to act in films and then faded away slowly because of the age factor, a decline in demand and a fall in the box-office returns of their films, their memories would have survived only in nostalgic articles and tributes and little more. But this did not happen and till this day, people have not stopped speculating about the possible answers to their social seclusion. This very mystique, intrigue and suspense have kept them alive even when they are no more. The details about Garbo and her life have been gleaned from a bunch of biographies on her that were published soon after her death.

In *Garbo: A Biography,*[4] Barry Paris unearths connections between the private woman and the public actress. Garbo's melancholy, self-obsession, her paradoxical need to perform and withdraw, manifested themselves in her teens, and these come across in the book. Recurring traumas of abandonment—the deaths of her father, Karl, a Stockholm landscapist, when she was fourteen, and of her beautiful actress sister Alva, victim of cancer at age twenty-three—shaped Garbo into a high-strung, hypersensitive recluse pathologically afraid of betrayal, of commitment, of pregnancy, according to Paris. After the Swedish beauty moved to Hollywood in 1925, she became 'the sex fantasy of the century', an androgynous, exotic persona on whom millions projected their desires, yet, according to Paris's account, she remained a largely celibate narcissist who longed for an idealized hearth and home.[5] Garbo found a substitute family in the home of her closest friend Salka Viertel's. Paris's biography draws on the correspondence between Garbo and Viertel, an Austrian actress and screenwriter, that lasted fifty long years and these form the research on the book. Other sources are Garbo's hundred hours of taped telephone conversations with her confidante, the New York art dealer Sam Green, who remained in touch during the last decade of her self-imposed exile in Manhattan and trips abroad.

Paris's biography tells the story of one of Hollywood's most enigmatic and legendary icons without resorting to hyperbole. Secondly, the meticulously researched work tells Garbo's story honestly, responsibly and thoroughly, including her mysterious days as New York's 'Most Famous Recluse'. Finally, the book digs deep into questions that made and continue to make Garbo one of the most enduring and mysterious figures in twentieth-century popular culture.

Mark A. Vieira's *Greta Garbo: A Cinematic Legacy*[6] is yet another book on Garbo. Mark Vieira is a photographer, a film historian and the author of the acclaimed *Hurrell's Hollywood Portraits, Sin in Soft Focus: Pre-Code Hollywood* and *Hollywood Horror: From Gothic to Cosmic*. As Vieira is a famous photographer, the images in the book ably complement the text and these are images one has never seen before. Vieira takes a close look at every single film Garbo featured in and appreciates her for her talent as an actress. Vieira throws up interesting possibilities on what really happened during her peculiar absences at the studio, the true causes of her conflict with a couple of her producers that lead one to wonder about the intrigue that defines Garbo.

Karen Swenson's *Greta Garbo: A Life Apart*[7] describes Garbo from a woman's perspective. Swenson is a noted entertainment writer and her book is the result of scrupulous research into a star who became a legend during her lifetime for her fiercely guarded privacy equalled by her haunting beauty and luminous acting in films like *Camille* (1936) and *Ninotchka* (1939). The book fleshes out the uniqueness of Greta Garbo's screen image vis-à-vis her earthier one off screen where she was shy yet blunt, devoted to her craft but indifferent to fame, sexually magnetic to men and women, and a loyal friend who mercilessly punished disloyalty. Swenson has double-checked the reportedly unreliable memories of Garbo's companions and lovers that dotted her unhappy and lonely life. Swenson's fact-finding and checking strategies are as precise and detailed as are a detective's and she offers a glimpse into who the mysterious Greta Garbo really was. Swenson's book takes us right into Garbo's relationships with her mentor Mauritz Stiller, her purported bisexuality, and her romantic attachments with John Gilbert, Mercedes De Acosta, Cecil Beaton, George Schlee and others.

Swenson revisits Garbo's childhood spent in a poverty-stricken home in Stockholm and her journey to become the extremely wealthy recluse in New York after her retirement from the silver screen in 1942 following the dismal failure of her last feature film *Two-Faced Woman*. Perhaps this is the only common ground with Suchitra Sen, who withdrew after her last film turned out to be a complete failure in 1978.

Greta Garbo: Divine Star[8] by David Bret investigates the two so-called missing periods in the life of Garbo. The first time she disappeared completely for several months was during the late 1920s, forcing the studio to employ a lookalike, and it was almost certainly to conceal a pregnancy. The second occurred during World War II, when Garbo was employed by British intelligence to track down Nazi sympathizers. Bret's work is backed by a large amount of previously unsourced material along with anecdotes from friends and colleagues not published before. He gives a complete picture of Garbo's childhood and young life in Sweden.

In *Walking with Garbo: Conversations and Recollections,*[9] author Raymond Daun and editor Vance Muse put together a collection of photographs of Garbo along with a running monologue taken down by Daun who was the curator of the Gloria Swanson Archives at the University of Texas, Austin. The text is by Muse who was a magazine editor with *Life* magazine. The book carries the remarkable and famous Garbo quote, 'I've always wanted two lives—one for movies, one for myself.' It contains quite of bit of biographical information, beautiful photographs, and interesting trivia and quotes about Garbo in relation to her film career. But what readers have found to be the most fascinating is the glimpse this book gives into Garbo's private life, her life after her film career had ended, her likes and dislikes, her habits, her sense of humour, her very human longings, and her observations of the anonymous others who were so busy observing her. The author extensively quotes from conversations with her. Critic Robert Floyd comments: 'She comes alive as a very warm and honest person. To her it would seem, her career as a film star was just a job. One that brought her fame that would follow her until the last days of her life when even as she was helped into her car to go to the hospital, she was hounded by photographers. When her time on the screen was over, she would have liked to just travel and enjoy her life. She never said, "I want to be alone." What she said was, "I want to be let alone."'

These markers in Garbo's life story bear no similarities at all with the life and career of Suchitra Sen. Nor was Sen ever called 'the sex fantasy of the century'. Sen belonged to a close-knit, fairly educated Bengali family with parents and several brothers and sisters. Her entry into films was post marriage and post motherhood. Her marriage to Dibanath Sen was an arranged one, negotiated by the two families. There were no reasons for her to feel 'abandoned' or 'lost' or to seek a 'substitute' family. Her husband Dibanath Sen ushered her into films; so, initially, there were no domestic conflicts about her entry into films. She brought up her daughter Moon Moon with great care and sent her to England, following it up with lessons in painting and a postgraduate degree from a university. She was never known to be androgynous and this trait among men or women was probably not known by the common public in India at that time.

She tried to be as much an ideal mother as she possibly could, which was quite tough considering the profession she was in. She was kept constantly in the limelight, was the centre of the media's attention, was a subject of gossip, and the unearthly hours of shooting she had to adhere to, not to talk of the constant mobility her work demanded. Garbo went for strolls and went window shopping after she retired from films and shifted to New York City. But Sen was never seen taking a stroll down the streets, though her biographer, friend and journalist Gopalkrishna Roy does report that she sometimes ventured out deep into the night when the streets were lonely and dark and even if someone spotted her, he or she would not be able to recognize her. Sen commanded a great deal of dignity when she was a top star. Garbo was the subject of a lot of gossip and controversy as reported gleefully by a gossip-hungry media. Sen kept her private life very private even when she was the top star. So whatever gossip the film glossies carried were not authenticated because she refused to respond to questions on her personal life.

OTHER VIEWS ON SEN'S WILFUL SOCIAL SECLUSION

Madhabi Mukherjee, Charu of Satyajit Ray's *Charulata*, known more for her histrionic abilities than for her star pull, does not like to be compared with Suchitra Sen. 'But I appreciate her supreme control over herself in being able to withdraw from the limelight and remain in seclusion for thirty-five years after having been the top star for more than two decades. I am not a contemporary of Suchitra Sen. I came several years after her entry into films and stayed several years after she had called it a day. If you want to know about the difference in our "styles", in her time, dialogues were delivered in a rather singsong tone, with an artificial drawl. Then, there was a middle way when heroines would cut their lines up into words, delivering their lines in a clipped manner. I introduced, perhaps with the help of Satyajit Ray, the natural way of speaking. That is, delivering dialogues like we speak in real life, no tone, no singsong changes of pitch, no clipped words, no drawl, nothing. A noted journalist once wrote: "Suchitra's era has ended and the Madhabi era has begun." I take that as a fine compliment,' says Madhabi.

Film-maker Tarun Majumdar says, 'Looking back, I feel that her decision to withdraw so completely from the screen was a private one. But it seems to have been a bit premature. However, looking at the state of Bengali films today, it also appears to have been a wise decision. Had she been active in films till now, she might have been forced to put in mediocre performances in mediocre films. We would not have discussed her the way we now do, turning her into a legend.'

According to film critic Pradeep Biswas, 'She was always an extremely withdrawn and shy person in private life. Her screen persona was in complete contrast to her personal one. The death of historian Bagishwar Jha, whom she looked up to as a father figure, shattered her emotionally. So did the death of close associate Manujendra Bhanja. There is no way of knowing in what way she would have contributed to Bengali cinema had she remained active. But we, her fans, would certainly have been happier than we now are.'

Ananya Chatterjee, film-maker, admires her great beauty but says, 'In terms of acting, I always thought she was highly theatrical. You can compare her with Uttam Kumar and discover that unlike Uttam Kumar, who brought a sea change in acting for the big screen, bringing in a whole new genre, Suchitra could do nothing of the kind. In this sense, it appears to have been a very intelligent decision on her part to withdraw when she did. Looking at the way the very concept of acting has changed today, I do not think she would have contributed in any way to cinema had she been active today. Her successors imitated her in terms of dress, make-up and hairstyle but even that is dated today.'

Ashok Viswanathan, film-maker, mentions Greta Garbo in the context of why and how Suchitra Sen withdrew from the big screen almost forty years ago. 'But the similarity between the two ends there. Suchitra Sen was not an actress with pre-eminent abilities. She had many mannerisms and unlike her screen partner Uttam Kumar, who kept on improving himself and innovating constantly, Suchitra failed to grow. She got caught in her own matrix of fiction. She had already transcended her peak because her last film, *Pronoy Pasha*, was a complete washout. In *Datta*, she was portraying a girl of seventeen, even though she was over forty, and was not able to carry that aura of a teenager at all. She was more conscious about her beautiful image than anything else. I do not think she would have contributed in any way to the cinema of today.'

Churni Ganguly, actress and director, feels that she probably withdrew to ensure that the image we have of her did not fade away or get lost. 'All actresses suffer from a sense of insecurity and Suchitra Sen was no exception. In this sense, it turned out to be an extremely wise decision. Her decision to withdraw so completely has sustained the aura of mystery about her. What more can a star-actress ask for? All actresses, including myself, grow every day. She, too, would have grown over the years, matured as a star performer. Had she been around today, she would have given much more of herself than she has. I miss the opportunity of interacting with her on a one-to-one level as an actress because she had so much to teach and I had so much to learn.'

CONCLUSION

Questions remain. Had she continued to act, would Suchitra Sen have reached the pinnacle of acting she always aspired to be at, at least in the latter part of her career? Or, would she have failed to survive the transition from the beautiful, charismatic star that held thousands of fans spellbound for many years by her beauty to the mortal entity she basically was thanks to the impact of ageing on screen and off it? As far as information goes, Suchitra Sen had no addiction to alcohol, drugs or tobacco. She led an austere life after retirement, though when she was the top star, her daughter Moon Moon Sen states she loved to party and enjoyed the flashlights of the cameras that flooded her existence. She kept her distance from her immediate family, though they lived under the same roof. Why did she not capitalize on the fame and power she had gained through hard work and success following the commercial disaster of *Pronoy Pasha*? Why did she not seek solidarity among her peers—actors, actresses, technicians and directors she had worked with? A few friends from the film industry would drop in initially but later faded out of her life. Why? She lived up to the ripe old age of eighty and beyond, but did not come out of her self-imposed social seclusion. Why? We will never know and will continue to be haunted by possible answers.

One can perhaps read Suchitra Sen's complete withdrawal from public life and from the screen as her individual way of keeping her star image alive so that her millions of fans and admirers, both male and female, and even children, would remember her screen persona. In this way, she intelligently skirted all possibilities of a collapse of the star image altogether and avoided the tensions between the star as a real person and the star as a constructed image that is often manipulated and created by magazines and the media, and the gossip mills. It was not that there was no gossip around her. There were questions about whether there was a real, off-screen relationship between herself and her hero Uttam Kumar. This was never substantiated by those who knew her and Uttam Kumar closely. Once, the grapevine went wild stating that Sen had cancer and had gone to London for treatment. This proved to be a red herring. The stories that concerned her fractured relationship with her husband, which she did not ever authenticate, are the ones believed to have emerged out of her lifestyle of almost a single mother responsible for the only child the marriage produced—Moon Moon Sen. Gossip about her unhappy life with husband Dibanath Sen, who was reportedly addicted to alcohol, horse-racing, etc., did the rounds but Suchitra Sen never ever substantiated these statements.

Gauri Chatterjee rightly concludes her tribute:[10] 'I don't understand why anyone who could choose to live as some sort of recluse wouldn't do so. It seems such a perfect, elegant expression of control: to occlude the flow of trivia in one's life; to accrue and manage fame on one's own terms; to engage with people you trust and appreciate. Mrs Sen did just that—and managed to do so even beyond her passing. She was, and always will be, incomparable.'

But questions will continue to nag us.

6

THE SUMMING UP

Besides her screen charisma, her popularity among the masses and the archival value of most of her films, Suchitra Sen's career features some elements exclusive to her screen persona. These are briefly detailed in this summing up. Before that, it would be in context to point out that the romantic and serious characters she portrayed confined her and typecast her in a romantic mould, at least in the films in which she acted opposite Uttam Kumar. The films that she did independently had serious storylines and plots and did not offer any scope to the actress to explore other areas of histrionics an actor looks for, such as comedy, noir and negative roles. She did not have the kind of comic timing that her peer Sabitri Chatterjee demonstrated in film after film. Her two films that belonged to the genre of comedy—*Saare Chuattar* and *Ekti Raat* (1956) became famous more because of Uttam Kumar's performance than for hers. Her films without Uttam Kumar were even more serious because even romance was peripheral to the characters she portrayed. When romance did exist, such as in *Datta*, it was low-key, subtle and restrained.

THE SUBMISSIVE WOMAN AND SUCHITRA SEN

The author has spoken to film personalities from different fields and some of Sen's contemporaries. The latter often mentioned her complete withdrawal from public space and speculated whether she would have still drawn packed theatres in West Bengal and sustained star charisma had she made a comeback. Interviews with her daughter Moon Moon Sen and her two granddaughters Riya and Raima Sen, the family spanning three generations in films as leading ladies, find place within the mapping of Mrs Sen's personal life and the impact she made on these three women.

The charisma of Suchitra Sen, with and without Uttam Kumar, evolved in the early 1950s. At the time, women, in films and in real life, were expected to be wives and mothers. They were not valued for their intelligence, nor were they encouraged to take up professional careers. Patriarchal modes of thinking and ideology ruled and any deviation from that ideology was considered blasphemy. The influx of refugees from East Pakistan (now Bangladesh) into West Bengal created pockets of refugee 'colonies' steeped in financial impoverishment. Extended families were slowly making way for nuclear families, urbanization was on the rise and the emergence of the working woman was a reality.

In films that showed the woman slighting or disowning her husband or lover, or leaving the husband for another man, the leading lady was made to realize, through the same man, that she was wrong and he was right. Among these films, one might mention *Agnipariksha, Indrani* and *Grihadaha*. In *Grihadaha*, the woman actually falls to her husband's feet begging him to forgive her. But this was the director being loyal to the original literary source, Sarat Chandra's classic novel. The commercial success of the film could be read as the audience's patriarchal mindset that felt happy with an apologetic woman who realizes her 'guilt' and her 'mistake'. It does not occur to us to question Mahim's close friend Suresh who plays a trick in the train to have Archana to himself. We do not sympathize with Archana even after she is violated by Suresh. Poetic justice happens when Suresh dies in the fire and Archana begs Mahim to forgive her. Suchitra Sen as Archana in *Grihadaha* offers a very convincing and histrionically impressive performance as she evolves from an extremely well-appointed, city-bred and educated Brahmo girl who falls in love with the very ordinary Hindu Mahim but cannot adjust to the poor surroundings of his village home. Archana is basically invested with the aura of a city-bred, educated woman. So, when Mahim's simple, straight-talking sister-in-law approaches her with the casualness and familiarity that is a part of her rural upbringing, Archana is not pleased and shows her discomfiture. She loves her husband but Suresh plays with her emotions and tries to pit her against Mahim. He tricks her so that she gets separated from him and is forced to go along with Suresh.

Agnipariksha was authored by Ashapurna Devi, a noted novelist of her time, while *Indrani* was written by Nripendra Krishna Chatterjee. The stories were structured to remove any possibility of the woman in the film rebelling against the ideology the film represented or in any way empowering the woman. These films fall within the pre-feminist era when patriarchy was idealized, practised and accepted. They could not have been any different unless the box-office prospects were to be risked by showing a rebellious woman as leading lady. Ironically and interestingly, these films, pairing Suchitra with Uttam Kumar, turned out to be box-office hits.

The most regressive and absurd portrait of a Bengali woman enacted by Suchitra Sen in her entire career is in *Sandhya Dweeper Sikha*, based on a serialized novel by the late Tarun Kumar Bhaduri. He was a noted journalist who first hit the headlines with a novel, *Abhishopto Chambal*, based on his first-hand experiences in the dreaded region of Chambal forests in Madhya Pradesh. The novel is a fictionalized account of his real-life experiences during his posting in the dreaded Chambal ravines. This novel first appeared in a serialized version in the noted literary magazine *Desh*. Since *Abhishopto Chambal* was one of the few novels that revealed the inside story of the dreaded dacoits of Chambal, the serialization became very popular and when it came out in the shape of a published novel, it was a big hit with the readers. *Sandhya Dweeper Sikha* is entirely fiction and did not go down half as well with the readers. It is therefore quite surprising that a producer thought of making a film adaptation of the novel, placing Suchitra Sen, then clearly past her prime, in the lead role.

Sandhya Dweeper Sikha is set against the 1962 Indo-China war. As the newly married bride of Major Anupam Banerjee, Suchitra Sen as Jayanti is the sole protagonist of the film. From a beautiful, house-proud wife of an army man who does not touch a drop of alcohol as a bride, she turns into an incurable alcoholic after her husband is killed in action somewhere in Ladakh. The news arrives on the day they are to celebrate their first wedding anniversary. The camera, beautifully handled by Bibhuti Laha, a top cinematographer of his time, captures the beauty of the star-actress in every angle possible, from long-shots to mid-long-shots to medium-close-ups to close-ups throughout the film. But in all its captivating moods, the film fails to capture the histrionic talents of Suchitra Sen, who remains extremely conscious of both the camera and her star charisma to be able to get under the skin of the character. But it is more the nondescript script and the extremely weak and melodramatic content that fail to bring out the best in her. A modern, educated young woman from Delhi, Jayanti approaching her in-laws for shelter, begging of her father-in-law to let her live by his feet, head covered like the traditional bahu, is downright absurd.

As a habitual alcoholic, her complexion comes out as peaches-and-cream without a line on her attractive face or any puffiness around the eyes. She looks beautiful in every scene and the only disturbance seen is in her dishevelled hair that falls across her face, enhancing her beauty instead of taking away from it. She climbs the snowy mountains of Leh to reach Lemchuk is search of her dead husband's grave without knowing how to climb mountains, how to cope with extreme weather conditions and without any mountaineering kit. She is finally shot to death next to the grave of an unknown soldier by a Chinese soldier and she says 'thank you'. The death of Jayanti Banerjee comes like a relief. The question that one feels like asking is: did Suchitra Sen's glamour and beauty come in the way of her performance in this and some other films? At that point of her career, was Suchitra Sen confused about the offers that came to her and gave her consent without understanding the impact of the film on her performance and on her career?

Directed by Haridas Bhattacharya when he was much past his prime and produced by actor Dilip Mukherjee who plays an observer half in love with this enigmatic woman, *Sandhya Dweeper Sikha* was a bad film and did nothing to add to the contribution of Suchitra Sen to Bengali cinema. As one watches the film, one is constantly dogged by questions like: is this the same Suchitra Sen who brought Rina Brown to life in *Saptapadi*? Or, is it the star Suchitra Sen who remained the star Suchitra Sen right through the film and, almost by design, refused to bring out the pain of the young widow with conviction? The dialogues are stilted and delivered with designed artifice that fails to convince. There is a scene where the camera focuses on a close-up of her beautiful face as a series of newspaper headlines pan across in. Her face remains almost completely shorn of expression in that scene where pain should have been evident.

LITERATURE, BENGALI CINEMA AND THE SUCHITRA SEN ERA

Though both literature and cinema are arts of narration, their ways of representation are completely different. Our texts reach out to local audiences only when they are modified in order to make them relevant to the cultural and ideological concerns of the new audiences that were far removed from the writer's vision. Besides, the language of the word and the language of cinema—expressed through visuals, dialogue, sound effects, editing, cinematography, acting and so on—are poles apart. Thirdly, a film-maker often picks a piece of literature to make a film on that which is distanced from his/her world in terms of time, if not in terms of place. Within the time-space paradigms, there are hundreds of permutations and combinations that make the director rethink about how he/she will approach the literary piece, treat it as he/she feels it should be treated and then present it to an audience.

The nexus between Bengali cinema and its narrative sources is something of a regional characteristic. While all Indian cinemas have, to varying degrees, derived their narrative impetus from popular and literary texts, Bengali film-makers and viewers have arguably placed more emphasis on textuality. The fact that Bengalis frequently call a movie *boi*—meaning book—highlights the Bengali's vested interest in the narrative source of the film.[1] Terms of negotiation between the word and the picture can assume a hundred permutations and combinations even for the same novel expressed in film by different film-makers at different times, but that is where the point of view comes across.

A director working in the year 2000 decides to adapt from a piece of literature that was created in, say, 1950. He could either make his adaptation into a period piece, just translating the story on celluloid, reflecting the time, the costume, the characters and their conflicts. Or, he might want to contemporize it and bring it to the present time and tweak the storyline accordingly. He may relocate the story to a different time and place without losing out on the essential message and core of the story. A very good example of the last one can be found in Vishal Bhardwaj's adaptations of Shakespeare's *Macbeth*, *Othello* and *Hamlet*, as *Maqbool*, *Omkara* and *Haider*. Another similar example is Satyajit Ray's *Ganashatru*, an Indianized adaptation of Henrik Ibsen's play, *Enemy of the People*.

A complete deconstruction of a famous literary piece that comes out with different resolutions and conflicts and even characterizations can also happen. Anurag Kashyap's *Dev D* (2009), a celluloid deconstruction of Sarat Chandra Chattopadhyay's *Devdas*, is an individualistic statement of the director who takes inspiration from an original classic piece of literature and then remoulds it differently to convey how he, as film-maker and writer, would like to tell the same story. Sanjay Leela Bhansali's *Devdas* (2002), on the other hand, is a rather distorted, highly glamourized and exaggerated melodrama that retains Sarat Chandra's original story but tells it very loudly, in typical Bollywood style featuring the larger-than-life Shah Rukh Khan in the title role with Aishwarya Rai playing Parvati and Madhuri Dixit doing the courtesan bit as Chandramukhi. The fact that there have been around fourteen different celluloid versions of *Devdas* in several Indian languages proves how versatile film-makers can be while telling the same story, transforming literature into cinema.

New Theatres' all-time hit, *Devdas*, directed by Pramathesh Chandra Barua who also played the title role in the Bengali version, choosing K.L. Saigal for the Hindi version as Barua was not confident about his knowledge of Hindi, remains a cult classic till today. It made Barua a star overnight and revolutionized the concept of cinema as entertainment into cinema of social concern and literature expressed through celluloid.

Barua used Sarat Chandra Chatterjee's novel as his raw material, creating his own structure and transforming what was purely verbal into an essentially visual form. Avoiding stereotypes and melodrama, Barua raised the film to the level of noble tragedy. The film's characters are not heroes and villains but ordinary people conditioned by a rigid and crumbling social system. Even the lead protagonist, Devdas, has no heroic dimensions to his character. What one sees are his weaknesses, his narcissism, his humanity as he is torn by driving passion and inner conflict. *Devdas* established Barua as a front-rank film-maker and New Theatres as a major studio.

Barua's *Devdas* left such a deep impression on its strapping young cameraman that when the latter, Bimal Roy, decided to make a Hindi version of the film twenty years later, his climax was the exact replica of the climax of New Theatres' *Devdas*. The difference between Barua's *Devdas* and Bimal Roy's *Devdas* is subtle, but strong. It lies in the style and interpretation of character through acting that had changed from Barua to Dilip Kumar, already established as the top tragic hero of Hindi cinema. Vyjayanthimala as Chandramukhi is embellished with her graceful dance style that evolves with her transition from a dancing woman to a woman, who, in love with Devdas, has unconsciously mutated to reflect the mainstream woman.

New Theatres, however, cannot be credited for bringing literature into Bengali cinema as this happened in the early years of its history. In 1928, Dhiren Ganguly (DG) founded the British Dominion Film Company along with Nitish Lahiri, the then manager of MGM. His first feature film *Bilet Ferat* (England Returned) was released at Russa Theatre in 1921. Under this banner, he brought together talented technicians and artists like Debaki Bose, P.C. Barua, Krishna Gopal and Sabita Devi. B.K. Ghose founded the Taj Mahal Film Company in 1922 along with lawyers and educated stage actors with a new agenda—to tap into Bengali literature as a source material.

New Theatres definitely took Bengali cinema based on literature to a new direction and gave it new meaning that also reinforced the 'Bengali' identity that lasted for many years to follow, well into the late 1980s and the beginning of 1990s, with actors like Kali Banerjee, Soumitra Chatterjee, Anil Chatterjee, Dipankar Dey and Ranjit Mullick complemented by Sabitri Chatterjee, Sharmila Tagore, Supriya Choudhuri, Tanuja and Aparna Sen, who ruled mainstream Bengali cinema. It was a time when literature was considered to be the most reliable source, for expression, interpretation and translation to cinematic language as well as for commercial success at the box office. Two qualities contributed to the compatibility between Bengali cinema and literature of the time. One was that many noted writers of those days doubled up to write scripts and screenplays of films and the other was that most film-makers were extremely well-educated and well-informed on literature and were completely aware of what writing to choose, why and how to convert it into a script with an ideal acting cast and technical crew. Music formed another important element of cinema with the emergence of some of the most outstanding music composers and singers contributing to the aesthetics, the story and the melodrama woven into all films of the time. In fact, it would be difficult to find a Bengali film at the time that was sourced to a direct screenplay and not to a piece of literature that already existed in the Bengali literary domain.

Within this socio-cultural scenario that defined Bengali cinema, therefore, it was natural for Suchitra Sen's films, with Uttam Kumar and without, to have been drawn from rich Bengali literary sources. This has been described by most critics and film scholars as one reason for the unique character of Bengali cinema as 'different' from Hindi cinema and other regional cinemas in the country. During the time Suchitra Sen reigned supreme, literature was the basic source for plot, storyline and screenplay in Bengali cinema. Three of her several Hindi films, too, were drawn from rich literary sources. These are *Devdas* (Sarat Chandra), *Mamta* (Nihar Ranjan Gupta) and *Aandhi* (Kamaleshwar).

The term 'parallel cinema' or 'art cinema' had not made its presence felt, and mainstream cinema's popularity was largely determined by the strength of its content. So, actors of her time were fortunate to realize historic characters from the written word to the cinema screen. Almost all feature films Sen acted in were based on or adapted from or were celluloid representations of literary works by noted Bengali littérateurs. Though the writers have been described and explained separately under the films based on their works, a passing glimpse would offer a grand galaxy of writers who have passed on but remain alive through their works. Two among them, namely Ashapurna Devi and Tarasankar Bandyopadhyay, were both Jnanpith awardees. Sen played the classic character of Rina Brown in *Saptapadi* by Tarasankar Bandyopadhyay and followed this up with one of the two leads in *Bipasha* and *Haar Mana Haar*. (Both stories are by Tarashankar Bandyopadhyay.)

She starred in several celluloid adaptations of Sarat Chandra Chattopadhyay's works, namely *Devdas* (Hindi), *Rajlakshmi O Sreekanto*, *Grihadaha*, *Datta*, *Kamallata* and *Chandranath*. *Saat Paake Bandha*, which fetched her Best Actress Award at the Third Moscow International Film Festival, was based on a novel by Ashutosh Mukherjee. *Deep Jele Jai* was also based on his *Nurse Mitra* and so was *Nabaraag*. *Ekti Raat* was adapted from a novel by Bonophool. *Sabar Uparey* was based on a 1953 novel by A.J. Cronin originally called *Beyond This Place*. *Hospital* and *Uttar Phalguni* were adapted from novels by the popular doctor-novelist Nihar Ranjan Gupta. *Smritituku Thaak* was based on a script by noted writer Premendra Mitra from a novel by Malabika Roy. She also portrayed the title role in *Debi Choudhurani*, a period classic by Bankim Chandra Chattopadhyay. *Aandhi* was adapted from a story by Kamaleshwar.

SUCHITRA SEN AND MENTAL ILLNESS IN FILMS

One interesting feature of Suchitra Sen's filmography is that she has often featured in films depicting mental illness of some kind, either directly as victim or indirectly in a corrective role, or, as 'agency' in a love relationship that in some way involves a mental illness. Let us take a brief look at these films.

In *Harano Sur*, Roma is a psychiatrist. She falls in love with Alok, an amnesiac, without knowing his name, address or identity. She even gives up her job at the nursing home and marries the man to take individual and intimate care of him in her own home because she feels that a wife can take better care of her husband than a doctor can take care of his/her patient. The way amnesia is dealt with in the film is not only very filmy and melodramatic but also lacking in medical logic. It is broadly addressed to an audience not interested in medical precision but only when it is used imaginatively as a strategy for romance. So, *Harano Sur* became a big box-office hit and no one ever raised questions about its ignorant 'treatment' and approach to amnesia. Amnesia worked as the 'agency' of love and marriage found-lost-rediscovered between Roma and Alok and that is all it was supposed to do. It also offered Suchitra Sen the challenge of actually portraying two polarized dimensions of a woman—the first as a psychiatrist committed to innovate curative therapies for mental diseases, and the second as a wife committed to saving her marriage that seems lost because her husband has forgotten all about her. *Harano Sur* must be commended for being the first-ever Bengali commercial film to bring amnesia to the fore as a 'character' in the film.

Deep Jele Jai is about a foreign-qualified, dedicated nurse, Radha Mitra, who is known for her special way of looking after mental patients who have a tendency for violence. But while caring for one especially violent patient who hates women because one has ditched him in love, Radha falls in love with him only to be shocked to discover that he does not love her back. Her mentor and the chief surgeon of the hospital keeps insisting that she is basically a nurse but she begins to realize that there is a woman craving for love under that starched, white uniform. When another similar patient arrives and is placed in the same room, she is asked by her chief to pretend that she is in love with the young man. 'I am not an actress, only a nurse,' she insists but no one is listening. The love is mutual this time but as loyalty towards her chief and mentor and as proof of her commitment, she refuses to step out of her room when the now recovered patient comes to bid goodbye before leaving. When the door is opened, Radha emerges, completely insane. The details of the mental illness are clouded in ambiguity and lack medical basis but this time, too, the strategy worked so well that Suchitra Sen's performance in the film is regarded to be one of her most outstanding ones ever. Her mental illness remains undiagnosed and whether she will be cured is left open to question. But that made no dent in the box-office returns of the film.

In *Alo Amar Alo*, Atashi, the very responsible, caring and beautiful eldest daughter of a refugee family steeped in poverty and living in a refugee colony with parents and five siblings is abducted by the goons of Nilendra, a two-faced industrialist. He is a generous philanthropist on one hand and a ruthless womanizer on the other who does not stop at kidnapping the girl he desires if she or her family do not bend to temptations of money or gifts in kind. Nilendra, with strong negative shades that slowly change when he falls in love with the girl he has arranged to kidnap for pleasure, is portrayed by Uttam Kumar while Suchitra Sen is convincing as a very young Atashi till she remains in the refugee colony. But as she is being forcibly taken away by Nilendra's goons, she fights back and in the melee, she is hit in the head and loses her memory. At Nilendra's mansion, she thinks Nilendra is a doctor treating her and begins to behave with exaggerated coquetry at times and like a spoilt brat at other times which stands in stark contrast to her character before she was kidnapped. The two fall in love but when she discovers who Nilendra really is and what he has done to her and her family, she is shocked. She insults him and goes away only to come back realizing that she has fallen in love with him. Her family back at Nabajiban Colony is left to fend for themselves. Uttam Kumar as Nilendra comes across much more powerfully in this film than Suchitra Sen does as Atashi. The amnesia element is once again glossed over with unrealistic and very cinematic dramaturgy aimed to please the box-office. It did.

In *Sabar Uparey*, as Rita, she provides a solid support system to Shankar all through his struggle to gain justice for his father's imprisonment for a murder he did not commit. Shankar finds himself all alone in the court, everyone having abandoned him in the pursuit of justice. Rita does not directly get involved in the insanity of Shankar's father but her support helps to boost his confidence when he is about to fall apart. Shankar's father has become insane and has also lost his memory due to the long sentence he has served, without having committed any crime. There is no diagnosis or treatment or explanation of the kind of mental illness he is suffering from and he regains his sanity when justice is served, that, too, without medical treatment or help.

The more affluent twin Utpola in *Smritituku Thaak* is involved in a train crash while returning from a friend's marriage from Patna to Kolkata. She loses her memory and does not remember her name, her identity, her family and her residential address. Her family is not bothered about locating her as they know nothing of the accident because her identical twin Shovana has taken her place in their home. She is taken to a nursing home where Dr Nag begins to treat her so that he can send her back to her family. In this case, Utpola's amnesia is total because she remembers absolutely nothing of her past. But the director treats her slow regaining of memory through a telling sound design of a rushing train followed by a resounding crash. There is the visual metaphor of an unfinished portrait she seemed to have been painting of a man—her fiancé Jayanta—which she cannot recognize right away. She feels that only when she finishes the portrait will she be able to regain her memory. 'The picture will be complete,' she says uncertainly. The picture that is complete in the end is a different one but she comes to terms with this loss in her life. Suchitra Sen captured in close-ups and tight close-ups during the phase of her amnesia puts in a very convincing though dramatic portrayal as Utpola who cannot respond to the emotional overtures of Dr Nag because at the back of her mind, she knows she loves another man.

Haar Mana Haar is the love story of Binu, a painter who also runs an orphanage, and Nira, who comes from an affluent family but runs away to escape a forced marriage. She begins to share in the work of the orphanage and the two fall in love. But there is a mental patient within the orphanage who is undergoing treatment. Her name is Protima and she is obsessively in love with Binu though he does not reciprocate her feelings. Protima, sensing that Nira and Binu are in love, tries to engineer misunderstandings between them and the gossip in the orphanage about Protima and Binu convinces Nira that there was something between them she does not know of. She goes away. The couple meets after several years when Nira learns about what Protima had done to destroy their relationship. By then, Protima is no more and Nira and Binu's love ends happily. But no one ever knows the mental illness Protima suffered from and how she came to suffer from this when she entered the orphanage as a normal woman.

There is little distinction made by film-makers, insist medical and psychiatric experts, between intellectual disability and psychotic disorder, and the characters end up with a bizarre depiction. The saddest part is that when we watch these films that are designed as powerful psychiatric melodramas, we respond with neither laughter nor fear, but pity for the bewildered victim. Indian cinema in general and Bengali cinema in particular has not known the difference between amnesia and partial memory loss, says Dr G.B. Daver, director, professional services, Hinduja Hospital, Mumbai. Countless films have revolved around the story of memory lost and regained. 'It is only in Hindi movies that the hero can be down with the worst possible fracture or ailment and be out of the hospital within a day,' says the doctor.

However, despite the ambiguous treatment of mental illness in these films, it needs to be mentioned that during the time these films were made, such ailments were almost unknown in celluloid and these films might mark a milestone in Bengali cinema for their introduction of mental illness either as 'character' or as 'strategy' or as 'agency' for breaking or cementing relationships. Placed against this backdrop, one must concede that considering the era in which these films were made and her ranking within the industry as a star and an actress, it goes to the credit of Suchitra Sen and is a signifier of her courage in doing roles that at that time could have been a big marketing risk. If they were not, part of the credit must go to Sen.

POSTERITY AND SUCHITRA SEN

In the 1930s, when English critic Cyril Connolly proposed a definition of posterity to measure whether a writer's work had stood the test of time, he suggested that posterity should be limited to ten years. The form and content of popular culture were changing too fast, he explained, to make any artist accountable for more than a decade.[2] The star charisma of Suchitra Sen has disproved this theory. Her withdrawal from public life and from her career in films continued to trigger curiosity among the media, among her fans and her audience, and among the film fraternity—old and new—dying to have her sign on the dotted line for a new film. This never happened. As a consequence, she lived through the repeat telecast of the films she had worked in, enchanting not only the audience that remained faithful to her but also a new generation of film buffs who were eager to see what Suchitra Sen was all about.

What Gloria Steinem wrote about Marilyn Monroe could be extended in a different way to apply to Suchitra Sen. Writes Steinem, 'Personalities and narratives projected onto the screen of our imaginations are far more haunting—and far more likely to be the stuff of conspiracies and conjuncture—if they have not been allowed to play themselves out to their logical or illogical ends.'[3] Steinem was referring to the sudden and tragic death of Monroe. This does not apply to Suchitra Sen. She did not die but lived in self-imposed seclusion, egging on the curiosity that naturally dogs a cinema-crazy and star-crazy public such as the one in Bengal.

Sen's power as a public figure not seen in public anymore remained as enduring as it was when she was at the top of her profession. Her star charisma and image did not differ between her on-screen and off-screen persona as she carried herself with great dignity and reflected class. This took away from her image any sign of vulnerability many stars are known for. Even in films in which her character was fleshed out as vulnerable and backed by audience sympathy, such as in the second half of *Harano Sur*, she embellished her performance and her image with a certain sense of dignity unmatched by her peers like Sabitri Chatterjee and later, Supriya Choudhury. Sabitri was a much more talented actress than Suchitra ever was because she was versatile, had perfect timing, a flair for comedy and posed a challenge to whoever was cast opposite her as hero. But she was not as beautiful and had less screen charisma than Suchitra Sen. Supriya Choudhury was not a highly rated actress and made it big by virtue of her robust voluptuousness and brazen sexuality, an image reportedly nurtured and constructed with great care by Uttam Kumar who, in later years, became her lover and mentor. As Supriya graduated from leading lady to character roles, she matured as an actress. But her sterling performances were in the two great Ghatak classics, *Meghe Dhaka Tara* (1960) and *Komal Gandhar* (1961).

The golden era of Bengali cinema was largely determined by several things: firstly, the Uttam Kumar-Suchitra Sen screen chemistry that graced around thirty-two films featuring them in the lead; secondly, the stories picked from Bengali literature that were adapted into films; thirdly, the melodious metaphors of songs and music; and, finally, the beautiful orchestration of the mise en scène created by the immensely innovative, talented and dedicated technical crew headed by the film-maker. The fact that these films, shot entirely in black-and-white, have stood the test of time against the tremendous advance modern cinema has made in terms of technology is proof that the golden era is a milestone in the history of Bengali cinema and will remain so for all time to come.

All the years I grew up on Uttam-Kumar-Suchitra Sen films, I was completely mesmerized by the charisma, screen presence and the killing good looks of Uttam Kumar. I came back from every film featuring the pair convinced that Uttam Kumar was certainly a much more superior actor than his screen partner. She was little more than a beautiful foil to the handsome hero, ready to fall into his arms, look into his eyes and always willing to leave everything she lived for to be with him in sickness and in pain and in happiness. I did not rate her very highly as an actress and felt she had more of the star in her than the actress. This was also perhaps because I too was deeply conditioned by the patriarchal mindset I was brought up in. But towards the end of her films with Uttam Kumar and in the films where she had meaningful roles without him, she began to exude a different aura as an actress worth watching.

It is difficult to draw a distinct dividing line between Suchtra Sen the Star and Suchitra Sen the Actress. Somewhere along the way, the two melded to become one. The glimmer we saw in *Harano Sur* began to gather its glow and shine to show up in strength through *Saptapadi, Hospital, Deep Jele Jai, Datta, Uttar Phalguni, Mamta, Aandhi, Devdas* and *Smrititukku Thaak*. Her photogenic face, her beauty, her feminine grace expressed through body language did not fade at all. In fact, it matured from one film to the next and acquired a different kind of beauty in films like *Uttar Phalguni*, *Smritituku Thaak* and *Aandhi* where she plays a greying woman perhaps in her mid-forties.

This book has been a journey searching for the 'cultural matrix of meaning and signification' of this 'mahanayika' because she is the only star-actress in Bengali cinema to get this tag and till this day, she remains the only one. She is a star and she is also an actress. In this, she never had to make a choice for the one at the cost of the other.

In the beginning of this book, I raised the question of whether this work is a biography or an analysis. For a star-actress of the calibre of Suchitra Sen, it would be difficult to honestly label it as either. An analysis of a selection of her films also charts out her biography in a manner of speaking. This is not the 'biography' one commonly understands from the term. An analysis of her films is also an analysis of the slow and steady evolution of this phenomenal woman who grew from a minuscule role in *Bhagaban Sri Sri Krishna Chaitanya* in 1953 to *Datta* in 1976 till the 'duality' of her existence finally merged to become one.

NOTES

INTRODUCTION

1 Maarten Reesink, 'Light Stars: Fame in Postmodern Times', 2008 (E-View, Vol. 2008, No. 1).

2 Richard Dyer, *Stars*, London: British Film Institute, 1979; and Dyer, *Heavenly Bodies*, London: British Film Institute, 1986.

3 Ibid, Dyer.

4 Kundu, Abhijit: 'Changing Iconography of the Women in Bengali Cinema (1950s to 1990s) – A Sociological Study of Some Select Films', Supervisor: Professor J.S. Gandhi, Jawaharlal Nehru University, 2002.

5 Moinak Biswas, 'The Couple and Their Spaces: *Harano Sur* as Melodrama Now', in R. Vasudevan (ed.), *Making Meaning in Indian Cinema,* New Delhi, Oxford University Press, 2000. Quoted by Abhijit Kundu, Chapter 4, Page 20.

6 'Post-Colonial Modernity: Melodrama and Self-Fashioning in Popular Bengali Cinema of the 1950s-70s', JNU, 2006-12.

7 http://www.india-seminar.com/2009/598/598_smita_mitra.htm

8 'Suchitra Sen: Biography of a Female Star', a talk by Dr Smita Mitra at Teen Murti House, Teen Murti Marg, 17 December 2013.

9 'Bengali Love Stories: Uttam-Suchitra and the Golden Era of Bengali Cinema', in Sharmistha Gooptu, *Bengali Cinema: An Other Nation*, Lotus Roli Books, 2010.

10 Ibid. p.157.

11 Ibid.

12 Bhaskar Sarkar, *Mourning the Nation: Indian Cinema in the Wake of Partition*, p. 69.

CHAPTER 2: UTTAM KUMAR AND SUCHITRA SEN: A MAGICAL SCREEN CHEMISTRY

1 *Television*, a Bengali monthly magazine brought out by Aaj Kaal publications, brought out several special nostalgia issues before it closed shop around the mid-1990s. Among these were two special issues on Uttam Kumar (January 1993 and July 1993), one on Uttam Kumar-Suchitra Sen (August 1992) and one on Suchitra Sen (February 1993) alone. These issues offered some rare insights into the psychology and mystique of Suchitra Sen as a star persona and Suchitra Sen as Uttam Kumar's female counterpart in films. Some quotes in this book are sourced from these special issues since the people quoted are no longer alive. I am deeply indebted to Anshuman Bhowmick for having made these archival documents available to me for the research of this book.

2 Ibid.

3 Ibid.

4 Bhaskar Sarkar, *Mourning the Nation: Indian Cinema in the Wake of Partition*, Chapter 3, p. 149, Duke University Press, Orient Blackswan Pvt. Ltd, 2010.

5 *Adhunika* means 'modern woman' in Bengali

6 Bhaskar Sarkar, *Mourning the Nation: Indian Cinema in the Wake of Partition*, Chapter 3, p. 152, Duke University Press, Orient Blackswan Pvt. Ltd, 2010.

7 Ibid. Chapter 3, p. 152.

8 Abhijit Kundu, 'Changing Iconography of Women in Bengali Cinema', PhD thesis, JNU, Chapter 4, 'Encounters with Modernity: Period of Recuperation, 1950s–1960s', 2002.

9 Ibid.

10 http://bethlovesbollywood.blogspot.in/2014/06/harano-sur.html, 22 June 2014.

11 Sharmistha Gooptu, *Bengali Cinema: An Other Nation*, p.168-69, Lotus Roli Books, 2010.

12 Abhijit Kundu, 'Changing Iconography of Women in Bengali Cinema', PhD Thesis, JNU, Chapter 4, 'Encounters with Modernity: Period of Recuperation, 1950s–1960s', 2002.

13 *The Rainmaker* (1956) is an American film directed by Joseph Anthony and adapted by N. Richard Nash from his play of the same name. The film tells the story of a middle-aged woman, suffering from unrequited love for the local town sheriff; however, she falls for a conman who comes to town with the promise that he can make it rain. This was later adapted into a Hindi film called *Thodasa Rumani Ho Jaaye* (1990) directed by Amol Palekar. The man who comes visiting claiming that he is a magician who can make it rain becomes a metaphor of everyone's dreams in this small hilly town and moves on when he thinks his work is over.

14 The inferences drawn by most social historians writing about this period in Bengal are that either the institution of Kulinism was so extreme that it lead to a great imbalance in the system, or that it was not Kulinism itself, but a combination of factors, perhaps just the general condition of Bengali society, that brought forth an abysmal picture on the status of women. The nineteenth century is considered to be a period of renaissance in Bengali society. During this period, old and evil customs were overthrown. The legal abolition of *sati*, however, did not alter the social conditioning of Bengali women in any real way.

15 The word *Kul* refers to the social and ceremonial position of the Kulin family in the hierarchy of Bengali Brahmins in terms of 'purity'. The term is closely associated with the Kulas—the extended family and

kin groups, or lineage. One's family name immediately revealed one's ranked position on the Kulin scales. Any Bengali having the family name Banerjee, Chatterjee, Mukherjee and Ganguly (changed by the British from their original denominations) could immediately be identified as the highest-ranking Brahmin, a Radi Kulin Brahmin. A group of Brahmins called Ghataks maintained family records. Their work was to note all births, deaths and marriages in the family to establish and sustain its purity. For this entire historical analysis of the Kulin factor among the Bengali Brahmin community, I am deeply indebted to Stutchbury's study of Michael Allen and S.N. Mukherjee's (ed.), 'Women in India and Nepal', in *Blood, Fire and Mediation: Human Sacrifice and Widow Burning in Nineteenth Century India*, Sterling Publishers India Ltd, 1990.

16 Tarasankar Bandopadhyay, *Amar Sahitya Jeebon*, Volume I, p. 19-20 (1963).

17 Ibid.

CHAPTER 3: FROM STAR TO ACTRESS: THE METAMORPHOSIS

1 Su Holmes, 'Starring Dyer?' in *Revisiting Star Studies and Contemporary Celebrity Culture*, Westminster Papers in Communication and Culture © 2005 (University of Westminster, London), Vol. 2(2): 6-21 ISSN 1744–6708 (Print); 1744–6716 (Online).

2 Richard Dyer, *Performing Arts*, British Film Institute, London, p. 204.

3 Maarten Reesink, 'Light Stars: Fame in Postmodern Times', *E-view*, Vol. 2008, No.1.

4 Christine Gledhill, 'Signs of Melodrama' in *Stardom: Industry of Desire*, London, Routledge, 1991.

5 Richard Dyer, *Stars*, London, British Film Institute, 1979 and *Heavenly Bodies*, London, British Film Institute, 1986.

6 P. McDonald, 'Reconceptualising Stardom', in Richard Dyer (ed.), *Stars* (second edition), London, British Film Institute, pp. 175–200, 1998.

7 Ibid.

8 Mary Ann Doane, *Pandora's Box,* G.W. Pabst (Dir.), Criterion Collection, 2006 (DVD commentary).

9 Somen Ghosh, *Bangla Cinemar Palabadal* (The Changing Phases of Bengali Cinema: An in-depth Study, Calcutta, Shyamal Prakashan, 1990.

10 Sue Holmes, see note 1.

11 Nasreen Munni Kabir, *Guru Dutt: A Life in Cinema*, New Delhi, OUP, 1997, p. 169.

12 http://www.kanandevi.com/index.php. Dr Jyotiprakash Guha is the owner and composer of this website.

13 Shoma A. Chatterji, *P.C. Barua: Legends of Indian Cinema*, SCB Distributors, 2008.

14 Ibid.

15 Smita Mitra, 'Mahanayika Madam', http://www.india-seminar.com/2009/598/598_smita_mitra.htm

16 Ashis Nandy, 'The Double in Hindi Cinema', *The Times of India*, 14 October 1979.

17 Ibid.

18 Neepa Majumdar, 'Doubling, Stardom and Melodrama in Indian Cinema: The "Impossible" Role of Nargis', *Post Script*, Vol. 22, No. 3, p. 90.

19 Ibid.

20 James Naremore, *Acting in the Cinema*, Berkeley, University of California Press, 1988, p. 72.

21 The title of the film is almost a carry-over of the title of the other big hit *Saptapadi* which basically means more or less the same thing. Within a Hindu marriage ritual, saptapadi signifies a special ritual that occurs soon after the father has performed the kanyadaan and the marriage mantras are chanted by the bride and groom. A senior relative from the bride's side ties a knot to join the end of the bride's sari to the groom's dhoti with another piece of cloth. Following this, the bride and groom stand up to take seven rounds around the holy

fire (agni kunda) along with the chanting of mantras by the priests conducting the rituals to bless the couple. These seven steps taken together are called the saptapadi and the knot tied to join the groom and the bride is referred to as saat paake bandha which signifies that the couple are now tied together not once but seven times and never mind how many rounds they take in the reverse direction, the knot can never be untied. Stated simply, it indicates that among Hindus, marriage is forever much like the Christian vows that end with the phrase, 'till death do us part'.

22 Gloria Goodwin Raheja, 'Crying When She's Born, and Crying When She Goes Away: Marriage and the Idiom of the Gift in Pahansu Song Performance' in Kindsay Harlan and Paul B. Courtright (eds.), *From the Margins of Hindu Marriage: Essays on Gender, Religion and Culture*, Oxford University Press, New York, 1995, p. 37.

23 Founded in 1828 by Raja Rammohan Roy in Kolkata, the Brahmo Samaj is a religious movement. At its centre is the belief that there is one God, who is omnipresent and omniscient. It initially evolved in India where it differed from existing practice, as it did not believe in idol worship or the caste system. The Brahmo religion is now practiced in many parts of the world. The Brahmo Samaj has played a significant role in the renaissance of India, and the roots of much of modern thinking in India can be traced back to the Brahmo movement. Rabindranath Tagore, the Nobel Laureate, was one of the luminaries of the Brahmo Samaj. As British rule consolidated in India during the 18th century, two factors contributed to the formation of the Brahmo Samaj in the following century. Firstly, the Hindu social system had begun to stagnate and placed too much of an emphasis on traditional rituals. Secondly, an English educated class of Indians began to emerge to fulfill the administrative and economic needs of British rule. Raja Ram Mohan Roy, a Bengali, was a product of the latter trend. (Source: Supriyo Chanda: http://www.chanda.freeserve.co.uk/brahmoframe.htm)

The reforms initiated by the Brahmo Samaj were social rather than religious, including the proscription of child marriage. However, this particular code was broken by Keshab Chandra

Sen, bringing about a permanent schism within the community of Brahmos.

24 For elaboration on the symbolism of hair, see Gananath Obeyesekere, 'Medusa's Hair: An Essay on Personal Symbols and Religious Experience', University of Chicago Press, 1981; and Alf Hiltebeitel, 'Draupadi's Hair' *Purusartha 5*, 1981, p. 179–214.

25 Lynn Bennett, *Dangerous Wives and Sacred Sisters: Social and Symbolic Roles of High-Caste Women in Nepal*, New York, Columbia University Press, 1983, pp. 224–29, 240–43.

26 Harlan and Courtright, op. cit., p. 12.

27 Neepa Majumdar, 'Doubling, Stardom and Melodrama in Indian Cinema: The Impossible Role of Nargis', *Post Script*, Vol. 22, No. 3, p. 89.

28 Bhaskar Sarkar, *Mourning the Nation: Indian Cinema in the Wake of Partition*, Duke University Press, Orient Blackswan Pvt. Ltd, 2009, p. 149.

29 'Suchitra Sen: Biography of A Female Star', a talk by Dr Smita Mitra at Teen Murti House, Teen Murti Marg, 17 December 2013.

CHAPTER 4: WORKING WOMEN, BENGALI CINEMA AND SUCHITRA SEN ENDNOTES

1 Esther Boserup, *Women's Role in Economic Development*, London, Geroge Allen and Unwin Ltd, 1975.

2 Kamla Bhasin and Nighat Said Khan, *Some Questions on Feminism and Its Relevance in Southeast Asia*, New Delhi, Kali for Women, 1986.

3 Ashapurna Devi, 'Indian Women: Myth and Reality', in Jasodhara Bagchi (ed.), *Indian Women: Myth and Reality*, New Delhi, Sangam Books, 1995, p. 19.

4 Diane Elson, 'Labour Markets as Gendered Institutions: Equality, Efficiency and Empowerment Issues', *World Development*, Vol. 27, No. 3, 1999, pp. 611–627.

5 Amartya Sen, 'Cooperation, Inequality and the Household', in McNicoll, Geofferey and Mead Cain (eds.), *Rural Development and Population: Institutions and Policy*, Oxford University Press for Population Council, New York, 1990, pp. 61–76.

6 Diane Elson, 'Labour Markets as Gendered Institutions: Equality, Efficiency and Empowerment Issues', *World Development*, Vol. 27, No. 3, 1999, pp. 611–627.

7 Bina Agarwal, *A Field of One's Own: Gender and Land Rights in South Asia*, Cambridge, Cambridge University Press, 1994; and Naila Kabeer, 'Resources, Agency, Achievements: Reflections on the Measurement of Women's Empowerment', in Birjitta Sevefjord and Berit Olsson (eds), *Discussing Women's Empowerment: Theory and Practice*, SIDA Studies No. 3, 2001.

8 Smita Mitra, *Mahanayika Madam*, http://www.india-seminar.com/2009/598/598_smita_mitra.htm

9 *Journal of Advanced Nursing*, Volume 29, Issue 1, pages 36–43, January 1999.

10 Shoma A. Chatterji, *Subject: Cinema, Object: Woman – A Study of the Portrayal of Women in Hindi Cinema*, Kolkata, Parumita Publications, 1998.

11 Shoma A. Chatterji, 'The Culture-Specific Use of Sound in Indian Cinema', paper presented at International Symposium on Sound in Cinema, organized by School of Sound, London, 15–19 April 1999.

12 The author is indebted to Karan Bali's review of *Uttar Phalguni* in his online magazine *upperstall.com* for his insights into the music of the Bengali film.

13 *The Hindu*, 20 July 2001.

14 Aarti went to study bar-at-law for which students go to Lincoln's Inn, not to Oxford. This appears to have been a bloomer by Gulzar but few seem to have noticed this anomaly.

CHAPTER 5: THE CONCEPT OF WILFUL SOCIAL SECLUSION AND SOCIAL ANXIETY DISORDER

1 For this section, I am indebted to Suman Gupta's reminiscences of Suchitra Sen, *Je Jon Aachhen Nirjone*, serialized in a Bengali monthly magazine for women called Sukhee Grihokone, April, 2002, pp. 80–82.

2 *OPEN* Magazine, 1 February 2014.

3 http://socialanxietydisorder.about.com/od/overviewofsad/a/overview.htm

4 Knopf, 1st edition, 21 February 1995.

5 Ibid.

6 Harry N. Abrams, August 2005.

7 Scribner, September 1997.

8 Robson Press, June 2012.

9 Harper Collins, August 1991.

10 Gauri Chatterjee, *OPEN* magazine, 1 February 2014.

CHAPTER 6: THE SUMMING UP

1 Rini Bhattacharya Mehta and Debali Mookerjea-Leonard (eds), *The Indian Partition in Literature and Films: History, Politics, Aesthetics*, Routledge Contemporary South Asia Series, 2014.

2 Gloria Steinem and George Barris (Photographer), *Marilyn*, This was first published in 1986 and later, in 1997 by MJA Books. In this sensitive, provocative portrait of Marilyn Monroe, Gloria Steinem reveals the woman behind the myth, the child Norma Jean, and the forces in America that shaped her into the fantasy and icon that has never died.

3 Ibid.

FILMOGRAPHY

Name of film	Director	Opposite
1953		
Saat Number Kayedi	Sukumar Dasgupta	Jahar Ganguly
Saare Chuattar	Nirmal Dey	Uttam Kumar
Kajori	Niren Lahiri	Biren Chattopadhyay
Bhagaban Sri Sri Krishna Chaitanya	Debakikumar Bose	Basanta Choudhury
1954		
Atom Bomb	Toru Mukhopadhyay	She was a bit player
Ora Thakey Odharey	Sukumar Dasgupta	Uttam Kumar
Dhuli	Pinaki Mukhopadhyay	Prasanta Kumar
Maraner Porey	Satish Dasgupta	Uttam Kumar
Sadanander Mela	Sukumar Dasgupta	Uttam Kumar
Annapurnar Mandir	Naresh Mitra	Uttam Kumar
Griha Prabesh	Ajoy Kar	Uttam Kumar
Boloygrash	Pinaki Mukhopadhyay	Not available
Agnipariksha	Agradoot (Bibhuti Laha)	Uttam Kumar

Name of film	Director	Opposite
1955		
Devdas (Hindi)	Bimal Roy	Dilip Kumar
Saanjher Pradip	Sudhangsu Mukherjee	Uttam Kumar
Saajghar	Debakikumar Bose	Bikash Roy
Shaap Mochan	Sudhir Mukhopadhyay	Uttam Kumar
Mejo Bou	Debnarayan Gupta	Bikash Roy
Bhalobasha	Debakikumar Bose	Bikash Roy
Sabar Uparey	Agradoot	Uttam Kumar
1956		
Sagarika	Agragami	Uttam Kumar
Trijama	Agradoot	Uttam Kumar
Shubhoratri	Sushil Majumdar	Basanta Choudhury
Ekti Raat	Chitta Bose	Kamal Mitra
Shilpi	Agragami	Uttam Kumar
Amar Bou	Khagen Roy	Bikash Roy
1957		
Musafir (Hindi)	Hrishikesh Mukherjee	Dilip Kumar
Harano Sur	Ajoy Kar	Uttam Kumar
Pathey Holo Deri	Agradoot	Uttam Kumar
Chandranath	Kartik Chattopadhyay	Uttam Kumar
Champakali (Hindi)	Nandalal Jaswantlal	Bharat Bhushan
Jeebon Trishna	Asit Sen	Uttam Kumar

Name of film	Director	Opposite
1958		
Rajlakshmi O Sreekanto	Haridas Bhattacharya	Uttam Kumar
Indrani	Niren Lahiri	Uttam Kumar
Suryatoran	Agradoot	Uttam Kumar
1959		
Chaoa Paoa	Jatrik	Uttam Kumar
Deep Jele Jai	Asit Sen	Basanta Choudhury
1960		
Hospital	Sushil Majumdar	Ashok Kumar
Smritituku Thaak	Jatrik	Bikash Roy, Asit Baran
Bambai Ka Babu (Hindi)	Raj Khosla	Dev Anand
Sarhad	Shankar Mukherjee	Dev Anand
1961		
Saptapadi	Ajoy Kar	Uttam Kumar
1962		
Bipasha	Agradoot	Uttam Kumar
1963		
Saat Paake Bandha	Ajoy Kar	Soumitra Chatterjee
Uttar Phalguni	Asit Sen	Bikash Roy, Dilip Mukherjee

Name of film	Director	Opposite
1964		
Sandhya Dweeper Shikha	Haridas Bhattacharya	Bikash Roy
1966		
Mamta (Hindi)	Asit Sen	Bikash Roy, Dilip Mukherjee
1967		
Grihadaha	Subodh Mitra	Uttam Kumar
1969		
Kamallata	Harisadhan Dasgupta	Uttam Kumar
1970		
Megh Kalo	Sushil Mukherjee	Basanta Choudhury
1971		
Fariyaad	Bijoy Bose	Utpal Dutt
Nabaraag	Bijoy Bose	Uttam Kumar
1972		
Alo Amar Alo	Pinaki Mukherjee	Uttam Kumar
Haar Mana Haar	Salil Sen	Uttam Kumar
1974		
Debi Choudhurani	Dinen Gupta	Ranjit Mullick
Sraban Sandhya	Bireshwar Bose	Samit Bhanja

Name of film	Director	Opposite
1975		
Priyo Bandhabi	Hiren Nag	Uttam Kumar
Aandhi (Hindi)	Gulzar	Sanjeev Kumar
1976		
Datta	Ajoy Kar	Soumitra Chatterjee
1978		
Pronoy Pasha	Mangal Chakabarty	Soumitra Chatterjee

(This filmography has been obtained from the special issue of *Television,* February 1993, pp. 52–55, where the credits for the filmography were attributed to Ramlal Nandi of Chhayabani Pvt. Ltd and to Pronob Kumar Bosu of Chandimata Films)

INDEX

BIBLIOGRAPHY

Books

Bandopadhyay, Tarasankar, *Amar Sahitya Jeebon*, Volume I, p. 19–20.

Bennett, Lynn, *Dangerous Wives and Sacred Sisters: Social and Symbolic Roles of High-Caste Women in Nepal*, Columbia University Press, New York, 1983. pp. 224–29, 240–43.

Bhasin, Kamla and Nighat Said Khan, *Some Questions on Feminism and Its Relevance in Southeast Asia*, Kali for Women, 1986.

Bhattacharya Mehta, Rini and Debali Mookerjea-Leonard (edited), *The Indian Partition in Literature and Films: History, Politics, Aesthetics*, Routledge Contemporary South Asia Series, 2014.

Biswas, Moinak, 'The Couple and their Spaces: *Harano Sur* as Melodrama Now', in R. Vasudevan (ed.), *Making Meaning in Indian Cinema*, New Delhi, Oxford University Press, 2000.

Boserup, Esther, *Women's Role in Economic Development*, London, Geroge Allen and Unwin Ltd, 1975.

Chatterji, Shoma A., *Subject-Cinema, Object-Woman: A Study of the Portrayal of Women in Hindi Cinema*, Parumita Publications, Kolkata, 1998.

Chatterji, Shoma A., 'The Culture-Specific Use of Sound in Indian Cinema', paper presented at International Symposium on Sound in Cinema, organized by School of Sound, London, 15–19 April 1999.

Chatterji, Shoma A., *P.C. Barua: Legends of Indian Cinema*, SCB Distributors, 2008.

Chattopadhyay Himangshu, *Tollywooder Greta Garbo*, Urbi Prakashan, 2005.

Chowdhury, Maitreyee, B.: *Uttam Kumar and Suchitra Sen: Bengali Cinema's First Couple*, Om Books International, 2013.

Dyer, Richard, *Stars*, London: British Film Institute, 1979

Dyer, Richard, *Heavenly Bodies*, London: British Film Institute, 1986

Gledhill, Christine, 'Signs of melodrama', in Christine Gledhill (ed.), *Stardom: Industry of Desire*, London: Routledge, 1991.

Gooptu, Sharmistha, *Bengali Cinema: An Other Nation*, Lotus Roli Books, 2010.

Kabir, Nasreen Munni, *Guru Dutt: A Life in Cinema*, OUP, Delhi, 1997.

Kanjilal, Phoolrani, *Amar Ballobondhu Mayanayika Suchitra Sen* (My Childhood Friend Suchitra Sen) in Bengali, Parumita Publications, 2004.

Kundu, Abhijit, 'Changing Iconography of Women in Bengali Cinema', PhD Thesis, JNU, 'Chapter 4, Encounters with Modernity: Period of Recuperation, 1950s–1960s', 2002.

McDonald, P., 'Reconceptualising Stardom', in Richard Dyer, *Stars* (second edition), London: BFI, 1998.

Mitra, Smita, 'Postcolonial Modernity: Melodrama and Self-Fashioning in Popular Bengali Cinema of the 1950s–1970s', PhD thesis, JNU 2006-2012.

Naremore, James, *Acting in the Cinema*, Berkeley: U of California P, 1988

Raheja, Gloria Goodwin, 'Crying When She's Born, and Crying When She Goes Away: Marriage and the Idiom of the Gift in Pahansu Song Performance', in Kindsay Harlan and Paul B. Courtright (ed.), *From the Margins of Hindu Marriage: Essays on Gender, Religion and Culture*, Oxford University Press, New York, 1995.

Sarkar, Bhaskar, *Mourning the Nation: Indian Cinema in the Wake of Partition*, Duke University Press, Orient Blackswan Pvt. Ltd, 2010

Sen, Amartya, 'Cooperation, Inequality and the Household', in McNicoll, Geofferey and Mead Cain (eds), Rural Development and Population: Institutions and Policy, Oxford University Press for Population Council, New York, 1990

Steinem, Gloria, *Marilyn Monroe: Still Life and Essay – The Woman Who Will Not Die*, 1986.

Magazines and Journals

Agarwal, Bina, *A Field of One's Own: Gender and Land Rights in South Asia*, Cambridge University Press, Cambridge, 1994.

Bhattacharya, Shankarlal, '*Smriti, Satta, Suchitra*', Bengali, *Anandalok*, 8 April 2002.

Chatterjee, Gauri, *OPEN Magazine*, 1 February 2014.

Deb, Dhiren, '*Phire Phire Chai*', Bengali, *Overland*, 11 June 1993.

Doane, Mary Ann, *Pandora's Box*, Dir. G.W. Pabst, Criterion Collection, 2006, DVD commentary.

Dyer, Richard, *Stars, Westminster Papers in Communication and Culture* © 2005, University of Westminster, London, Vol. 2 (2): 6–21, ISSN 1744–6708 (Print); 1744–6716 (Online)

Elson, Diane, 'Labour Markets as Gendered Institutions: Equality, Efficiency and Empowerment Issues', *World Development*, Vol. 27, No. 3, 1999.

Gupta, Suman, *Je Jon Aachen Nirjone*, Serialized in April 2002

Holmes, Su, 'Starring Dyer?': Revisiting Star Studies and Contemporary Celebrity Culture', University of Kent, *Westminster Papers in Communication and Culture* © 2005, University of Westminster, London, Vol. 2 (2): 6–21, ISSN 1744-6708 (Print); 1744–6716 (Online)

Maaren, Reesink, *Light Stars: Fame in Postmodern Times*, E-View, Vol. No. 1, 2008.

Majumdar, Neepa, 'Doubling, Stardom and Melodrama in Indian Cinema: The "Impossible" Role of Nargis', *Post Script*, Vol. 22, No. 3

Mitra, Smita, 'Suchitra Sen: Biography of a Female Star', Talk delivered at Teen Murti House, Teen Murti Marg, 17 December 2013

Mitra, Smita, 'Mahanayika Madam', http://www.india-seminar.com/2009/598/598_smita_mitra.htm

Nandy, Ashis, 'The Double in Hindi Cinema', The *Times of India*, 14 October 1979.

Obeyesekere, Gananath, 'Medusa's Hair: An Essay on Personal Symbols and Religious Experience, Chicago: University of Chicago Press, 1981; and Alf Hiltebeitel, 'Draupadi's Hair', *Purusartha 5* (1981): 179–214.

Television, a Bengali monthly magazine published by the AAJ KAAL group of publications, brought out several special nostalgia issues before it closed shop around the mid-1990s. Among these, were two special issues on Uttam Kumar (January 1993 and July 1993), one on the Uttam Kumar-Suchitra Sen (August 1992) and one on Suchitra Sen (February 1993) alone. These magazines were a great source of research material for this book.

http://bethlovesbollywood.blogspot.in/2014/06/harano-sur.html, 22 June 2014.

ACKNOWLEDGEMENTS

A small two-page note thanking everyone in connection with an entire book hardly does justice to the people involved in the process. But justice or not, it is imperative to document their contribution before, during and after writing the book purely for the emotional satisfaction of knowing that thanks has been extended. It has been like climbing a mountain which is tougher at seventy-two than it was at thirty-five when this writer's journey as an author began. But once one has taken a decision, the mountain evens out into a plateau, metaphorically and symbolically, and everything else falls in place.

Writing a book on a living enigma like Suchitra Sen who, during the last years of her life, kept away from any kind of direct or indirect interaction was dependent on many factors. My first thanks go to Shantanu Ray Chaudhuri for accepting my proposal of writing an entire book on the legendary actress who lives on through her films and the stories that revolve around her life spent in self-seclusion. There are hardly any books in English on Suchitra Sen and so this was a project undertaken to reach out to the English-reading audience in India and beyond. I had written a slim volume on Suchitra Sen more than a decade ago under a different imprint but always felt dissatisfied because of the small coverage of an actress who had worked in more than sixty films during her career and made a very significant contribution to the Golden Age of Bengali cinema. I also thank Shantanu, one of the best editors in the country, for going through the proofs with a fine-toothed comb so that the finished book does justice to the subject – Suchitra Sen.

HarperCollins India deserves a bouquet full of thanks for accepting the proposal and going ahead with it and for this too, I have Shantanu to offer a special note of thanks to. Amitava Nag, friend, film scholar and editor *Silhouette*, deserves my gratitude for having put me in touch with Shantanu so that I could spread my wings to reach out to publishers other than the ones who had already published my works. I also extend my deep gratitude to Sunayna Saraswat of HarperCollins India for painstakingly having gone through the final proofs to prepare for the press which demands great patience and commitment. My very young friend Anugyan Nag, a research scholar at the JNU who is doing his PhD in cinema and has just been awarded a Fulbright scholarship, needs to be thanked because he went through the rough draft of the first chapter and encouraged me to go on with the project.

My thanks include Suchitra Sen's daughter Moon Moon Sen and her two beautiful granddaughters, Raima and Ria, who shed considerable light on the actress in two long interviews I had with them on their personal experiences. Other film personalities – film-maker Tarun Majumdar, film-maker Ashok Viswanathan, actress-director Churni Ganguly, film-maker Ananya Chatterjee and actress Madhabi Mukherjee – deserve a thanks for their free and personal response to the issue of the actress's withdrawal from the film industry and from public life which find place in this book. I am also deeply obligated to Gulzar Saab who happily granted me a telephonic interview to share his experiences with the actress he addressed as 'Sir'.

Over the years, I have written dozens of articles, profiles, analyses and explorations on Suchitra Sen. I extend my thanks to the editors of these print and online publications like *Screen*, www.IndiaTogether.com, *One India One People*, *Vogue India*, *Swagat*,

Vidura, The *Times of India* and the entire editorial and publishing team of Rupa Publication (2002) which published my earlier book on Suchitra Sen under their Charitavali Series. This book is different from that earlier one which was a short monograph of approximately 10,000 words.

My deep gratitude to two very important individuals namely, Subhash Chheda and S.M.M. Ausaja, noted archivists of cinema posters, lobby cards, images and stills for use in this book purely for the love of the subject. This book would never have been possible without their help.

My husband Ajoy has always hovered in the backdrop, helping me by just being there, and allowing me to explore my space the way I wanted to. Having shared fifty years of our lives together, I must concede that nothing of the little I have done would have seen the light of day without him, and this book is just one pebble among the several I have cast in the ocean of writing on Indian cinema and cinema personalities. My grandson Ishaan Agarwal, all of fourteen and preparing for his board exams, has cheered me up with his spells of mischief every now and then, though these were more to annoy and irritate me which they did. But looking back, they had wonderful entertainment value as moments of happy relief from heavy work.

I owe readers who will read this book a generous dose of gratitude for bearing with my very individual explorations of the works of an actress I have never met or interacted with in any way.